EMPLOYMENT PROTECTION LEGISLATION

EMPLOYMENT PROTECTION LEGISLATION

R V UPEX, MA, LLB (Cantab)

of The Middle Temple, Barrister, Lecturer in Law at Kingston Polytechnic

OYEZ PUBLISHING LIMITED

Oyez Publishing Limited
Norwich House, 11/13 Norwich Street,
London EC4A 1AB

ISBN 0 85120 389 2

Printed in Great Britain by Oyez Press Limited
(a subsidiary of The Solicitor's Law Stationery Society, Limited)
at their works, 27 Crimscott Street, London SE1 5TT

PREFACE

Although a consolidation measure, the Employment Protection (Consolidation) Act 1978 has had a surprisingly chequered career. The first attempt to steer it through Parliament, towards the end of the 1977 session, failed; and, as the end of the 1978 session approached, one began to fear that a similar fate was awaiting it. Fortunately, it was possible for it to complete its progress, and it received the Royal Assent on 31 July. A welcome and much-needed consolidation measure has thus reached the Statute Book, which will, it is hoped, simplify the task of those involved in this area of the law. Whilst all the ends will not be tied up until the collective aspects of the legislation are consolidated, it is at least possible to anticipate that some of the nightmarish problems of cross-referencing, experienced since the enactment of the Employment Protection Act 1975, will be eliminated.

The aim of the annotations is to give guidance to those who are relatively unfamiliar with this field, as well as to provide as detailed a commentary as possible on the law, by indicating both the areas which are problematical and the relevant and up-to-date case-law. Although it is hoped that this book will be of particular benefit to all those involved in problems relating to individual employment (not only lawyers), it is intended that it should also assist students and teachers of labour law.

I am grateful to my publishers for compiling the Tables and the Index, and to my brother for his assistance with the typing. The text of the Act is reproduced by kind permission of Her Majesty's Stationery Office.

The law is stated as at 1 August, 1978.

Robert Upex

Old Square,
Lincoln's Inn.
October, 1978.

CONTENTS

Employment Protection (Consolidation) Act 1978

PART I

PARTICULARS OF TERMS OF EMPLOYMENT

PART II

RIGHTS ARISING IN COURSE OF EMPLOYMENT

Part IV

Termination of Employment

Part V

Unfair Dismissal

Right not to be unfairly dismissed

Meaning of unfair dismissal

Exclusion of section 54

Remedies for unfair dismissal

Amount of compensation

PAGE

Section

Interim relief

Teachers in aided schools

PART VI

REDUNDANCY PAYMENTS

Right to redundancy payment

Redundancy Fund

Contents

TABLE OF CASES

TABLE OF STATUTES

PAGE

PAGE

TABLE OF STATUTORY INSTRUMENTS

TABLE OF ABBREVIATIONS

ACTS

1965	The Redundancy Payments Act 1965
1972	The Contracts of Employment Act 1972
1974	The Trade Union and Labour Relations Act 1974 (The reference to 'para' indicates a paragraph of Schedule 1 to the Act)
1975	The Employment Protection Act 1975

STATUTORY INSTRUMENTS

1977 Order	Redundancy Payments (Variation of Rebates) Order 1977
1977 Order (No 2)	Employment Protection (Variation of Limits) Order 1977

GENERAL

EAT	Employment Appeal Tribunal

INTRODUCTION

The Employment Protection (Consolidation) Act 1978 is the latest in a series of enactments dating back to the Contracts of Employment Act 1963, which deal with the rights of individual employees in their employment. Since, however, unlike its predecessors, it is a consolidation measure, it effects no substantive changes.

It covers most of the rights conferred upon employees as individuals. It does not include, however, any of the relevant provisions of the Equal Pay Act 1970, the Sex Discrimination Act 1975 or the Race Relations Act 1976.

Part I of the Act contains the provisions relating to particulars of the terms of employment, that is written statements under what was s 4 of the Contracts of Employment Act 1972 and itemised pay statements under s 81 of the Employment Protection Act 1975. Part II contains the provisions which relate to the employee's rights arising in the course of his employment: guarantee payments (ss 12 to 18); suspension from work on medical grounds (ss 19 to 22); trade union membership and activities (ss 23 to 26); and time off work (ss 27 to 32). Part III contains the provisions relating to maternity; Part IV those relating to the termination of the employment (including the right to a minimum period of notice, and the employee's right to a written statement of the reasons for his dismissal); Part V those relating to unfair dismissal; Part VI those relating to redundancy payments; and Part VII those relating to the employer's insolvency. Part VIII deals with the resolution of disputes relating to employment. Part IX contains the miscellaneous and supplemental provisions, of which the more important are: s 137, which gives the power to extend the employment protection legislation; s 138, which relates to Crown employment; s 139, which relates to House of Commons staff; s 140, which contains the provisions relating to contracting out of the Act; and ss 141 to 147, which exclude certain classes of employment.

Of the seventeen Schedules, the more important are: Sched 2, which contains supplementary provisions relating to maternity; Scheds 4, 6 and 7, which provide for the calculation of redundancy payments, redundancy rebates and payments to employees out of the Redundancy Fund respectively; Scheds 9 and 11, which relate to industrial tribunals and the Employment Appeal Tribunal respectively; Sched 12, which makes provision for the death of the employer or the employee; Sched 13, which provides the method of computation of the employee's period of employment; and Sched 14, which provides for the calculation of the employee's normal working hours and a week's pay.

Nearly all the Act came into effect on 1 November, 1978. Section 139, and other consequential provisions relating to the House of Commons, will come into effect on 1 January, 1979.

PART I

PARTICULARS OF TERMS OF EMPLOYMENT

WRITTEN PARTICULARS OF TERMS OF EMPLOYMENT

1. Written particulars of terms of employment

(1) Not later than thirteen weeks after the beginning of an employee's period of employment with an employer, the employer shall give to the employee a written statement in accordance with the following provisions of this section.

(2) An employer shall in a statement under this section—

(*a*) identify the parties;

(*b*) specify the date when the employment began;

(*c*) state whether any employment with a previous employer counts as part of the employee's continuous period of employment, and, if so, specify the date when the continuous period of employment began.

(3) A statement under this section shall contain the following particulars of the terms of employment as at a specified date not more than one week before the statement is given, that is to say—

(*a*) the scale or rate of remuneration, or the method of calculating remuneration,

(*b*) the intervals at which remuneration is paid (that is, whether weekly or monthly or by some other period),

(*c*) any terms and conditions relating to hours of work (including any terms and conditions relating to normal working hours),

(*d*) any terms and conditions relating to—

(i) entitlement to holidays, including public holidays, and holiday pay (the particulars given being sufficient to enable the employee's entitlement, including any entitlement to accrued holiday pay on the termination of employment, to be precisely calculated),

(ii) incapacity for work due to sickness or injury, including any provision for sick pay,

(iii) pensions and pension schemes,

(*e*) the length of notice which the employee is obliged to give and entitled to receive to determine his contract of employment, and

(*f*) the title of the job which the employee is employed to do:

Provided that paragraph (*d*)(iii) shall not apply to the employees of any body or authority if the employees' pension rights depend on the terms of a pension scheme established under any provision contained in or having effect under an Act of Parliament and the body or authority are required by any such provision to give to new employees information concerning their pension rights, or concerning the determination of questions affecting their pension rights.

(4) Subject to subsection (5), every statement given to an employee under this section shall include a note—

(*a*) specifying any disciplinary rules applicable to the employee, or referring to a document which is reasonably accessible to the employee and which specifies such rules;

(*b*) specifying, by description or otherwise—

(i) a person to whom the employee can apply if he is dissatisfied with any disciplinary decision relating to him; and

(ii) a person to whom the employee can apply for the purpose of seeking redress of any grievance relating to his employment,

and the manner in which any such application should be made;

(*c*) where there are further steps consequent upon any such application, explaining those steps or referring to a document which is reasonably accessible to the employee and which explains them; and

(*d*) stating whether a contracting-out certificate is in force for the employment in respect of which the statement is given.

(5) The provisions of paragraphs (*a*) to (*c*) of subsection (4) shall not apply to rules, disciplinary decisions, grievances or procedures relating to health or safety at work.

(6) The definition of week given by section 153(1) does not apply for the purposes of this section.

NOTES

Derivation: 1972, s 4 (1), (2), (2A); 1975, Sched 16, Pt II, paras 4, 5, 6; Social Security Pensions Act 1975, s 30 (5).

General Note: this section and ss 2 to 7 require the employer to give the employee a written statement containing particulars of certain terms of his employment. Section 4 deals with the situation where the terms of employment are changed; s 5 excludes the employer from the obligation where he gives the employee a written contract complying with the requirements of that section; s 6 gives the Secretary of State power to require additional particulars to be given; s 7 gives him power to vary the number of hours necessary to qualify the employee for the rights (see also s 3); and s 11 provides the procedure to enforce the rights. See also the General Notes to ss 3, 4 and 5 and the provisions of ss 137, 149, 151 (2) and 157.

Exclusions:

(i) certain part-timers (ss 3 and 7);
(ii) certain written contracts of employment (s 5);
(iii) Crown employment (s 138);
(iv) employment outside Great Britain (s 141 (1));
(v) mariners (s 144 (1));
(vi) dock workers, except when engaged in work which is not dock work (s 145 (1) and (5));
(vii) employment by spouse (s 146 (1)).

Note ss 139 (which deals with House of Commons staff) and 147.

Employee: see s 153 (1), and *Ready Mixed Concrete (South East) Ltd* v *Minister of Pensions and National Insurance* [1968] 2 QB 497; *Ferguson* v *John Dawson and Partners (Contractors) Ltd* [1976] IRLR 346; and *Davis* v *New England College of Arundel* [1977] ICR 6. The most important recent case is *Massey* v *Crown Life Insurance Co* [1978] ICR 590, which was decided by the Court of Appeal. The previous Court of Appeal decision in *Ferguson* v *Dawson* was distinguished. Other recent cases are: *Tyne and Clyde*

Warehouses Ltd v *Hamerton* (1978) 13 ITR 66 (agents); *Folami* v *Nigerline (UK) Ltd* [1978] ICR 277 and *Parsons* v *Albert J Parsons & Sons Ltd* [1978] ICR 456 (directors); *102 Social Club and Institute Ltd* v *Bickerton* [1977] ICR 911 (club secretary); and *Gadhok* v *Commonwealth Secretariat* (1977) 12 ITR 440 (employee of the Commonwealth Secretariat).

Employer: see s 153 (1). It is possible to become an employer by estoppel: see *Smith* v *Blandford Gee Cementation Company Ltd* [1970] 3 All ER 154. For a case on employing oneself, see *Rowley, Holmes & Co* v *Barber* [1977] ICR 387. Note the provisions of s 138 on Crown employment and those of s 139, particularly subss (4) to (9), in relation to House of Commons staff.

Written statement: the exact status of such written statements is uncertain: see *Turriff Construction Ltd* v *Bryant* (1967) 2 ITR 292 and *Owens* v *Multilux Ltd* [1974] IRLR 113, and contrast *Gascol Conversions Ltd* v *Mercer* [1974] ICR 420. Presumably, inaccuracies in the particulars, or the matters required to be stated by subs (2) could lead to an estoppel against the employer: see *Smith* v *Blandford Gee*, above, and *Evenden* v *Guildford City Association Football Club* [1975] ICR 367. Note the requirement in s 2 (2) that if the contract is for a fixed term, the statement must state the date when the contract expires; note also s 142.

Continuous period of employment: since many of the rights in the Act depend upon a minimum period of continuous employment (eg four weeks for the right to claim a guarantee payment (s 143 (1)), twenty-six weeks for the right not to be unfairly dismissed (s 64 (1))), it is important for the employee to know for how long he has been continuously employed. For the provisions for ascertaining the length of an employee's period of employment, and whether the employment has been continuous, see s 151 and Sched 13, and the notes to those provisions.

Provision for sick pay: see *Roberts* v *BICC Ltd* [1976] IRLR 404.

Length of notice: see s 49.

Title of job: see *Churcher* v *Weyside Engineering Ltd* [1976] IRLR 402.

Subsection (4): 'document which is reasonably accessible': see note to s 2 (3).

Definitions: 'employee', 'employer', 'written statement' and 'continuous period of employment': see above; 'employment' and 'job': see s 153 (1); 'week': note that the definition in s 153 (1) does not apply (s 1 (6)).

2. Supplementary provisions relating to statements under s 1

(1) If there are no particulars to be entered under any of the heads of paragraph (*d*) of subsection (3) of section 1, or under any of the other provisions of section 1(2) and (3), that fact shall be stated.

(2) If the contract is for a fixed term, the statement given under section 1 shall state the date when the contract expires.

(3) A statement given under section 1 may, for all or any of the particulars to be given by the statement, refer the employee to some document which the employee has reasonable opportunities of reading in the course of his employment or which is made reasonably accessible to him in some other way.

(4) If not more than six months after the termination of an employee's period of employment, a further period of employment is begun with the same employer, and the terms of employment are the same, no statement need be given under section 1 in respect of the second period of employment, but without prejudice to the operation of subsection (1) of section 4 if there is a change in the terms of employment.

NOTES

Derivation: 1972, s 4 (3) to (6).

General Note: see the General Note to s 1, and note the exclusions listed in the notes to s 1.

Subsection (3): this provision may facilitate the incorporation of collectively agreed terms into the individual's contract: see *Camden Exhibition and Display Ltd* v *Lynott* [1966] 1QB 155; *Burroughs Machines Ltd* v *Timmoney* [1977] IRLR 404; and *British Leyland UK Ltd* v *McQuilken* [1978] IRLR 245. The Courts in such cases have tended to assume that a reference to a reasonably accessible document automatically incorporates it. This assumption is questionable. For what is a 'reasonably accessible' document, see *King* v *Post Office* [1973] ICR 120 and *Green* v *Moyses Stevens* [1974] IRLR 274.

Definitions: 'employee' and 'employer': see note to s 1; 'employment': see s 153 (1).

3. Certain hours of employment to be disregarded

(1) Subject to the following provisions of this section, no account shall be taken under section 1 of employment during any period when the hours of employment are normally less than sixteen hours weekly.

(2) If the employee's relations with his employer cease to be governed by a contract which normally involves work for sixteen hours or more weekly and become governed by a contract which normally involves employment for eight hours or more, but less than sixteen hours, weekly, the employee shall nevertheless for a period of twenty-six weeks (computed in accordance with subsection (3)) be treated for the purposes of subsection (1) as if his contract normally involved employment for sixteen hours or more weekly.

(3) In computing the said period of twenty-six weeks no account shall be taken of any week—

(*a*) during which the employee is in fact employed for sixteen hours or more;

(*b*) during which the employee takes part in a strike (as defined in paragraph 24 of Schedule 13) or is absent from work because of a lock-out (as so defined) by his employer; or

(*c*) during which there is no contract of employment but which, by virtue of paragraph 9(1) of Schedule 13, counts in computing a period of continuous employment.

(4) An employee whose relations with his employer are governed by a contract of employment which normally involves employment for eight hours or more, but less than sixteen hours, weekly shall nevertheless, if he has been continuously employed for a period of five years or more, be treated for the purposes of subsection (1) as if his contract normally involved employment for sixteen hours or more weekly.

NOTES:

Derivation: 1972, s 4(7) to (10); 1975, Sched 16, Pt II, paras 7, 8.

General Note: the obligations under s 1 only arise where the employee is employed for more than sixteen hours a week. The provisions of this section deal with the situation where the employee's hours fall below sixteen a week, but not below eight: for twenty-six weeks he is treated as if his normal hours were sixteen per week. Subsection (3) provides that in the computation of the twenty-six weeks mentioned in subs (2) certain weeks are to be disregarded. Subsection (4) provides for employees who normally work more than eight, but less than sixteen, hours per week and have been continuously employed for five years or more. See also the notes to s 1. Note the power given to the Sectetary of State by s 7 to amend this section.

Continuous employment, continuously employed: see note to s 1.

Definitions: 'employee' and 'employer': see note to s 1; 'contract of employment' and 'employment': see s 153 (1); 'strike' and 'lock-out': note subs (3) (b) and Sched 13, para 24.

4. Changes in terms of employment

(1) If after the date to which a statement given under section 1 relates there is a change in the terms of employment to be included, or referred to, in that statement the employer shall, not more than one month after the change, inform the employee of the nature of the change by a written statement and, if he does not leave a copy of the statement with the employee, shall preserve the statement and ensure that the employee has reasonable opportunities of reading it in the course of his employment, or that it is made reasonably accessible to him in some other way.

(2) A statement given under subsection (1) may, for all or any of the particulars to be given by the statement, refer the employee to some document which the employee has reasonable opportunities of reading in the course of his employment, or which is made reasonably accessible to him in some other way.

(3) If, in referring in the statement given under section 1 or under subsection (1) of this section to any such document, the employer indicates to the employee that future changes in the terms of which the particulars are given in the document will be entered up in the document (or recorded by some other means for the information of persons referring to the document), the employer need not under subsection (1) inform the employee of any such change if it is duly entered up or recorded not later than one month after the change is made.

(4) Where, after an employer has given to an employee a written statement in accordance with section 1—

(*a*) the name of the employer (whether an individual or a body corporate or partnership) is changed, without any change in the identity of the employer, or

(*b*) the identity of the employer is changed, in such circumstances that, in accordance with section 139(7) or paragraph 17 or paragraph 18 of Schedule 13, the continuity of the employee's period of employment is not broken,

and (in either case) the change does not involve any change in the terms (other than the names of the parties) included or referred to in the statement, then, the person who, immediately after the change, is the employer shall not be required to give to the employee a statement in accordance with section 1, but, subject to subsection (5), the change shall be treated as a change falling within subsection (1) of this section.

(5) A written statement under this section which informs an employee of such a change in his terms of employment as is referred to in subsection (4)(*b*) shall specify the date on which the employee's continuous period of employment began.

NOTES

Derivation: 1972, s 5; 1975, Sched 16, Pt II, para 9; House of Commons (Administration) Act 1978, Sched 2, para 4.

General Note: this section is complementary to s 1, and deals with the situation where the terms of employment change. Failure to give a new notice does not invalidate the change itself: see *Parkes Classic Confectionery Ltd* v *Ashcroft* (1973) 8 ITR 43. See also the notes to s 1. Note ss 146 (1), 147, 151 (2) and 157.

Reasonably accessible: see the note to s 2 (3).

Subsection (3): the effect of *Gascol Conversions Ltd* v *Mercer* [1974] ICR 420 is that, if an employee signs a written statement, he is bound by what he signs. Presumably, therefore, if he signs a statement containing provisions similar to those in this subsection, he will be taken to have signed away his right to object to future changes.

Subsection (4): in a situation covered by Sched 13, para 17, it will be necessary to consider whether the change in the identity of the employer means that the new employer is put into possession of a 'going concern': see *Kenmir Ltd* v *Frizzell* [1968] 1 WLR 329; *Woodhouse* v *Peter Brotherhood Ltd* [1972] ICR 197; *Crompton* v *Truly Fair (International) Ltd* [1975] ICR 359; *Dhami* v *Top Spot Night Club* [1977] IRLR 231; and *Rastill* v *Automatic Refreshment Services Ltd* [1978] ICR 289. See also *Rowley, Holmes and Co* v *Barber* [1977] ICR 387, a case decided under what is now para 17 (4); and the notes to paras 17 and 18. The latter deals with employment by an associated employer of the original employer.

Definitions: 'employer', 'employer' and 'continuous period of employment': see note to s 1; 'employment': see s 153 (1).

5. Exclusion of certain contracts in writing

Sections 1 and 4 shall not apply to an employee if and so long as the following conditions are fulfilled in relation to him, that is to say—

(*a*) the employee's contract of employment is a contract which has been reduced to writing in one or more documents and which contains express terms affording the particulars to be given under each of the paragraphs in subsection (3) of section 1, and under each head of paragraph (*d*) of that subsection;

(*b*) there has been given to the employee a copy of the contract (with any variations made from time to time), or he has reasonable opportunities of reading such a copy in the course of his employment, or such a copy is made reasonably accessible to him in some other way; and

(*c*) such a note as is mentioned in section 1(4) has been given to the employee or he has reasonable opportunities of reading such a note in the course of his employment or such a note is made reasonably accessible to him in some other way:

Provided that if at any time after the beginning of an employee's period of employment these conditions cease to be fulfilled in relation to him, the employer shall give the employee a written statement under section 1 not more than one month after that time.

NOTES

Derivation: 1972, s 6.

General Note: if the conditions in this section are fulfilled, the employer is not obliged to give a written statement under s 1 or a notice of any change under s 4. See also the notes to s 1. Note section 157.

Reasonably accessible: see the note to s 2 (3).

Definitions: 'employee' and 'employer': see note to s 1; 'contract of employment', and 'continuous employment': see s 153 (1).

6. Power of Secretary of State to require further particulars

The Secretary of State may by order provide that section 1 shall have effect as if such further particulars as may be specified in the order were included in the particulars to be included in a statement under that section, and, for that purpose, the order may include such provisions amending section 1(1), (2) and (3) as appear to the Secretary of State to be expedient.

NOTES

Derivation: 1972, s 7 (1), (2).

Orders under this section: none had been made at the time of going to press.

7. Power to vary number of weekly hours of employment necessary to qualify for rights

(1) The Secretary of State may by order provide that this Part and Schedule 13 shall have effect as if—

(*a*) for each of the references to sixteen hours in section 3 and in paragraphs 3 to 7 of Schedule 13 there were substituted a reference to such other number of hours less than sixteen as may be specified in the order; and

(*b*) as if for each of the references to eight hours in section 3 and in paragraphs 6 and 7 of Schedule 13 there were substituted a reference to such other number of hours less than eight as may be specified in the order.

(2) An order under subsection (1) shall not be made unless a draft of the order has been laid before Parliament and approved by resolution of each House.

NOTES

Derivation: 1972, s 10 (1), (4); 1975, Sched 16, Pt II, para 11.

General Note: note sections 149 and 157.

Orders under this section: none had been made at the time of going to press.

ITEMISED PAY STATEMENTS

8. Right to itemised pay statement

Every employee shall have the right to be given by his employer at or before the time at which any payment of wages or salary is made to him an itemised pay statement, in writing, containing the following particulars, that is to say—

(*a*) the gross amount of the wages or salary;

(*b*) the amounts of any variable and, subject to section 9, any fixed deductions from that gross amount and the purposes for which they are made;

(*c*) the net amount of wages or salary payable; and

(*d*) where different parts of the net amount are paid in different ways, the amount and method of payment of each part-payment.

NOTES

Derivation: 1975, s 81.

General Note: this section and ss 9 and 10 give the employee the right to an itemised pay statement, containing certain particulars, to be given to him by his employer at the time any payment of wages or salary is made to him.

Section 9 deals with the giving of a standing statement of fixed deductions; s 10 gives the Secretary of State power to amend ss 8 and 9; and s 11 provides the procedure for the employee to enforce his rights under these sections. Provision is also made for conciliation: see s 133 (1) (a) and (2) to (7). There is no minimum qualifying period before an employee is entitled to his rights under ss 8 to 10. Persons in Crown employment, and House of Commons staff, are not excluded (see ss 138 and 139). See also s 150 and Sched 12, Pt I, which make provision for the death of the employer or employee. Note sections 137, 149 and 157.

Exclusions:

(i) employment outside Great Britain (s 141 (2) and (5));
(ii) share fishermen (s 144 (2));
(iii) merchant seamen (s 144 (4) and (5));
(iv) employment by spouse (s 146 (1));
(v) employment in police service (s 146 (2) and (3));
(vi) part-timers (s 146 (4) to (7)).

Deductions: any deductions made will have to comply with the requirements of the Truck Acts 1831-1940.

Definitions: 'employee' and 'employer': see note to s 1.

9. Standing statement of fixed deductions

(1) A pay statement given in accordance with section 8 need not contain separate particulars of a fixed deduction if it contains instead an aggregate amount of fixed deductions, including that deduction, and the employer has given to the employee, at or before the time at which that pay statement is given, a standing statement of fixed deductions, in writing, which contains the following particulars of each deduction comprised in that aggregate amount, that is to say,—

(*a*) the amount of the deduction;

(*b*) the intervals at which the deduction is to be made; and

(*c*) the purpose for which it is made,

and which, in accordance with subsection (4), is effective at the date on which the pay statement is given.

(2) A standing statement of fixed deductions may be amended, whether by addition of a new deduction or by a change in the particulars or cancellation of an existing deduction, by notice in writing, containing particulars of the amendment, given by the employer to the employee.

(3) An employer who has given to an employee a standing statement of fixed deductions shall, within the period of twelve months beginning with the date on which the first standing statement was given and at intervals of not more than twelve months thereafter, re-issue it in a consolidated form incorporating any amendments notified in accordance with subsection (2).

(4) A standing statement of fixed deductions shall become effective, for the purposes of subsection (1), on the date on which it is given to the employee and shall cease to have effect on the expiration of the period of twelve months beginning with that date, or, where it is re-issued in accordance with subsection (3), the expiration of the period of twelve months beginning with the date on which it was last re-issued.

NOTES

Derivation: 1975, s 82.

Definitions: 'employee' and 'employer': see note to s 1.

10. Power to amend ss 8 and 9

The Secretary of State may by order—

(*a*) vary the provisions of sections 8 and 9 as to the particulars which must be included in a pay statement or a standing statement of fixed deductions by adding items to or removing items from the particulars listed in those sections or by amending any such particulars; and

(*b*) vary the provisions of section 9(3) and (4) so as to shorten or extend the periods of twelve months referred to in those subsections, or those periods as varied from time to time under this section.

NOTES

Derivation: 1975, s 83.

Orders under this section: none had been made at the time of going to press.

ENFORCEMENT OF RIGHTS UNDER PART I

11. References to industrial tribunals

(1) Where an employer does not give an employee a statement as required by section 1 or 4(1) or 8, the employee may require a reference to be made to an industrial tribunal to determine what particulars ought to have been included or referred to in a statement so as to comply with the requirements of the relevant section.

(2) Where—

(*a*) a statement purporting to be a statement under section 1 or 4(1), or

(*b*) a pay statement, or a standing statement of fixed deductions, purporting to comply with section 8 or 9(1),

has been given to an employee, and a question arises as to the particulars which ought to have been included or referred to in the statement so as to comply with the requirements of this Part, either the employer or the employee may require that question to be referred to and determined by an industrial tribunal.

(3) Where a statement under section 1 or 4(1) given by an employer to an employee contains such an indication as is mentioned in section 4(3), and

(*a*) any particulars purporting to be particulars of a change to which that indication relates are entered up or recorded in accordance with that indication, and

(*b*) a question arises as to the particulars which ought to have been so entered up or recorded,

either the employer or the employee may require that question to be referred to and determined by an industrial tribunal.

(4) In this section, a question as to the particulars which ought to have been included—

(*a*) in a pay statement, or in a standing statement of fixed deductions, does not include a question solely as to the accuracy of an amount stated in any such particulars;

(*b*) in a note under section 1(4), does not include any question whether the employment is, has been or will be contracted-out employment for the purposes of Part III of the Social Security Pensions Act 1975.

(5) Where, on a reference under subsection (1), an industrial tribunal determines particulars as being those which ought to have been included or referred to in a statement given under section 1 or 4(1) the employer shall be deemed to have given to the employee a statement in which those particulars were included, or referred to, as specified in the decision of the tribunal.

(6) On determining a reference under subsection (2)(*a*), an industrial tribunal may either confirm the particulars as included or referred to in the statement given by the employer, or may amend those particulars, or may substitute other particulars for them, as the tribunal may determine to be appropriate; and the statement shall be deemed to have been given by the employer to the employee in accordance with the decision of the tribunal.

(7) On determining a reference under subsection (3), an industrial tribunal may either confirm the particulars to which the reference relates, or may amend those particulars or may substitute other particulars for them, as the tribunal may determine to be appropriate; and particulars of the change to which the reference relates shall be deemed to have been entered up or recorded in accordance with the decision of the tribunal.

(8) Where on a reference under this section an industrial tribunal finds that an employer has failed to give an employee any pay statement in accordance with section 8 or that a pay statement or standing statement of fixed deductions does not, in relation to a deduction, contain the particulars required to be included in that statement by that section or section 9(1)—

(*a*) the tribunal shall make a declaration to that effect; and

(*b*) where the tribunal further finds that any unnotified deductions have been made from the pay of the employee during the period of thirteen weeks immediately preceding the date of the application for the reference (whether or not the deductions were made in breach of the contract of employment), the tribunal may order the employer to pay the employee a sum not exceeding the aggregate of the unnotified deductions so made.

In this subsection " unnotified deduction " means a deduction made without the employer giving the employee, in any pay statement or standing statement of fixed deductions, the particulars of that deduction required by section 8 or 9(1).

(9) An industrial tribunal shall not entertain a reference under this section in a case where the employment to which the reference relates has ceased unless an application requiring the reference to be made was made before the end of the period of three months beginning with the date on which the employment ceased.

NOTES

Derivation: 1972, s 8; 1975, s 84; Social Security Pensions Act 1975, s 30 (5).

Reference: a reference to an industrial tribunal is to be made in accordance with regulations under s 128 and Sched 9. See also the provisions for conciliation in s 133 (1) (a) and (2) to (7) in relation to references under s 8. So far as itemised pay statements are concerned, the tribunal may order the employer to repay unnotified deductions made from the pay of the employee during the thirteen weeks before his application for the reference: see subs (8) (b). Otherwise, in the case of both written statements given under ss 1 and 4, and itemised pay statements, if there is no statement, or the statement is defective, the tribunal determines what the statement ought to have said and the employer is deemed to have complied with that determination. If the employer fails to comply, presumably the employee would sue him for breach of contract in the ordinary courts, at least until s 131 is brought into effect. There is no decided case on this point, however. The recent case of *Construction Industry Training Board* v *Leighton* [1978] ICR577 shows the limitations of this section. See also *Owens* v *Multilux Ltd* [1974] IRLR 113 and *Cuthbertson* v *AML Distributors Ltd* [1975] IRLR 228.

Appeals: These lie to the Employment Appeal Tribunal, and thence to the Court of Appeal: see ss 135 and 136.

Definitions: 'employee' and 'employer': see note to s 1; 'employment': see s 153 (1); 'unnotified deduction': note subs (8) (b).

PART II

RIGHTS ARISING IN COURSE OF EMPLOYMENT

Guarantee payments

12. Right to guarantee payment

(1) Where an employee throughout a day during any part of which he would normally be required to work in accordance with his contract of employment is not provided with work by his employer by reason of—

(*a*) a diminution in the requirements of the employer's business for work of the kind which the employee is employed to do, or

(*b*) any other occurrence affecting the normal working of the employer's business in relation to work of the kind which the employee is employed to do,

he shall, subject to the following provisions of this Act, be entitled to be paid by his employer a payment, referred to in this Act as a guarantee payment, in respect of that day, and in this section and sections 13 and 16—

(i) such a day is referred to as a " workless day ", and

(ii) " workless period " has a corresponding meaning.

(2) In this section and sections 13 to 17, " day " means the period of twenty-four hours from midnight to midnight, and where a period of employment begun on any day extends over midnight into the following day, or would normally so extend, then—

(*a*) if the employment before midnight is, or would normally be, of longer duration than that after midnight, that period of employment shall be treated as falling wholly on the first day; and

(*b*) in any other case, that period of employment shall be treated as falling wholly on the second day.

Notes

Derivation: 1975, s 22 (1), (2).

General Note: this section and ss 13 to 18 cover the employee's right to a guarantee payment in respect of a 'workless day'. Section 13 contains general exclusions

from the right; s 14 provides the method of calculating a guarantee payment; s 15 imposes limits on the amount of and entitlement to a guarantee payment; s 16 contains supplementary provisions; s 17 provides the remedy for a failure to pay a guarantee payment; s 18 deals with exemption orders. See also ss 121 and 122 which confer priority on debts owed in respect of guarantee payments by employers on insolvency and give employees the right to be paid such debts out of the Redundancy Fund, s 132 which makes provision for the recoupment of certain benefits, s 133 (1) (*a*) and (2) to (7) which make provision for conciliation, and s 150 and Sched 12, which make provision for the death of the employer or the employee. Persons in Crown employment and House of Commons staff are not excluded (see ss 138 and 139).
Note sections 137, 140 (2)(*a*), 149 and 157.

Exclusions:

(i) employee with no normal working hours on workless day (s 14 (1));
(ii) employment outside Great Britain (s 141 (2) and (5));
(iii) employees continuously employed for less than four weeks (s 143 (1));
(iv) employment under a fixed-term contract of twelve weeks or less, unless the employee has been continuously employed for more than twelve weeks (s 143 (3) (*a*) and (4));
(v) temporary employment where the task is not expected to last more than twelve weeks, and the employee has not been continuously employed for twelve weeks (s 143 (3) (*b*) and (4));
(vi) share fishermen (s 144 (2));
(vii) registered dock workers, except when wholly or mainly engaged in work which is not dock work (s 145 (2) and (5));
(viii) employment by spouse (s 146 (1));
(ix) employment in police service (s 146 (2) and (3)).

See also the general exclusions in section 13.

Subsection (1): Industrial tribunal decisions on this subsection are: *Robinson* v *Claxton and Garland* (*Teesside*) *Ltd* [1977] IRLR 159; *Clemens* v *Peter Richards Ltd, t/a John Bryan* [1977] IRLR 332; *Daley* v *Strathclyde Regional Council* [1977] IRLR 414; *North* v *Pavleigh Ltd* [1977] IRLR 461; and *York and Reynolds* v *Colledge Hosiery Ltd* [1978] IRLR 53. The theme which runs through them all is that it is necessary to determine what are the terms (express, implied or customary) of the employee's contract. Note that subs (1) does not apply to a failure to provide work in consequence of a trade dispute involving any employee of the employer or an associated employer: see s 13 (1). The only reported EAT case is *Mailway* (*Southern*) *Ltd* v *Willsher* [1978] ICR 511.

Subsection (1) (*a*): see *North* v *Pavleigh Ltd* [1977] IRLR 461, where it was held that employees laid off because of a Jewish holiday were not entitled to guarantee payments, since the reason for the lay-off was not a dimunition in the requirements of the employer's business.

Subsection (1) (*b*): see *North* v *Pavleigh Ltd* [1977] IRLR 461, where it was held that a Jewish holiday which causes a lay-off is not an 'occurrence' and that the word must be given a more restricted meaning; restricted to cases 'such as power failures which directly affect the working of the factory'.

Subsection (2): the meaning of the word 'day' in this subsection has been considered in *Trevethan* v *Sterling Metals Ltd* [1977] IRLR 416, where it was held that an employee who started work at 8 pm on Monday and finished at 6.30 am on Friday normally worked four days in a week, not five. Note the Secretary of State's power to modify and adapt the provisions of this subsection: see s 16 (4).

Definitions: 'employee' and 'employer': see note to s 1; 'workless day', 'workless period': see subs (1); 'day': see note above and note subs (2); 'contract of employment' and 'business': see s 153 (1).

13. General exclusions from right under s 12

(1) An employee shall not be entitled to a guarantee payment in respect of a workless day if the failure to provide him with work occurs in consequence of a trade dispute involving any employee of his employer or of an associated employer.

(2) An employee shall not be entitled to a guarantee payment in respect of a workless day if—

(*a*) his employer has offered to provide alternative work for that day which is suitable in all the circumstances whether or not work which the employee is under his contract employed to perform, and the employee has unreasonably refused that offer; or

(*b*) he does not comply with reasonable requirements imposed by his employer with a view to ensuring that his services are available.

NOTES

Derivation: 1975, s 23.

Subsection (1): see *Thompson* v *Priest* (*Lindley*) *Ltd* [1978] IRLR 99, where it was held, in effect, that the trade dispute does not have to be the only cause of the lay-off, if it can be said to be the immediate cause.

Subsection (2) (*a*): see *Purdy* v *Willowbrook International Ltd* [1977] IRLR 388, where work outside the employee's own particular trade, which demanded an equivalent type and level of practical skill, and upon which he had been engaged for a period of some five months previously, was held to be suitable. It was pointed out, *obiter*, in *North* v *Pavleigh Ltd* [1977] IRLR 461 that 'alternative work for that day' means 'work to be performed on that day but of a different nature from the employee's contractual work', not contractual work performed on different days.

Subsection (2) (*b*): for an example of a reasonable requirement see *Meadows* v *Faithful Overalls Ltd* [1977] IRLR 330.

Definitions: 'employee' and 'employer': see note to s 1; 'guarantee payment', 'workless day': see s 12 (1); for 'day', see s 12 (2); 'trade dispute': see s 153 (1); for 'associated employer', see s 153 (4).

14. Calculation of guarantee payment

(1) Subject to the limits set by section 15, the amount of a guarantee payment payable to an employee in respect of any day shall be the sum produced by multiplying the number of normal working hours on that day by the guaranteed hourly rate, and, accordingly, no guarantee payment shall be payable to an employee in whose case there are no normal working hours on the day in question.

(2) Subject to subsection (3), the guaranteed hourly rate in relation to an employee shall be the amount of one week's pay divided by—

(*a*) the number of normal working hours in a week for that employee when employed under the contract of employment in force on the day in respect of which the guarantee payment is payable; or

(*b*) where the number of such normal working hours differs from week to week or over a longer period, the average number of such hours calculated by dividing by twelve the total number of the employee's normal working hours during the period of twelve weeks ending with the last complete week before the day in respect of which the guarantee payment is payable; or (*c*) in a case falling within paragraph (*b*) but where the employee has not been employed for a sufficient period to enable the calculation to be made under that paragraph, a number which fairly represents the number of normal working hours in a week having regard to such of the following considerations as are appropriate in the circumstances, that is to say,—

(i) the average number of normal working hours in a week which the employee could expect in accordance with the terms of his contract;

(ii) the average number of such hours of other employees engaged in relevant comparable employment with the same employer.

(3) If in any case an employee's contract has been varied, or a new contract has been entered into, in connection with a period of short-time working, subsection (2) shall have effect as if for the reference to the day in respect of which the guarantee payment is payable there was substituted a reference to the last day on which the original contract was in force.

NOTES

Derivation: 1975, s 24 (1), (2), (4).

Normal working hours and week's pay: see s 152 and Sched 14, and the cases cited there. Note Sched 14, para 7 (1) (*a*).

Modifications and adaptations: note the Secretary of State's power to modify and adapt the provisions of this section (see s 16 (4)).

Definitions: 'employee' and 'employer': see note to s 1; 'normal working hours' and 'week's pay': see above; 'guaranteed hourly rate': see subsection (2); 'week': see s 153 (1); 'guarantee payment': see s 12 (1); 'contract of employment' and 'employment': see s 153 (1).

15. Limits on amount of and entitlement to guarantee payment

(1) The amount of a guarantee payment payable to an employee in respect of any day shall not exceed £6·60.

(2) An employee shall not be entitled to guarantee payments in respect of more than the specified number of days in any one of the relevant periods, that is to say, the periods of three months commencing on 1st February, 1st May, 1st August and 1st November in each year.

(3) The specified number of days for the purposes of subsection (2) shall be, subject to subsection (4),—

(*a*) the number of days, not exceeding five, on which the employee normally works in a week under the contract of employment in force on the day in respect of which the guarantee payment is claimed; or

(*b*) where that number of days varies from week to week or over a longer period, the average number of such days, not exceeding five, calculated by dividing by twelve the total number of such days during the period of twelve weeks ending with the last complete week before the day in respect of which the guarantee payment is claimed, and rounding up the resulting figure to the next whole number; or

(*c*) in a case falling within paragraph (*b*) but where the employee has not been employed for a sufficient period to enable the calculation to be made under that paragraph, a nnmber which fairly represents the number of the employee's normal working days in a week, not exceeding five, having regard to such of the following considerations as are appropriate in the circumstances, that is to say,—

(i) the average number of normal working days in a week which the employee could expect in accordance with the terms of his contract;

(ii) the average number of such days of other employees engaged in relevant comparable employment with the same employer.

(4) If in any case an employee's contract has been varied, or a new contract has been entered into, in connection with a period of short-time working, subsection (3) shall have effect as if for the references to the day in respect of which the guarantee payment is claimed there were substituted references to the last day on which the original contract was in force.

(5) The Secretary of State may vary any of the limits referred to in this section, and may in particular vary the relevant periods referred to in subsection (2), after a review under section 148, by order made in accordance with that section.

NOTES

Derivation: 1975, s 25; 1977 Order (No 2) Art 2.

General Note: The Secretary of State has power to vary the limits referred to in this section (see subs (5)) and the duty to review the limits annually (see s 148).

Subsection (3): note the Secretary of State's power to modify and adapt the provisions of this subsection (see s 16 (4)).

Definitions: 'employee' and 'employer': see note to s 1; 'guarantee payment': see s 12 (1); 'relevant periods': see subs (2); 'contract of employment' and 'week': see s 153 (1).

16. Supplementary provisions relating to guarantee payments

(1) Subject to subsection (2), a right to a guarantee payment shall not affect any right of an employee in relation to remuneration under his contract of employment (in this section referred to as " contractual remuneration ").

(2) Any contractual remuneration paid to an employee in respect of a workless day shall go towards discharging any liability of the employer to pay a guarantee payment in respect of that day, and conversely any guarantee payment paid in respect of a day shall go towards discharging any liability of the employer to pay contractual remuneration in respect of that day.

(3) For the purposes of subsection (2), contractual remuneration shall be treated as paid in respect of a workless day—

(*a*) where it is expressed to be calculated or payable by reference to that day or any part of that day, to the extent that it is so expressed; and

(*b*) in any other case, to the extent that it represents guaranteed remuneration, rather than remuneration for work actually done, and is referable to that day when apportioned rateably between that day and any other workless period falling within the period in respect of which the remuneration is paid.

(4) The Secretary of State may by order provide that in relation to any description of employees the provisions of sections 12(2), 14 and 15(3) (as originally enacted or as varied under section 15(5)) and of subsections (1) to (3), and, so far as they apply for the purposes of those provisions, the provisions of Schedule 14 shall have effect subject to such modifications and adaptations as may be prescribed by the order.

NOTES

Derivation: 1975, s 26.

Subsections (1) *to* (3): note the Secretary of State's power to modify and adapt these provisions (see s 16 (4)).

Definitions: 'employee' and 'employer'; see note to s 1; 'contract of employment': see s 153 (1); 'guarantee payment', 'workless day', and 'workless period': see s 12 (1); 'day': see s 12 (2); 'contractual remuneration': see subs (1).

Orders under this section: none had been made at the time of going to press.

17. Complaint to industrial tribunal

(1) An employee may present a complaint to an industrial tribunal that his employer has failed to pay the whole or any part of a guarantee payment to which the employee is entitled.

(2) An industrial tribunal shall not entertain a complaint relating to a guarantee payment in respect of any day unless the complaint is presented to the tribunal before the end of the period of three months beginning with that day or within such further period as the tribunal considers reasonable in a case where it is satisfied that it was not reasonably practicable for the complaint to be presented within the period of three months.

(3) Where an industrial tribunal finds a complaint under subsection (1) well-founded, the tribunal shall order the employer to pay the complainant the amount of guarantee payment which it finds is due to him.

NOTES

Derivation: 1975, s 27.

Complaint: a complaint to an industrial tribunal is to be made in accordance with regulations under s 128 and Sched 9. See also the provisions for conciliation in s 133 (1) (*a*) and (2) to (7).

Appeals: these lie to the Employment Appeal Tribunal, and thence to the Court of Appeal: see ss 135 and 136.

Reasonable . . . reasonably practicable . . . : see the note to s 67 (2).

Definitions: 'employee' and 'employer': see note to s 1; 'guarantee payment': see s 12 (1); 'day': see s 12 (2).

18. Exemption orders

(1) If at any time there is in force a collective agreement, or a wages order, whereby employees to whom the agreement or order relates have a right to guaranteed remuneration and on the application of all the parties to the agreement or, as the case may be, of the council or Board making the order, the appropriate Minister, having regard to the provisions of the agreement or order, is satisfied that section 12 should not apply to those employees, he may make an order under this section excluding those employees from the operation of that section.

(2) In subsection (1), a wages order means an order made under any of the following provisions, that is to say—

(*a*) section 11 of the Wages Councils Act 1959;
(*b*) section 3 of the Agricultural Wages Act 1948;
(*c*) section 3 of the Agricultural Wages (Scotland) Act 1949.

(3) In subsection (1), " the appropriate Minister " means—

(*a*) as respects a collective agreement or such an order as is referred to in subsection (2)(*a*) or (*c*), the Secretary of State;
(*b*) as respects such an order as is referred to in subsection (2)(*b*), the Minister of Agriculture, Fisheries and Food.

(4) The Secretary of State shall not make an order under this section in respect of an agreement unless—

(*a*) the agreement provides for procedures to be followed (whether by arbitration or otherwise) in cases where an employee claims that his employer has failed to pay the whole or any part of any guaranteed remuneration to which the employee is entitled under the agreement, and that those procedures include a right to arbitration or adjudication by an independent referee or body in cases where (by reason of an equality of votes or otherwise) a decision cannot otherwise be reached; or
(*b*) the agreement indicates that an employee to whom the agreement relates may present a complaint to an industrial tribunal that his employer has failed to pay the whole or any part of any guaranteed remuneration to which the employee is entitled under the agreement;

and where an order under this section is in force in respect of such an agreement as is described in paragraph (*b*) an industrial tribunal shall have jurisdiction over such a complaint as if it were a complaint falling within section 17.

(5) Without prejudice to section 154(4), an order under this section may be varied or revoked by a subsequent order thereunder, whether in pursuance of an application made by all or any of the parties to the agreement in question, or, as the case may be, by the council or Board which made the order in question, or without any such application.

NOTES

Derivation: 1975, s 28.

General Note: note the provisions of ss 140 (2) (*a*) and 154.

Complaint: see note to s 17.

Definitions: 'employee' and 'employer': see the note to s 1; 'collective agreement': see s 153 (1); 'wages order': see subs (2); 'appropriate Minister': see subs (3).

Orders under this section: at the time of going to press, eighteen orders had been made under s 28 of the 1975 Act (the predecessor of this section): see SI 1977 Nos 156, 157, 158, 208, 902, 1096, 1158, 1322, 1349, 1522, 1523, 1583, 1601, 2032 and SI 1978 Nos 153, 429, 737 and 826.

SUSPENSION FROM WORK ON MEDICAL GROUNDS

19. Right to remuneration on suspension on medical grounds

(1) An employee who is suspended from work by his employer on medical grounds in consequence of—

(*a*) any requirement imposed by or under any provision of any enactment or of any instrument made under any enactment, or

(*b*) any recommendation in any provision of a code of practice issued or approved under section 16 of the Health and Safety at Work etc. Act 1974,

which is a provision for the time being specified in Schedule 1 shall, subject to the following provisions of this Act, be entitled to be paid by his employer remuneration while he is so suspended for a period not exceeding twenty-six weeks.

(2) For the purposes of this section and sections 20 to 22 and 61, an employee shall be regarded as suspended from work only if, and so long as, he continues to be employed by his employer, but is not provided with work or does not perform the work he normally performed before the suspension.

(3) The Secretary of State may by order add provisions to or remove provisions from the list of specified provisions in Schedule 1.

NOTES

Derivation: 1975, s 29 (1) to (3).

General Note: this section and ss 20 to 22 give the employee the right to remuneration when suspended from work on 'medical grounds'. Section 20 contains general exclusions from the right; s 21 provides the method of calculating the remuneration; s 22 provides the remedy for failure to pay remuneration. See also s 121, which gives priority to debts owed in respect of such remuneration by employers on insolvency; s 122, which gives the employee the right to be paid such debts out of the Redundancy Fund; s 132 which makes provision for the recoupment of certain benefits; s 133 (1) (*a*) and (2) to (7), which make provision for conciliation, and s 150 and Sched 12, Pt I, which make provision for the death of the employer or the employee. Persons in Crown employment and House of Commons staff are not excluded from these provisions (see ss 138 and 139). Section 61 (2) deals with the situation where a replacement for a suspended employee is dismissed. Given the exclusion contained in s 20 (1), it seems unlikely that the provisions will be particularly wide in their coverage. Note also ss 137, 149 and 157.

Exclusions:

(i) employee incapable of work by reason of disease or bodily or mental disablement (s 20 (1));
(ii) employment outside Great Britain (s 141 (2) and (5));
(iii) employee continuously employed for a period of less than four weeks ending with the last complete week before the day on which the suspension begins (s 143 (2));
(iv) employment under a fixed-term contract of twelve weeks or less, unless the employee has been continuously employed for more than twelve weeks (s 143 (3) (*a*) and (4));
(v) temporary employment where the task is not expected to last more than twelve weeks, and the employee has not been continuously employed for twelve weeks (s 143 (3) (*b*) and (4));
(vi) share fishermen (s 144 (2));
(vii) registered dock workers, except when wholly or mainly employed in work which is not dock work (s 145 (2) and (5));
(viii) employment by spouse (s 146 (1));
(ix) employment in police service (s 146 (2) and (3)).

Note also the exclusions in section 20 (2).

Employee, Employer: see note to s 1.

Suspended from work ....: this section does not confer any right on the employer to suspend on medical grounds. The employer's power of suspension depends upon the contract of employment.

Subsection (1): note the provisions of s 64 (2) in relation to dismissals.

Orders under this section: see the Employment Protection (Medical Suspension) Order 1976 (SI 1976 No 659).

20. General exclusions from right under s 19

(1) An employee shall not be entitled to remuneration under section 19 in respect of any period during which he is incapable of work by reason of disease or bodily or mental disablement.

(2) An employee shall not be entitled to remuneration under section 19 in respect of any period during which—

(*a*) his employer has offered to provide him with suitable alternative work, whether or not work which the employee is under his contract, or was under the contract in force before the suspension, employed to perform, and the employee has unreasonably refused to perform that work; or

(*b*) he does not comply with reasonable requirements imposed by his employer with a view to ensuring that his services are available.

NOTES

Derivation: 1975, s 30 (2), (3).

Subsection (2): see the note to s 13 (2), but note the differences in wording between the two subsections.

Definitions: 'employee' and 'employer': see note to s 1; 'suspension': see s 19(2).

21. Calculation of remuneration

(1) The amount of remuneration payable by an employer to an employee under section 19 shall be a week's pay in respect of each week of the period of suspension referred to in subsection (1) of that section, and if in any week remuneration is payable in respect only of part of that week the amount of a week's pay shall be reduced proportionately.

(2) Subject to subsection (3), a right to remuneration under section 19 shall not affect any right of an employee in relation to remuneration under his contract of employment (in this section referred to as " contractual remuneration ").

(3) Any contractual remuneration paid by an employer to an employee in respect of any period shall go towards discharging the employer's liability under section 19 in respect of that period, and conversely any payment of remuneration in discharge of an employer's liability under section 19 in respect of any period shall go towards discharging any obligation of the employer to pay contractual remuneration in respect of that period.

NOTES

Derivation: 1975, s 31 (1), (3), (4).

Week's pay: see s 152 and Sched 14, Pt II and the cases cited there. Note Sched 14, para 7 (1) (*b*).

Definitions: 'employee' and 'employer': see the note to s 1; 'suspension': see s 19 (2); 'contract of employment' and 'week': see s 153 (1); 'contractual remuneration': see subs (2).

22. Complaint to industrial tribunal

(1) An employee may present a complaint to an industrial tribunal that his employer has failed to pay the whole or any part of remuneration to which the employee is entitled under section 19.

(2) An industrial tribunal shall not entertain a complaint relating to remuneration under section 19 in respect of any day unless the complaint is presented to the tribunal before the end of the period of three months beginning with that day, or within such further period as the tribunal considers reasonable in a case where it is satisfied that it was not reasonably practicable for the complaint to be presented within the period of three months.

(3) Where an industrial tribunal finds a complaint under subsection (1) well-founded the tribunal shall order the employer to pay the complainant the amount of remuneration which it finds is due to him.

NOTES

Derivation: 1975, s 32.

Complaint: a complaint to an industrial tribunal is to be made in accordance with regulations under s 128 and Sched 9. See also the provisions for conciliation in ss 133 (1) (*a*) and (2) to (7).

Appeals: these lie to the Employment Appeal Tribunal, and thence to the Court of Appeal: see ss 135 and 136.

Reasonable . . . reasonably practicable . . . : see the note to s 67 (2).

Definitions: 'employee' and 'employer': see note to s 1.

TRADE UNION MEMBERSHIP AND ACTIVITIES

23. Trade union membership and activities

(1) Subject to the following provisions of this section, every employee shall have the right not to have action (short of dismissal) taken against him as an individual by his employer for the purpose of—

(*a*) preventing or deterring him from being or seeking to become a member of an independent trade union, or penalising him for doing so; or

(*b*) preventing or deterring him from taking part in the activities of an independent trade union at any appropriate time, or penalising him for doing so; or

(*c*) compelling him to be or become a member of a trade union which is not independent.

(2) In this section " appropriate time ", in relation to an employee taking part in any activities of a trade union, means time which either—

(*a*) is outside his working hours, or

(*b*) is a time within his working hours at which, in accordance with arrangements agreed with, or consent given by his employer, it is permissible for him to take part in those activities;

and in this subsection " working hours ", in relation to an employee, means any time when, in accordance with his contract of employment, he is required to be at work.

(3) The provisions of subsection (4) shall have effect in relation to an employee—

(*a*) of the same class as employees for whom it is the practice in accordance with a union membership agreement to belong to a specified independent trade union or to one of a number of specified independent trade unions; or

(*b*) not of the same class as described in paragraph (*a*) but of the same grade or category as such employees as are referred to in that paragraph.

(4) In relation to such an employee the right conferred by subsection (1)(*b*) in relation to the activities of an independent trade union shall extend to activities on the employer's premises only if that union is a specified union.

(5) For the purposes of this section a trade union—

(*a*) shall be taken to be specified for the purposes of, or in relation to, a union membership agreement if it is specified in the agreement or is accepted by the parties to the agreement as being the equivalent of a union so specified; and

(*b*) shall also be treated as so specified if—

(i) the Advisory, Conciliation and Arbitration Service has made a recommendation for recognition of that union covering the employee in question which is operative within the meaning of section 15 of the Employment Protection Act 1975; or

(ii) the union has referred a recognition issue covering that employee to the Advisory, Conciliation and Arbitration Service under section 11 of the said Act of 1975 and the Service has not declined to proceed on the reference under section 12 of that Act, the union has not withdrawn the reference, or from the reference, and the issue has not been settled or reported on under that section.

(6) An employee who genuinely objects on grounds of religious belief to being a member of any trade union whatsoever shall have the right not to have action (short of dismissal) taken against him by his employer for the purpose of compelling him to belong to a trade union.

(7) In this section, unless the context otherwise requires, references to a trade union include references to a branch or section of a trade union.

Notes

Derivation: 1975, s 53.

General Note: this provision is complementary to s 58, and the cumulative effect of the two provisions is that an employee may neither be discriminated against in his employment, nor dismissed from it, for (a) being or seeking to become a member of an independent trade union, (b) taking part in its activities, or (c) refusing to become a member of a non-independent trade union, without a contravention of the Act. Employees who genuinely object on grounds of religious belief to being a member of any trade union whatsoever are, however, protected. It is interesting to note that the only sanction provided for an infringement by an employer of the employee's rights under this section is an order of compensation; the tribunal has no jurisdiction to order the employer to desist.

Section 23 defines the right; s 24 provides the remedy for infringement of the right; s 25 contains provisions supplementary to those of s 24; and s 26 provides the method of assessing the compensation awarded on a complaint under s 24. There is no minimum qualifying period for the rights under these sections, nor are part-timers excluded. See s 132 which makes provision for the recoupment of certain benefits, s 133 (1) (*a*) and (2) to (7), which make provision for conciliation and s 150 and Sched 12, Pt I, which make provision for the death of the employer or the employee. Persons in Crown employment and House of Commons staff are not excluded from these provisions (see ss 138 and 139). Note sections 137, 140 (2) (*b*) (i), 149 and 157.

Exclusions:

(i) employment outside Great Britain (s 141 (2) and (5));
(ii) share fishermen (s 144 (2));
(iii) employment by spouse (s 146 (1));
(iv) employment in police service (s 146 (2) and (3)).

Employee, Employer: see note to s 1.

Action: the EAT doubted, *obiter*, in *Brassington* v *Cauldon Wholesale Ltd* [1978] ICR 405 whether 'action' could consist of a threat.

Appropriate time: see subs (2); *PO* v *Crouch* [1974] ICR 378; *Robb* v *Leon Motor Services Ltd* [1978] ICR 506; and *The Marley Tile Co Ltd* v *Shaw* [1978] IRLR 238.

Union membership agreement: see s 153 (1); *Sarvent* v *Central Electricity Generating Board* [1976] IRLR 66; *Home Counties Dairies Ltd* v *Woods* [1977] ICR 463; *Gayle* v *John Wilkinson & Sons (Saltley) and TGWU* [1978] ICR 154; and *Jeffrey* v *Laurence Scott & Electromotors Ltd* [1977] IRLR 466. Reference may also be made to the notes on s 58.

Subsection (6): for recent cases on objections on religious grounds, see the note to s 58 (3).

Definitions: 'employee', 'employer', 'appropriate time' and 'union membership agreement': see above; for 'action', 'contract of employment' and 'independent trade union': see s 153 (1); 'specified trade union': note subs (5); 'trade union': see s 153 (1); 'recognition issue': see s 11 (3) of the Employment Protection Act 1975; 'the Advisory, Conciliation and Arbitration Service': see s 1 (1) of the Employment Protection Act 1975.

24. Complaint to industrial tribunal

(1) An employee may present a complaint to an industrial tribunal on the ground that action has been taken against him by his employer in contravention of section 23.

(2) An industrial tribunal shall not entertain a complaint under subsection (1) unless it is presented to the tribunal before the end of the period of three months beginning with the date on which there occurred the action complained of, or where that action is part of a series of similar actions, the last of those actions, or within such further period as the tribunal considers reasonable in a case where it is satisfied that it was not reasonably practicable for the complaint to be presented within the period of three months.

(3) Where the tribunal finds the complaint well-founded it shall make a declaration to that effect and may make an award of compensation, calculated in accordance with section 26, to be paid by the employer to the employee in respect of the action complained of.

NOTES

Derivation: 1975, s 54.

Complaint: a complaint to an industrial tribunal is to be made in accordance with regulations under s 128 and Sched 9. See also the provisions for conciliation in ss 133 (1) (*a*) and (2) to (7). Note Sched 9, para 2.

Appeals: these lie to the Employment Appeal Tribunal, and thence to the Court of Appeal: see ss 135 and 136.

Reasonable . . . reasonably practicable . . . : see the note to s 67 (2).

Compensation: see s 26 for the provisions on assessing compensation.

Definitions: 'employee' and 'employer': see the note to s 1.

25. Supplementary provisions relating to complaints under s 24

(1) On a complaint under section 24 it shall be for the employer to show—

(*a*) the purpose for which action was taken against the complainant; and

(*b*) that the purpose was not such a purpose as is referred to in section 23(1)(*a*) to (*c*) or (6).

(2) In determining on a complaint under section 24, any question as to whether action was taken by the complainant's employer or the purpose for which it was taken, no account shall be taken of any pressure which, by calling, organising, procuring or financing a strike or other industrial action, or threatening to do so, was exercised on the employer to take the action complained of, and that question shall be determined as if no such pressure had been exercised.

NOTES

Derivation: 1975, s 55 (1), (2).

It shall be for the employer to show . . . : the employee will first have to show that discriminatory action was taken against him, and then the burden will pass to the employer. If he fails to discharge it under subs (1), the employee's complaint will succeed.

Employer: see note to s 1.

Subsection (2): note similar provisions in s 63 in relation to unfair dismissal.

26. Assessment of compensation on a complaint under s 24

(1) The amount of the compensation awarded by a tribunal on a complaint under section 24 shall be such amount as the tribunal considers just and equitable in all the circumstances having regard to the infringement of the complainant's right under section 23 by the employer's action complained of and to any loss sustained by the complainant which is attributable to that action.

(2) The said loss shall be taken to include—

(*a*) any expenses reasonably incurred by the complainant in consequence of the action complained of, and

(*b*) loss of any benefit which he might reasonably be expected to have had but for that action.

(3) In ascertaining the said loss the tribunal shall apply the same rule concerning the duty of a person to mitigate his loss as applies to damages recoverable under the common law of England and Wales or of Scotland, as the case may be.

(4) In determining the amount of compensation to be awarded under subsection (1), no account shall be taken of any pressure as is referred to in section 25(2), and that question shall be determined as if no such pressure had been exercised.

(5) Where the tribunal finds that the action complained of was to any extent caused or contributed to by any action of the complainant it shall reduce the amount of the compensation by such proportion as it considers just and equitable having regard to that finding.

NOTES

Derivation: 1975, s 56.

Subsection (1): in *Brassington* v *Cauldon Wholesale Ltd* [1978] ICR 405, the EAT said that the object of s 23 to 26 is to compensate an employee for the injury sustained as a result of the infringement of his rights, not to impose a fine on the employer.

Subsection (4): cf s 63, which deals with pressure exercised on the employer to dismiss unfairly, and the cases cited there.

Subsection (5): see the notes to ss 73 (7) and 74 (6) and the cases cited there.

Definitions: 'employer': see note to s 1; 'action'; see s 153 (1) and note to s 23.

TIME OFF WORK

27. Time off for carrying out trade union duties

(1) An employer shall permit an employee of his who is an official of an independent trade union recognised by him to take time off, subject to and in accordance with subsection (2), during the employee's working hours for the purpose of enabling him—

(*a*) to carry out those duties of his as such an official which are concerned with industrial relations between his employer and any associated employer, and their employees; or

(*b*) to undergo training in aspects of industrial relations which is—

(i) relevant to the carrying out of those duties; and

(ii) approved by the Trades Union Congress or by the independent trade union of which he is an official.

(2) The amount of time off which an employee is to be permitted to take under this section and the purposes for which, the occasions on which and any conditions subject to which time off may be so taken are those that are reasonable in all the circumstances having regard to any relevant provisions of a Code of Practice issued by the Advisory, Conciliation and Arbitration Service under section 6 of the Employment Protection Act 1975.

(3) An employer who permits an employee to take time off under this section for any purpose shall, subject to the following provisions of this section, pay him for the time taken off for that purpose in accordance with the permission—

(*a*) where the employee's remuneration for the work he would ordinarily have been doing during that time does not vary with the amount of work done, as if he had worked at that work for the whole of that time;

(*b*) where the employee's remuneration for that work varies with the amount of work done, an amount calculated by reference to the average hourly earnings for that work.

(4) The average hourly earnings referred to in subsection (3)(*b*) shall be the average hourly earnings of the employee concerned or, if no fair estimate can be made of those earnings, the average hourly earnings for

work of that description of persons in comparable employment with the same employer or, if there are no such persons, a figure of average hourly earnings which is reasonable in the circumstances.

(5) Subject to subsection (6), a right to be paid any amount under subsection (3) shall not affect any right of an employee in relation to remuneration under his contract of employment (in this section referred to as " contractual remuneration ").

(6) Any contractual remuneration paid to an employee in respect of a period of time off to which subsection (1) applies shall go towards discharging any liability of the employer under subsection (3) in respect of that period, and conversely any payment of any amount under subsection (3) in respect of a period shall go towards discharging any liability of the employer to pay contractual remuneration in respect of that period.

(7) An employee who is an official of an independent trade union recognised by his employer may present a complaint to an industrial tribunal that his employer has failed to permit him to take time off as required by this section or to pay him the whole or part of any amount so required to be paid.

NOTES

Derivation: 1975, s 57 (1), (2), (4) to (8).

General Note: s 27 gives certain trade union officials the right to take time off for carrying out trade union duties; s 28 gives the members of 'appropriate trade unions' the right to take time off for trade union activities; s 29 gives employees the right to take time off for certain public duties; s 30 provides the remedy for an infringement of these rights.

See s 121 which gives priority to payments owed under s 27 (3) by an employer on insolvency, and s 122 which gives employees the right to be paid such debts out of the Redundancy Fund; see also s 132 which makes provision for the recoupment of certain benefits, s 133 (1) (*a*) and (2) to (7), which make provision for conciliation, and s 150 and Sched 12 Pt I, which make provision for the death of the employer or the employee. Note sections 137, 149 and 157.

There is no minimum qualifying period for the rights under ss 27 to 29, but certain part-timers are excluded (see s 146 (4) and (5) to (7)). Persons in Crown Employment and House of Commons staff are not excluded (see ss 138 and 139).

It is interesting to note that the only sanction for an employer's infringement of these sections (as of s 23 above) is financial.

Exclusions:

(i) employment outside Great Britain (s 141 (2) and (5));

(ii) share fishermen (s 144 (2));

(iii) (sections 29 and 31 only) merchant seamen (s 144 (4) and (5));

(iv) (section 31 only) registered dock workers, except when wholly or mainly employed in work which is not dock work (see s 145 (2) and (5));

(v) employment by spouse (s 146 (1));

(vi) employment in police service (s 146 (2) and (3));

(vii) (sections 27 to 29 only) certain part-timers (s 146 (4) to (7)).

Employee, Employer: see note to s 1.

Subsection (2): see also s 29 (4).

Code of Practice: see Code of Practice on Time Off for Trade Union Duties and Activities, prepared by the Advisory, Conciliation and Arbitration Service.

Complaint: see, further, s 30.

Definitions: 'employee' and 'employer': see above; 'official': see s 153 (1); 'independent trade union': see s 153 (1); 'recognised': see s 32; 'working hours': see s 32 (1) (*b*); 'associated employer': see s 153 (4); 'the Advisory, Conciliation and Arbitration Service': see s 1 (1) of the Employment Protection Act 1975; 'trade union': see s 153 (1); 'contractual remuneration': see subs (5).

28. Time off for trade union activities

(1) An employer shall permit an employee of his who is a member of an appropriate trade union to take time off, subject to and in accordance with subsection (3), during the employee's working hours for the purpose of taking part in any trade union activity to which this section applies.

(2) In this section " appropriate trade union ", in relation to an employee of any description, means an independent trade union which is recognised by his employer in respect of that description of employee, and the trade union activities to which this section applies are—

(*a*) any activities of an appropriate trade union of which the employee is a member; and

(*b*) any activities, whether or not falling within paragraph (*a*), in relation to which the employee is acting as a representative of such a union,

excluding activities which themselves consist of industrial action whether or not in contemplation or furtherance of a trade dispute.

(3) The amount of time off which an employee is to be permitted to take under this section and the purposes for which, the occasions on which and any conditions subject to which time off may be so taken are those that are reasonable in all the circumstances having regard to any relevant provisions of a Code of Practice issued by the Advisory, Conciliation and Arbitration Service under section 6 of the Employment Protection Act 1975.

(4) An employee who is a member of an independent trade union recognised by his employer may present a complaint to an industrial tribunal that his employer has failed to permit him to take time off as required by this section.

NOTES

Derivation: 1975, s 58 (1) to (3), (5).

General Note: see General Note to s 27.

In contemplation or furtherance of a trade dispute: see *Conway* v *Wade* [1909] AC 506; *Dallimore* v *Williams* (1912) 29 TLR 67; (1914) 30 TLR 432; *Bent's Brewery Co Ltd* v *Hogan* [1945] 2 All ER 570; *Huntly* v *Thornton* [1957] 1 WLR 321; *BBC* v *Hearn* [1977] ICR 685; and *Beaverbrook Newspapers Ltd* v *Keys* [1978] ICR 582.

Trade dispute: see the cases mentioned above and s 153 (1).

Subsection (3): see also s 29 (4).

Code of practice: see notes to s 27.

Complaint: see, further, s 30.

Definitions: 'employee' and 'employer': see note to s 1; 'working hours': see s 32 (1) (*b*); 'independent trade union': see s 153 (1); 'trade union': see s 153 (1); 'recognised': see s 32; 'the Advisory, Conciliation and Arbitration Service': see s 1 (1) of the Employment Protection Act 1975; 'trade dispute': see above.

29. Time off for public duties

(1) An employer shall permit an employee of his who is—

(*a*) a justice of the peace;

(*b*) a member of a local authority;

(*c*) a member of any statutory tribunal;

(*d*) a member of, in England and Wales, a Regional Health Authority or Area Health Authority or, in Scotland, a Health Board;

(*e*) a member of, in England and Wales, the managing or governing body of an educational establishment maintained by a local education authority, or, in Scotland, a school or college council or the governing body of a central institution or a college of education; or

(*f*) a member of, in England and Wales, a water authority or, in Scotland, river purification board,

to take time off, subject to and in accordance with subsection (4), during the employee's working hours for the purposes of performing any of the duties of his office or, as the case may be, his duties as such a member.

(2) In subsection (1)—

(*a*) " local authority " in relation to England and Wales includes the Common Council of the City of London but otherwise has the same meaning as in the Local Government Act 1972, and in relation to Scotland has the same meaning as in the Local Government (Scotland) Act 1973;

(*b*) " Regional Health Authority " and " Area Health Authority " have the same meaning as in the National Health Service Act 1977, and " Health Board " has the same meaning as in the National Health Service (Scotland) Act 1972;

(*c*) " local education authority " means the authority designated by section 192(1) of the Local Government Act 1972, " school or college council " means a body appointed under section 125(1) of the Local Government (Scotland) Act 1973, and " central institution " and " college of education " have the meanings assigned to them by section 145(10) and (14) respectively of the Education (Scotland) Act 1962; and

(*d*) " river purification board " means a board established under section 135 of the Local Government (Scotland) Act 1973.

(3) For the purposes of subsection (1) the duties of a member of a body referred to in paragraphs (*b*) to (*f*) of that subsection are:—

(*a*) attendance at a meeting of the body or any of its committees or sub-committees;

(*b*) the doing of any other thing approved by the body, or anything of a class so approved, for the purpose of the discharge of the functions of the body or of any of its committees or sub-committees.

(4) The amount of time off which an employee is to be permitted to take under this section and the occasions on which and any conditions subject to which time off may be so taken are those that are reasonable in all the circumstances having regard, in particular, to the following:—

(*a*) how much time off is required for the performance of the duties of the office or as a member of the body in question, and how much time off is required for the performance of the particular duty;

(*b*) how much time off the employee has already been permitted under this section or sections 27 and 28;

(*c*) the circumstances of the employer's business and the effect of the employee's absence on the running of that business.

(5) The Secretary of State may by order—

(*a*) modify the provisions of subsection (1) by adding any office or body to, or removing any office or body from, that subsection or by altering the description of any office or body in that subsection; and

(*b*) modify the provisions of subsection (3).

(6) An employee may present a complaint to an industrial tribunal that his employer has failed to permit him to take time off as required by this section.

NOTES

Derivation: 1975, s 59.

General Note: see General Note to s 27. Note s 138 (8). There is only one reported EAT decision on this section, *Corner* v *Buckinghamshire County Council* [1978] IRLR 320. The EAT emphasised there that industrial tribunals only have power to declare whether or not there has been a failure to permit the employee to take time off. They do not have power to impose a condition upon the parties as to the way in which the time off should be granted. See also *Emmerson* v *Commissioners of Inland Revenue* [1977] IRLR 458 and *Ratcliffe* v *Dorset County Council* [1978] IRLR 191.

Subsection (4): see ss 27 (2) and 28 (3).

Complaint: see further s 30.

Definitions: 'employee' and 'employer': see note to s 1; 'working hours': see s 32 (1) (*b*). NB the definitions in subs (2).

Orders under this section: none had been made at the time of going to press.

30. Provisions as to industrial tribunals

(1) An industrial tribunal shall not consider—

(*a*) a complaint under section 27, 28 or 29 that an employer has failed to permit an employee to take time off; or

(*b*) a complaint under section 27 that an employer has failed to pay an employee the whole or part of any amount required to be paid under that section;

unless it is presented within three months of the date when the failure occurred or within such further period as the tribunal considers reasonable in a case where it is satisfied that it was not reasonably practicable for the complaint to be presented within the period of three months.

(2) Where an industrial tribunal finds any complaint mentioned in

subsection (1)(*a*) well-founded, the tribunal shall make a declaration to that effect and may make an award of compensation to be paid by the employer to the employee which shall be of such amount as the tribunal considers just and equitable in all the circumstances having regard to the employer's default in failing to permit time off to be taken by the employee and to any loss sustained by the employee which is attributable to the matters complained of.

(3) Where on a complaint under section 27 an industrial tribunal finds that the employer has failed to pay the employee the whole or part of the amount required to be paid under that section, the tribunal shall order the employer to pay the employee the amount which it finds due to him.

NOTES

Derivation: 1975, s 60.

Complaint: a complaint to an industrial tribunal is to be made in accordance with regulations under s 128 and Sched 9. See also the provisions for conciliation in ss 133 (1) (*a*) and (2) to (7).

Reasonable . . . reasonably practicable: see the note to s 67 (2).

Appeals: these lie to the Employment Appeal Tribunal, and thence to the Court of Appeal: see ss 135 and 136.

Definitions: 'employee' and 'employer': see note to s 1.

31. Time off to look for work or make arrangements for training

(1) An employee who is given notice of dismissal by reason of redundancy shall, subject to the following provisions of this section, be entitled before the expiration of his notice to be allowed by his employer reasonable time off during the employee's working hours in order to look for new employment or make arrangements for training for future employment.

(2) An employee shall not be entitled to time off under this section unless, on whichever is the later of the following dates, that is to say,—

(*a*) the date on which the notice is due to expire; or

(*b*) the date on which it would expire were it the notice required to be given by section 49(1),

he will have been or, as the case may be, would have been continuously employed for a period of two years or more.

(3) An employee who is allowed time off during his working hours under subsection (1) shall, subject to the following provisions of this section, be entitled to be paid remuneration by his employer for the period of absence at the appropriate hourly rate.

(4) The appropriate hourly rate in relation to an employee shall be the amount of one week's pay divided by—

(*a*) the number of normal working hours in a week for that employee when employed under the contract of employment in force on the day when notice was given; or

(*b*) where the number of such normal working hours differs from week to week or over a longer period, the average number of such hours calculated by dividing by twelve the total number of the employee's normal working hours during the period of twelve weeks ending with the last complete week before the day on which notice was given.

(5) If an employer unreasonably refuses to allow an employee time off from work under this section, the employee shall, subject to subsection (9), be entitled to be paid an amount equal to the remuneration to which he would have been entitled under subsection (3) if he had been allowed the time off.

(6) An employee may present a complaint to an industrial tribunal on the ground that his employer has unreasonably refused to allow him time off under this section or has failed to pay the whole or any part of any amount to which the employee is entitled under subsection (3) or (5).

(7) An industrial tribunal shall not entertain a complaint under subsection (6) unless it is presented to the tribunal within the period of three months beginning with the day on which it is alleged that the time off should have been allowed, or within such further period as the tribunal considers reasonable in a case where it is satisfied that it was not reasonably practicable for the complaint to be presented within the period of three months.

(8) If on a complaint under subsection (6) the tribunal finds the grounds of the complaint well-founded it shall make a declaration to that effect and shall order the employer to pay to the employee the amount which it finds due to him.

(9) The amount—

(*a*) of an employer's liability to pay remuneration under subsection (3); or

(*b*) which may be ordered by a tribunal to be paid by an employer under subsection (8),

or, where both paragraphs (*a*) and (*b*) are applicable, the aggregate amount of the liabilities referred to in those paragraphs, shall not exceed, in respect of the notice period of any employee, two-fifths of week's pay of that employee.

(10) Subject to subsection (11), a right to any amount under subsection (3) or (5) shall not affect any right of an employee in relation to remuneration under the contract of employment (in this section referred to as " contractual remuneration ").

(11) Any contractual remuneration paid to an employee in respect of a period when he takes time off for the purposes referred to in subsection (1) shall go towards discharging any liability of the employer to pay remuneration under subsection (3) in respect of that period, and conversely any payment of remuneration under subsection (3) in respect of a period shall go towards discharging any liability of the employer to pay contractual remuneration in respect of that period.

NOTES

Derivation: 1975, s 61 (1) to (4), and (7) to (13).

General Note: this section gives the employee who is under notice for redundancy the right to take time off to look for new employment, or make arrangements for training for future employment; it also provides the remedy for an infringement of these rights. See s 121 which gives priority to debts owed under s 31 (3) by an employer on insolvency, and s 122 which gives employees the right to be paid such debts out of the Redundancy Fund. See also s 132 which makes provision for the recoupment of certain benefits, s 133 (1) (*a*) and (2) to (7), which make provision for conciliation, and s 150 and Sched 12, Pt I, which make provision for the death of the employer or the employee. Persons in Crown employment and House of Commons staff are not excluded from these provisions: see ss 138 and 139. Note ss 137, 149 and 157, and Sched 14, para 7 (1) (*c*). It is, perhaps, surprising that these provisions only apply to those dismissed for redundancy. The only reported decision on this section is one of the EAT: see *Dutton* v *Hawker Siddeley Aviation Ltd*, The Times, 7 July, 1978.

Exclusions: see note to s 27.

Redundancy: see s 153 (2), and note to s 81 (2) and the cases cited there.

Subsection (2): 'continuously employed for . . . two years or more': see s 151 (1) and Sched 13 for the method of ascertaining the length of an employee's period of employment and whether it has been continuous, and see the cases cited in the notes to Sched 13.

Subsection (4): 'week's pay and normal working hours': see s 152 and Sched 14, and the cases cited in the notes to those provisions.

Subsection (5): in *Dutton* v *Hawker Siddeley Aviation Ltd*, The Times, 7 July, 1978, the EAT said that it was unreasonable of the employers to require the employee to produce evidence of interviews or appointments before paying him, though it might be relevant to ask whether he had an appointment but no more.

Complaint: a complaint to an industrial tribunal is to be made in accordance with regulations under s 128 and Sched 9. See also the provisions for conciliation in ss 133 (1) (*a*) and (2) to (7).

Appeals: these lie to the EAT, and thence to the Court of Appeal: see ss 135 and 136.

Reasonable . . . reasonably practicable: see note to s 67 (2).

Definitions: 'employee' and 'employer': see note to s 1; 'dismissal': see ss 153 (2) and 81; 'redundancy' and 'continuously employed': see above; 'working hours: see s 32 (1) (*b*); 'week' and 'contract of employment': see s 153 (1); 'appropriate hourly rate' and 'contractual remuneration': see subs (4) and (10) above; 'normal working hours' and 'week's pay': see above.

32. Provisions supplementary to ss 27 to 31

(1) For the purposes of sections 27 to 31—

(*a*) a trade union shall be treated as recognised not only if it is recognised for the purposes of collective bargaining, but also if the Advisory, Conciliation and Arbitration Service has made a recommendation for recognition which is operative within the meaning of section 15 of the Employment Protection Act 1975; and

(*b*) the working hours of an employee shall be taken to be any time when, in accordance with his contract of employment, he is required to be at work.

(2) In subsection (1)—

" collective bargaining " means negotiations related to or connected with one or more of the matters specified in section 29(1) of the Trade Union and Labour Relations Act 1974;

" recognised " means recognised by an employer, or two or more associated employers, to any extent for the purposes of collective bargaining.

NOTES

Derivation: 1975, ss 62 (*a*), (*b*), and 126 (1).

Definitions: 'trade union': see s 153 (1); 'the Advisory, Conciliation and Arbitration Service': see s 1 (1) of the Employment Protection Act 1975; 'employee' and 'employer': see note to s 1; 'contract of employment': see s 153 (1); 'associated employers': see s 153 (4).

PART III

MATERNITY

GENERAL PROVISIONS

33. Rights of employee in connection with pregnancy and confinement

(1) An employee who is absent from work wholly or partly because of pregnancy or confinement shall, subject to the following provisions of this Act,—

(*a*) be entitled to be paid by her employer a sum to be known as maternity pay; and

(*b*) be entitled to return to work.

(2) Schedule 2 shall have effect for the purpose of supplementing the following provisions of this Act in relation to an employee's right to return to work.

(3) An employee shall be entitled to the rights referred to in subsection (1) whether or not a contract of employment subsists during the period of her absence but, subject to subsection (4), she shall not be so entitled unless—

(*a*) she continues to be employed by her employer (whether or not she is at work) until immediately before the beginning of the eleventh week before the expected week of confinement;

(*b*) she has at the beginning of that eleventh week been continuously employed for a period of not less than two years; and

(*c*) she informs her employer (in writing if he so requests) at least twenty-one days before her absence begins or, if that is not reasonably practicable, as soon as reasonably practicable,—

(i) that she will be (or is) absent from work wholly or partly because of pregnancy or confinement, and

(ii) in the case of the right to return, that she intends to return to work with her employer.

(4) An employee who has been dismissed by her employer for a reason falling within section 60(1)(*a*) or (*b*) and has not been re-engaged in accordance with that section, shall be entitled to the rights referred to in subsection (1) of this section notwithstanding that she has thereby ceased to be employed before the beginning of the eleventh week before the expected week of confinement if, but for that dismissal, she would at the beginning of that eleventh week have been continuously employed for a period of not less than two years, but she shall not be entitled to the right to return unless she informs her employer (in writing if he so

requests), before or as soon as reasonably practicable after the dismissal takes effect, that she intends to return to work with him.

In this subsection " dismiss " and " dismissal " have the same meaning as they have for the purposes of Part V.

(5) An employee shall not be entitled to either of the rights referred to in subsection (1) unless, if requested to do so by her employer, she produces for his inspection a certificate from a registered medical practitioner or a certified midwife stating the expected week of her confinement.

(6) The Secretary of State may by order vary the periods of two years referred to in subsections (3) and (4), or those periods as varied from time to time under this subsection, but no such order shall be made unless a draft of the order has been laid before Parliament and approved by resolution of each House of Parliament.

NOTES

Derivation: 1975, ss 35, 50 (2).

General Note: the rights given to employees in respect of maternity are twofold: they are entitled to be paid maternity pay; and they are entitled to return to work after the confinement. Section 33 provides the general conditions which have to be fulfilled to enable an employee to be entitled to either right; ss 34 to 44 relate to maternity pay, and ss 45 to 48 relate to the right to return to work. See also s 60 which deals with dismissals on the ground of pregnancy, s 61 which deals with the dismissal of replacements, s 132 which makes provision for the recoupment of certain benefits, s 133 (1) (*a*) and (2) to (7) which make provision for conciliation; Sched 2, which contains supplementary provisions relating to maternity; and s 150 and Sched 12, Pt I, which make provision for the death of the employer or the employee. Persons in Crown employment and House of Commons staff are not excluded from these provisions, apart from s 44 (see ss 138 and 139). Note sections 137, 149 and 157.

Exclusions:

(i) employees not continuously employed for two years at the beginning of the eleventh week before the expected week of confinement (s 33 (3) (*b*));
(ii) employment outside Great Britain (s 141 (2) and (5));
(iii) share fisherwomen (s 144 (2));
(iv) employment by spouse (s 146 (1));
(v) employment in police service (s 146 (2) and (3)).

Note the requirements of s 33 (3) to (5), and the provisions of Sched 2, Pt I, para 2 (4).

Employee, Employer: see note to s 1.

Continuously employed for . . . two years: see s 151 and Sched 13, which contains provisions for ascertaining the length of an employee's period of employment and whether it has been continuous; see also the cases cited in the notes to Sched 13.

Subsection (3): see *Hughes* v *Gwynedd Area Health Authority* [1978] ICR 161, where the EAT suggested that if an employee resigns before the eleventh week before the expected week of confinement, she will be outside the scope of these provisions. It also pointed out that a notice of resignation by an employee must be specific and must specify the date when it is to take effect or make it feasible for the date to be deduced with certainty from what is said. Note the Secretary of State's power to vary the two-year period: see s 33 (6).

Subsection (4): it is not entirely clear whether the dismissal referred to in this subsection is intended to be an unfair or a fair dismissal. See the note to s 60 for a discussion of this point. Note the Secretary of State's power to vary the two-year period: see s 33 (6).

Orders under this section: none had been made at the time of going to press.

Definitions: 'employee' and 'employer': see above; 'confinement': see s 153 (1); 'maternity pay': see ss 153 (1) and 33 (1); 'return to work': see s 153 (3); 'contract of employment', 'expected week of confinement' and 'week': see s 153 (1); 'dismiss' and 'dismissal'; see subs (4) and s 55; 'registered medical practitioner'; see Medical Act 1956, ss 52 (2) and 54 (1); 'certified midwife': see s 153 (1).

MATERNITY PAY

34. Maternity pay

(1) Maternity pay shall be paid in respect of a period not exceeding, or periods not exceeding in the aggregate, six weeks during which the employee is absent from work wholly or partly because of pregnancy or confinement (in this section and sections 35 and 36 referred to as the payment period or payment periods).

(2) An employee shall not be entitled to maternity pay for any absence before the beginning of the eleventh week before the expected week of confinement, and her payment period or payment periods shall be the first six weeks of absence starting on or falling after the beginning of that eleventh week.

(3) The Secretary of State may by order vary the periods of six weeks referred to in subsections (1) and (2), or those periods as varied from time to time under this subsection, but no such order shall be made unless a draft of the order has been laid before Parliament and approved by resolution of each House of Parliament.

(4) Where an employee gives her employer the information required by section 33(3)(*c*) or produces any certificate requested under section 33(5) after the beginning of the payment period or the first of the payments periods, she shall not be entitled to maternity pay for any part of that period until she gives him that information or certificate, but on giving him the information or, as the case may be, producing the certificate, she shall be entitled to be paid in respect of that part of the period or periods which fell before the giving of the information or the production of the certificate.

NOTES

Derivation: 1975, s 36.

General Note: s 33 gives employees the right to maternity pay and prescribes the general conditions that need to be fulfilled. Section 34 makes further provision for the entitlement to maternity pay; s 35 provides the method of calculating it; s 36 provides the remedy for the employer's failure to pay; ss 37 to 44 provide for the administration and financing of the Maternity Pay Fund. See also General Notes to ss 33 and 37.

Exclusions: see note to s 33.

Six weeks: these periods may be varied by order under subs (3).

Definitions: 'employee' and 'employer': see note to s 1; 'maternity pay': see ss 153 (1) and 33 (1); 'week', 'confinement', 'expected week of confinement'; see s 153 (1).

Orders under this section: none had been made at the time of going to press.

35. Calculation of maternity pay

(1) The amount of maternity pay to which an employee is entitled as respects any week shall be nine-tenths of a week's pay reduced by the amount of maternity allowance payable for the week under Part I of Schedule 4 to the Social Security Act 1975, whether or not the employee in question is entitled to the whole or any part of that allowance.

(2) Maternity pay shall accrue due to an employee from day to day and in calculating the amount of maternity pay payable for any day—

(*a*) there shall be disregarded Sunday or such other day in each week as may be prescribed in relation to that employee under section 22(10) of the Social Security Act 1975 for the purpose of calculating the daily rate of maternity allowance under that Act; and

(*b*) the amount payable for any other day shall be taken as one-sixth of the amount of the maternity pay for the week in which the day falls.

(3) Subject to subsection (4), a right to maternity pay shall not affect any right of an employee in relation to remuneration under any contract of employment (in this section referred to as " contractual remuneration ").

(4) Any contractual remuneration paid to an employee in respect of a day within a payment period shall go towards discharging any liability of the employer to pay maternity pay in respect of that day, and conversely any maternity pay paid in respect of a day shall go towards discharging any liability of the employer to pay contractual remuneration in respect of that day.

NOTES

Derivation: 1975, s 37 (1) to (4).

Week's pay: see s 152 and Sched 14, Pt II, and the cases cited in the notes to those provisions. Note Sched 14, Para 7 (1) (*d*).

Definitions: 'employee' and 'employer': see note to s 1; 'payment period': see s 34 (1); 'contractual remuneration': see subs (3).

36. Complaint to industrial tribunal

(1) A complaint may be presented to an industrial tribunal by an employee against her employer that he has failed to pay her the whole or any part of the maternity pay to which she is entitled.

(2) An industrial tribunal shall not entertain a complaint under subsection (1) unless it is presented to the tribunal before the end of the period of three months beginning with the last day of the payment period or, as the case may be, the last ot the payment periods, or within such further period as the tribunal considers reasonable in a case where it is satisfied that it was not reasonably practicable for the complaint to be presented within the period of three months.

(3) Where an industrial tribunal finds a complaint under subsection (1) well-founded, the tribunal shall order the employer to pay the complainant the amount of maternity pay which it finds is due to her.

NOTES

Derivation: 1975, s 38.

Complaint: a complaint to an industrial tribunal is to be made in accordance with regulations under s 128 and Sched 9. See also the provisions for conciliation in s 133 (1) and (2) to (7).

Appeals: these lie to the Employment Appeal Tribunal, and thence to the Court of Appeal: see ss 135 and 136.

Reasonable . . . reasonably practicable . . . : see the note to s 67 (2).

Definitions: 'employee', and 'employer': see note to s 1; 'maternity pay': see s 33 (1).

37. Maternity Pay Fund

(1) The Secretary of State shall continue to have the control and management of the Maternity Pay Fund established under section 39 of the Employment Protection Act 1975, and payments shall be made out of that fund in accordance with the following provisions of this Part and section 156(1).

(2) The Secretary of State shall prepare accounts of the Maternity Pay Fund in such form as the Treasury may direct and shall send them to the Comptroller and Auditor General not later than the end of the month of November following the end of the financial year to which the accounts relate; and the Comptroller and Auditor General shall examine and certify every such account and shall lay copies thereof, together with his report thereon, before Parliament.

(3) Any money in the Maternity Pay Fund may from time to time be paid over to the National Debt Commissioners and invested by them, in accordance with such directions as may be given by the Treasury, in any such manner as may be specified by an order of the Treasury for the time being in force under section 22(1) of the National Savings Bank Act 1971.

NOTES

Derivation: 1975, s 39.

General Note: the purpose of the Maternity Pay Fund is to provide a means of financing the maternity pay to which employees are entitled under ss 33 to 35. Section 37 provides for the management of the fund; s 38 provides for advances to be made out of the National Loans Fund; s 39 provides for rebates to be paid to employers who have paid maternity pay to an employee; s 40 enables employees to apply to the Secretary of State for a payment of maternity pay out of the Fund in certain circumstances; ss 41 and 42 contain provisions supplementary to s 40; s 43 provides enforcement procedures in relation to rebates under s 39 and payments under s 40. See the General Notes to ss 33 and 34. Note also the provisions in s 156 which relate to payments from the Maternity Pay Fund and the Redundancy Fund into the Consolidated Fund.

38. Advances out of National Loans Fund

(1) Subject to the provisions of subsections (2) to (4), the Treasury may from time to time advance out of the National Loans Fund to the Secretary of State for the purposes of the Maternity Pay Fund such sums as the Secretary of State may request; and any sums advanced to the Secretary of State under this section shall be paid into the Maternity Pay Fund.

(2) The aggregate amount outstanding by way of principal in respect of sums advanced to the Secretary of State under subsection (1) shall not at any time exceed £4 million, or such larger sum, not exceeding £10 million, as the Secretary of State may by order made with the consent of the Treasury determine.

(3) No order under subsection (2) shall be made unless a draft of the order has been laid before Parliament and approved by resolution of each House of Parliament.

(4) Any sums advanced to the Secretary of State under subsection (1) shall be re-paid by the Secretary of State out of the Maternity Pay Fund into the National Loans Fund in such manner and at such times, and with interest thereon at such rate, as the Treasury may direct.

NOTES

Derivation: 1975, s 41.

National Loans Fund: see National Loans Act 1968, s 1 (1).

Orders made under this section: none had been made at the time of going to press.

39. Maternity pay rebate

(1) Subject to any regulations made under this section, the Secretary of State shall pay out of the Maternity Pay Fund to every employer who makes a claim under this section and who, being liable to pay, has paid maternity pay to an employee, an amount equal to the full amount of maternity pay so paid (in this section and sections 42 and 43 referred to as a " maternity pay rebate ").

(2) The Secretary of State may if he thinks fit, and if he is satisfied that it would be just and equitable to do so having regard to all the relevant circumstances, pay such a rebate to an employer who makes a claim under this section and who has paid maternity pay to an employee in circumstances in which, by reason of the time limit provided for in section 36(2) a complaint by the employee has been dismissed, or would not be entertained, by an industrial tribunal.

(3) For the purposes of subsections (1) and (2), a payment of contractual remuneration by an employer shall be treated as a payment of maternity pay to the extent that, by virtue of section 35(4),—

(*a*) it extinguishes the employer's liability to pay maternity pay; or

(*b*) in a case falling within subsection (2), it would extinguish that liability if a complaint by the employee were not time-barred as described in that subsection.

(4) The Secretary of State shall make provision by regulations as to the making of claims for maternity pay rebates under this section and such regulations may in particular—

(*a*) require a claim to be made within such time limit as may be prescribed; and

(*b*) require a claim to be supported by such evidence as may be prescribed.

NOTES

Derivation: 1975, s 42 .

Further provisions: see ss 41, 42 (2) and 43; also s 44 (4) in relation to offences.

Definitions: 'employee', and 'employer': see note to s 1; 'maternity pay'; see s 33 (1); 'maternity pay rebate': see subs (1); 'contractual remuneration': see s 35 (4).

Regulations under this section: see the Maternity Pay (Rebate) Regulations 1977 (SI 1977 No 322), amended by the Maternity Pay (Rebate) (Amendment) Regulations 1977 (SI 1977 No 668). See also the Social Security (Contributions) (Employment Protection) Regulations 1977 (SI 1977 No 622).

40. Payments to employees out of Maternity Pay Fund

(1) Where an employee claims that her employer is liable to pay her maternity pay and—

(*a*) that she has taken all reasonable steps (other than proceedings to enforce a tribunal award) to recover payment from the employer; or

(*b*) that her employer is insolvent (as defined in section 127 for the purposes of sections 122 to 126);

and that the whole or part of the maternity pay remains unpaid, the employee may apply to the Secretary of State under this section.

(2) If the Secretary of State is satisfied that the claim is well-founded the Secretary of State shall pay the employee out of the Maternity Pay Fund the amount of the maternity pay which appears to the Secretary of State to be unpaid.

(3) A payment made by the Secretary of State to an employee under this section shall, for the purpose of discharging any liability of the employer to the employee, be treated as if it had been made by the employer.

NOTES

Derivation: 1975, s 43.

Tribunal award: ie under s 36.

Further provisions: see also ss 41 and 42 (1). A person who has applied to the Secretary of State for a payment under this section, may present a complaint to an industrial tribunal under s 43 if no payment is made, or if the amount paid is less than it should have been. See also s 44, which makes provision as to the information the Secretary of State may require in connection with an application made under s 40; see subs (4) in relation to offences.

Definitions: 'employee' and 'employer': see note to s 1; 'maternity pay': see s 33 (1); insolvent': see subs (1) (*b*) and s 127.

41. Unreasonable default by employer

(1) Where the Secretary of State makes a payment to an employee in respect of unpaid maternity pay in a case falling within section 40(1)(*a*) and it appears to the Secretary of State that the employer's default in payment was without reasonable excuse, the Secretary of State may recover from the employer such amount as the Secretary of State considers appropriate, not exceeding the amount of maternity pay which the employer failed to pay.

(2) Where a sum is recovered by the Secretary of State by virtue of this section that sum shall be paid into the Maternity Pay Fund.

NOTES

Derivation: 1975, s 44.

Appeals: an employer may appeal from a determination by the Secretary of State under this section to an industrial tribunal: see s 43 (4) and (5).

Definitions: 'employee' and 'employer': see note to s 1; 'maternity pay': see s 33(1).

42. Supplementary provisions relating to employer's insolvency

(1) Where the Secretary of State makes a payment to an employee under section 122 (which provides for payments out of the Redundancy

Fund in respect of certain debts where an employer is insolvent) and that payment, in whole or in part, represents arrears of pay, then, in ascertaining for the purpose of section 40 the amount of any unpaid maternity pay, section 35(4) shall apply as if the arrears of pay in question had been duly paid by the employer to the employee in accordance with the contract of employment.

(2) Where the Secretary of State makes a payment to an employee out of the Redundancy Fund under section 122 which, if it had been made by the employer to the employee, would have attracted a maternity pay rebate from the Maternity Pay Fund in accordance with section 39, then, the Secretary of State shall make a payment out of the Maternity Pay Fund into the Redundancy Fund of an amount corresponding to the amount of rebate which would have been so payable.

NOTES

Derivation: 1975, s 45.

Redundancy Fund: see s 103, and, generally ss 103 to 109 and the notes to those provisions.

Definitions: 'employee' and 'employer': see note to s 1; 'maternity pay': see s 33 (1); 'contract of employment': see s 153 (1); 'maternity pay rebate': see ss 153 (1) and 39; 'insolvent': see s 127.

43. Complaints and appeals to industrial tribunal

(1) A person who has—

(*a*) made a claim for a maternity pay rebate under section 39, in a case to which subsection (1) of that section applies; or

(*b*) applied for a payment under section 40,

may, subject to subsection (5), present a complaint to an industrial tribunal that—

(i) the Secretary of State has failed to make any such payment; or

(ii) any such payment made by the Secretary of State is less than the amount which should have been paid.

(2) Where an industrial tribunal finds that the Secretary of State ought to make any such payment or further payment, it shall make a declaration to that effect and shall also declare the amount of any such payment which it finds the Secretary of State ought to make.

(3) An employer who has made a claim for a maternity pay rebate under section 39, in a case to which subsection (2) of that section applies, may, subject to subsection (5), appeal to an industrial tribunal on the ground that—

(*a*) the Secretary of State has refused to pay a maternity pay rebate; or

(*b*) any rebate paid by the Secretary of State is less than the amount which should have been paid,

and if on any such appeal the tribunal is satisfied that it is just and equitable having regard to all the relevant circumstances that a maternity pay rebate should be paid or, as the case may be, finds that a further payment by way of rebate should be made, the tribunal shall determine accordingly, and the Secretary of State shall comply with the determination.

(4) Where the Secretary of State determines that an amount is recoverable from an employer under section 41, the employer may, subject to

subsection (5), appeal to an industrial tribunal; and if on any such appeal the tribunal is satisfied that no amount should be recovered from the employer, or that a lesser or greater amount should be recovered (but in any case not exceeding the amount of maternity pay which the employer failed to pay) the tribunal shall determine accordingly and the amount, if any, so determined shall be the amount recoverable from the employer by the Secretary of State.

(5) An industrial tribunal shall not entertain a complaint or appeal under this section unless it is presented to the tribunal within the period of three months beginning with the date on which the relevant decision of the Secretary of State was communicated to the complainant or appellant or within such further period as the tribunal considers reasonable in a case where it is satisfied that it was not reasonably practicable for the complaint or appeal to be presented within the period of three months.

NOTES

Derivation: 1975, s 46.

Complaint: a complaint to an industrial tribunal is to be made in accordance with regulations under s 128 and Sched 9.

Appeals: these lie to the Employment Appeal Tribunal, and thence to the Court of Appeal: see ss 135 and 136.

Reasonable . . . reasonably practicable . . . : see the note to s 67 (2).

Definitions: 'employee' and 'employer': see note to s 1; 'maternity pay rebate': see ss 153 (1) and 39; 'maternity pay': see s 33 (1).

44. Provisions as to information

(1) Where an application is made to the Secretary of State by an employee under section 40, the Secretary of State may require—

(*a*) the employer to provide him with such information as the Secretary of State may reasonably require for the purpose of determining whether the employee's application is well-founded; and

(*b*) any person having the custody or control of any relevant records or other documents to produce for examination on behalf of the Secretary of State any such document in that person's custody or under his control which is of such a description as the Secretary of State may require.

(2) Any such requirement shall be made by a notice in writing given to the person on whom the requirement is imposed and may be varied or revoked by a subsequent notice so given.

(3) If a person refuses or wilfully neglects to furnish any information or produce any document which he has been required to furnish or produce by a notice under this section he shall be liable on summary conviction to a fine not exceeding £100.

(4) If any person in making a claim under section 39 or an application under section 40 or in purporting to comply with a requirement of a notice under this section knowingly or recklessly makes any false statement he shall be liable on summary conviction to a fine not exceeding £400.

NOTES

Derivation: 1975, s 47.

Further provisions: note s 155.

Crown Employment: see ss 138 and 139, which exclude the application of s 44 to Crown employment and House of Commons staff. Note, however, ss 138 (5) and 139 (1).

Definitions: 'employee' and 'employer': see note to s 1.

RIGHT TO RETURN TO WORK

45. Right to return to work

(1) The right to return to work of an employee who has been absent from work wholly or partly because of pregnancy or confinement is, subject to the following provisions of this Act, a right to return to work with her original employer, or, where appropriate, his successor, at any time before the end of the period of twenty-nine weeks beginning with the week in which the date of the confinement falls, in the job in which she was employed under the original contract of employment and on terms and conditions not less favourable than those which would have been applicable to her if she had not been so absent.

(2) In subsection (1) " terms and conditions not less favourable than those which would have been applicable to her if she had not been so absent " means, as regards seniority, pension rights and other similar rights, that the period or periods of employment prior to the employee's absence shall be regarded as continuous with her employment following that absence.

(3) If an employee is entitled to return to work in accordance with subsection (1), but it is not practicable by reason of redundancy for the employer to permit her so to return to work she shall be entitled, where there is a suitable available vacancy, to be offered alternative employment with her employer (or his successor), or an associated employer, under a new contract of employment complying with subsection (4).

(4) The new contract of employment must be such that—

(*a*) the work to be done under the contract is of a kind which is both suitable in relation to the employee and appropriate for her to do in the circumstances; and

(*b*) the provisions of the new contract as to the capacity and place in which she is to be employed and as to the other terms and conditions of her employment are not substantially less favourable to her than if she had returned to work in accordance with subsection (1).

NOTES

Derivation: 1975, s 48 (1), (2), (4), (5).

General Note: s 33 gives employees the right to return to work after pregnancy or confinement and prescribes the general conditions that need to be fulfilled. Section 45 further defines the right to return to work; s 46 provides the remedies for an infringement of an employee's rights under s 45; s 47 contains provisions dealing with the exercise of the employee's right to return to work; s 48 deals with the situation where an employee has a contractual right to return to work. See also ss 56 and 86, by virtue of which a failure to permit a woman to return to work after confinement is treated as a dismissal for the purposes of the unfair dismissal and redundancy payments provisions respectively; and see the General Note to s 33, and Sched 2. The only reported EAT decision on this section is *Bovey* v *The Board of Governors of the Hospital for Sick Children* [1978] IRLR 241, in which the EAT upheld the industrial tribunal's decision that where an employee was given the choice of returning to her full-time employment in her original job or taking a part-time job on a lower grade, she could not claim a composite right to return to her original job on a part-time basis See also *McFadden* v *Greater Glasgow Passenger Transport Executive* [1977] IRLR 327 and *Edgell* v *Lloyd's Register of Shipping* [1977] IRLR 463.

Exclusions: see note to s 33.

Redundancy: see s 81 (2), and the cases cited in the notes to it, s 86 and Sched 2, Pt II, paras 4 and 5

Entitled . . . to be offered alternative employment: see Sched 2, Pt I, para 2 (2).

Definitions: 'employee' and 'employer': see note to s 1; 'confinement': see s 153 (1); 'successor': see s 153 (1); 'week' and 'original contract of employment': see s 153 (1); 'associated employer': see s 153 (4); 'redundancy': see above.

46. Enforcement of rights under s 45

The remedies of an employee for infringement of either of the rights mentioned in section 45 are those conferred by or by virtue of the provisions of sections 47, 56 and 86 and Schedule 2.

NOTES

Derivation: 1975, s 48 (6).

General Note: note s 48 (2).

Definitions: 'employee': see note to s 1.

47. Exercise of right to return to work

(1) An employee shall exercise her right to return to work by notifying the employer (who may be her original employer or a successor of that employer) at least seven days before the day on which she proposes to return of her proposal to return on that day (in this section referred to as the " notified day of return ").

(2) An employer may postpone an employee's return to work until a date not more than four weeks after the notified day of return if he notifies her before that day that for specified reasons he is postponing her return until that date, and accordingly she will be entitled to return to work with him on that date.

(3) Subject to subsection (4), an employee may—

(*a*) postpone her return to work until a date not exceeding four weeks from the notified day of return, notwithstanding that that date falls after the end of the period of twenty-nine weeks mentioned in section 45(1); and

(*b*) where no day of return has been notified to the employer, extend the time during which she may exercise her right to return in accordance with subsection (1), so that she returns to work not later than four weeks from the expiration of the said period of twenty-nine weeks;

if before the notified day of return or, as the case may be, the expiration of the period of twenty-nine weeks she gives the employer a certificate from a registered medical practitioner stating that by reason of disease or bodily or mental disablement she will be incapable of work on the notified day of return or the expiration of that period, as the case may be.

(4) Where an employee has once exercised a right of postponement or extension under subsection (3)(*a*) or (*b*), she shall not again be entitled to exercise a right of postponement or extension under that subsection in connection with the same return to work.

(5) If an employee has notified a day of return but there is an interruption of work (whether due to industrial action or some other reason) which renders it unreasonable to expect the employee to return to work on the notified day of return, she may instead return to work when work resumes after the interruption or as soon as reasonably practicable thereafter.

(6) If no day of return has been notified and there is an interruption of work (whether due to industrial action or some other reason) which renders it unreasonable to expect the employee to return to work before the expiration of the period of twenty-nine weeks referred to in section 45(1), or which appears likely to have that effect, and in consequence the employee does not notify a day of return, the employee may exercise her right to return in accordance with subsection (1) so that she returns to work at any time before the end of the period of fourteen days from the end of the interruption notwithstanding that she returns to work outside the said period of twenty-nine weeks.

(7) Where the employee has either—

(*a*) exercised the right under subsection (3)(*b*) to extend the period during which she may exercise her right to return; or

(*b*) refrained from notifying the day of return in the circumstances described in subsection (6),

the other of those subsections shall apply as if for the reference to the expiration of the period of twenty-nine weeks there were substituted a reference to the expiration of the further period of four weeks or, as the case may be, of the period of fourteen days from the end of the interruption of work.

(8) Where—

(*a*) an employee's return is postponed under subsection (2) or (3)(*a*), or

(*b*) the employee returns to work on a day later than the notified day of return in the circumstances described in subsection (5),

then, subject to subsection (4), references in those subsections and in sections 56 and 86 and Schedule 2 to the notified day of return shall be construed as references to the day to which the return is postponed or, as the case may be, that later day.

NOTES

Derivation: 1975, s 49.

Right to return to work: see ss 33, 45 and 48.

Notified day of return: see subs (1) and note Sched 2, Pt I, para 2 (3). Note subs (8).

Definitions: 'employee' and 'employer': see note to s 1; 'successor': see s 153 (1); 'week': see s 153 (1); 'registered medical practitioner': see Medical Act 1956, ss 52 (2) and 54 (1).

48. Contractual right to return to work

(1) An employee who has a right both under this Act and under a contract of employment, or otherwise, to return to work, may not exercise

the two rights separately but may in returning to work take advantage of whichever right is, in any particular respect, the more favourable.

(2) The provisions of sections 45, 46, 47, 56 and 86 and paragraphs 1 to 4 and 6 of Schedule 2 shall apply, subject to any modifications necessary to give effect to any more favourable contractual terms, to the exercise of the composite right described in subsection (1) as they apply to the exercise of the right to return conferred solely by this Part.

NOTES

Derivation: 1975, Sched 3, para 5.

General Note: note the power given by Sched 2, Pt III, para 7 to the Secretary of State to amend this section.

Definition: 'employee': see note to s 1.

PART IV

TERMINATION OF EMPLOYMENT

49. Rights of employer and employee to a minimum period of notice

(1) The notice required to be given by an employer to terminate the contract of employment of a person who has been continuously employed for four weeks or more—

(*a*) shall be not less than one week's notice if his period of continuous employment is less than two years;

(*b*) shall be not less than one week's notice for each year of continuous employment if his period of continuous employment is two years or more but less than twelve years; and

(*c*) shall be not less than twelve weeks' notice if his period of continuous employment is twelve years or more.

(2) The notice required to be given by an employee who has been continuously employed for four weeks or more to terminate his contract of employment shall be not less than one week.

(3) Any provision for shorter notice in any contract of employment with a person who has been continuously employed for four weeks or more shall have effect subject to the foregoing subsections, but this section shall not be taken to prevent either party from waiving his right to notice on any occasion, or from accepting a payment in lieu of notice.

(4) Any contract of employment of a person who has been continuously employed for twelve weeks or more which is a contract for a term certain of four weeks or less shall have effect as if it were for an indefinite period and, accordingly, subsections (1) and (2) shall apply to the contract.

(5) It is hereby declared that this section does not affect any right of either party to treat the contract as terminable without notice by reason of such conduct by the other party as would have enabled him so to treat it before the passing of this Act.

(6) The definition of week given by section 153(1) does not apply for the purposes of this section.

NOTES

Derivation: 1972, s 1 (1) to (4), and (6); 1975 Sched 16, Pt II, paras 1, 2, 3.

General Note: this section gives the employee the right to certain minimum periods of notice, the length of notice depending upon how long he has been continuously employed by his employer; he is also required to give a minimum amount of notice to his employer. See s 122, which gives employees the right to be paid debts arising under s 122 (3) (*b*) (ie in respect of any amounts which the employer is liable to pay the employee for the notice period or for failure to give the requisite notice) out of the Redundancy Fund, and ss 137, 149 and 157.

Exclusions:

(i) (except s 53) employees continously employed for less than four weeks (s 49 (1));
(ii) (s 53 only) employees continuously employed for less than twenty-six weeks (s 53 (2));
(iii) (except s 53) persons in Crown employment (s 138);
(iv) (except s 53) House of Commons staff (s 139);
(v) work outside Great Britain (s 141 (1), (2) and (5));
(vi) employment under a contract made in contemplation of the performance of a specific task which is not expected to last for more than twelve weeks (s 143 (3));
(vii) (ss 49 to 51 only) mariners (s 144 (1));
(viii) (s 53 only) share fishermen (s 144 (2));
(ix) dock workers, with certain exceptions (s 145 (1), (2) and (5));
(x) (s 53 only) employment by spouse (s 146 (1));
(xi) (s 53 only) employment in police service (s 146 (2) and (3)).

Employee, Employer: see note to s 1.

Continuously employed . . . : see s 151 and Sched 13, which contain provisions for ascertaining the length of an employee's period of employment and whether it has been continuous; see also the cases cited in the notes to Sched 13.

Subsection (3): *quaere* whether the employee may refuse to accept wages in lieu of notice. *Konski* v *Peet* [1915] 1 Ch 530 suggests that he may not.

Subsection (5): for cases on what conduct suffices to enable the other party to the contract to treat it as terminable without notice, see *Clouston & Co* v *Corry* [1906] AC 122, 129; *Laws* v *London Chronicle* [1959] 2 All ER 285; *Sinclair* v *Neighbour* [1967] 2 QB 279; *Pepper* v *Webb* [1969] 2 All ER 216; *Wilson* v *Racher* [1974] ICR 428; *Marriott* v *Oxford & District Co-operative Society Ltd* (*No* 2) [1969] 3 All ER 1126. See also *Boston Deep Sea Fishing* v *Ansell* (1888) 39 ChD 339 and *Cyril Leonard & Co* v *Simo Securities Trust Ltd* [1971] 3 All ER 1313, which establish that 'where an employee has in fact been guilty of uncondoned misconduct so grave that it justifies instant dismissal, the employer can rely on that misconduct in defence of any action for wrongful dismissal, even if at the date of dismissal the action was not known to him' (per Sachs LJ in the latter case).

Definitions: 'employee' and 'employer': see above; 'contract of employment': see s 153 (1); 'continuously employed . . . ': see above; 'week': note subs (6).

50. Rights of employee in period of notice

(1) If an employer gives notice to terminate the contract of employment of a person who has been continuously employed for four weeks or more, the provisions of Schedule 3 shall have effect as respects the liability of the employer for the period of notice required by section 49(1).

(2) If an employee who has been continuously employed for four weeks or more gives notice to terminate his contract of employment, the pro-

visions of Schedule 3 shall have effect as respects the liability of the employer for the period of notice required by section 49(2).

(3) This section shall not apply in relation to a notice given by the employer or the employee if the notice to be given by the employer to terminate the contract must be at least one week more than the notice required by section 49(1).

NOTES

Derivation: 1972, s 2 (1) to (3); 1975, Sched 16, Pt II, para 1.

General Note: this section, together with Sched 3, gives the employee the right to be paid during his period of notice, whether the notice was given by the employer or the employee. See also the notes to Sched 3. Note s 110 (4).

Exclusions: see the note to s 49.

Definitions: 'employee' and 'employer': see note to s 1; 'contract of employment': see s 153 (1); 'continuously employed': see note to s 49.

51. Measure of damages in proceedings against employers

If an employer fails to give the notice required by section 49, the rights conferred by section 50 (with Schedule 3) shall be taken into account in assessing his liability for breach of the contract.

NOTES

Derivation: 1972, s 3.

General Note: see *Secretary of State for Employment* v *Wilson* [1978] ICR 200.

Definition: 'employer' see note to s 1.

52. Statutory contracts

Sections 49 and 50 shall apply in relation to a contract all or any of the terms of which are terms which take effect by virtue of any provision contained in or having effect under an Act of Parliament, whether public or local, as they apply in relation to any other contract; and the reference in this section to an Act of Parliament includes, subject to any express provision to the contrary, an Act passed after this Act.

NOTES

Derivation: 1972, s 11 (2).

General Note: note s 149 (2).

53. Written statement of reasons for dismissal

(1) An employee shall be entitled—

(*a*) if he is given by his employer notice of termination of his contract of employment;

(*b*) if his contract of employment is terminated by his employer without notice; or

(*c*) if, where he is employed under a contract for a fixed term, that term expires without being renewed under the same contract,

to be provided by his employer, on request, within fourteen days of that request, with a written statement giving particulars of the reasons for his dismissal.

(2) An employee shall not be entitled to a written statement under subsection (1) unless on the effective date of termination he has been, or

will have been, continuously employed for a period of twenty-six weeks ending with the last complete week before that date.

(3) A written statement provided under this section shall be admissible in evidence in any proceedings.

(4) A complaint may be presented to an industrial tribunal by an employee against his employer on the ground that the employer unreasonably refused to provide a written statement under subsection (1) or that the particulars of reasons given in purported compliance with that subsection are inadequate or untrue, and if the tribunal finds the complaint well-founded—

(*a*) it may make a declaration as to what it finds the employer's reasons were for dismissing the employee; and

(*b*) it shall make an award that the employer pay to the employee a sum equal to the amount of two weeks' pay.

(5) An industrial tribunal shall not entertain a complaint under this section relating to the reasons for a dismissal unless it is presented to the tribunal at such a time that the tribunal would, in accordance with section 67(2) or (4), entertain a complaint of unfair dismissal in respect of that dismissal presented at the same time.

NOTES

Derivation: 1975, s 70 (1) to (5).

General Note: the employee's right to be given a written statement with particulars of the reason for his dismissal can be regarded as a facet of the developing right to be given information in relation to one's employment. Its particular significance here is in relation to unfair dismissal: an employer who commits himself to certain reasons for the dismissal in his written statement under this section may be prevented from relying on other reasons at the hearing of the complaint of unfair dismissal. See s 57 and the cases mentioned in the notes. See also s 132, which makes provision for the recoupment of certain benefits, s 133 (1) (*a*) and (2) to (7), which make provision for conciliation, and s 150 and Sched 12, Pt I, which make provision for the death of the employer or the employee. Persons in Crown employment and House of Commons staff are not excluded (see ss 138 and 139). Note ss 137, 149 and 157.

Exclusions:
- (i) employees not continuously employed for twenty-six weeks (s 53 (2));
- (ii) employment outside Great Britain (s 141 (2) and (5));
- (iii) share fishermen (s 144 (2));
- (iv) employment as registered dock worker, other then employment by virtue of which the employee is wholly or mainly engaged in work which is not dock work (s 145 (2) and (5));
- (v) employment by spouse (s 146 (1));
- (vi) employment in police service (s 146 (2) and (3)).

Further provisions: note Sched 14, para 7 (1) (*f*) and (*g*).

Employee, Employer: see note to s 1.

Effective date of termination: see ss 153 (1), 55 (4) and (5).

Continuously employed: see note to s 49.

Written statement: for decided cases on this provision, see *Joines* v *B & S (Burknall) Ltd* [1977] IRLR 83; *Keen* v *Dymo Ltd* [1977] IRLR 118; and *Horsley Smith & Sherry Ltd* v *Dutton* [1977] ICR 594. In *Charles Lang & Sons Ltd* v *Aubrey* [1978] ICR 168 the EAT said that s 53 ought to be strictly construed and only applied where the evidence clearly indicated that there had been an unreasonable refusal to provide the written statement. Delay or inaction does not necessarily amount to unreasonable refusal.

Complaint: a complaint to an industrial tribunal is to be made in accordance with regulations under s 128 and Sched 9. See also the provisions for conciliation in ss 133 (1) (*a*) and (2) to (7).

Appeals: these lie to the Employment Appeal Tribunal, and thence to the Courts of Appeal: see ss 135 and 136.

Definitions: 'employee' and 'employer': see note above; 'contract of employment': see s 153 (1); 'effective date of termination': see note above; 'week's pay': see s 152 and Sched 14, Pt III.

PART V

UNFAIR DISMISSAL

Right not to be unfairly dismissed

54. Right of employee not to be unfairly dismissed

(1) In every employment to which this section applies every employee shall have the right not to be unfairly dismissed by his employer.

(2) This section applies to every employment except in so far as its application is excluded by or under any provision of this Part or by section 141 to 149.

Notes

Derivation: 1974, para 4.

General Note: this section, and ss 55 to 80, deal with the employee's right not to be unfairly dismissed. The provisions started life in the Industrial Relations Act 1971; on the repeal of that Act, they were re-enacted, in an amended form, in Sched 1 of the Trade Union and Labour Relations Act 1974, whence they are derived.

In relation to what may be called an 'ordinary' complaint of unfair dismissal, four questions have to be asked:

(i) Was the complainant dismissed? (If not, then the complaint will fail *in limine*) (s 55)

(ii) What was the reason for the dismissal? (s 57 (1) (*a*))

(iii) Was it a 'fair' reason? (s 57 (1) (*b*) and (2))

(iv) Did the employer act fairly in treating that fair reason as sufficient for dismissing the employee? (s 57 (3))

Apart from the 'ordinary' situation, there are certain special situations:

(*a*) dismissals relating to trade union membership (s 58);

(*b*) dismissals on grounds of redundancy (s 59);

(*c*) dismissals on grounds of pregnancy (s 60);

(*d*) dismissals of employees engaged to replace employees absent because of pregnancy or confinement (s 61);

(*e*) dismissals in connection with a lock-out, strike or other industrial action (s 62);

(*f*) situations where pressure is exercised on the employer to dismiss unfairly (s 63).

Exclusions are dealt with in ss 64 to 66 and ss 141 to 149 (and see note Exclusions). Section 67 deals with the presentation of complaints to industrial tribunals; ss 68 to 76 prescribe the remedies; ss 77 to 79 provide for a special remedy where the employee complains of an unfair dismissal on the grounds of union membership or activities; s 80 deals with teachers in aided schools.

See also s 132, which makes provision for the recoupment of certain benefits, s 134, which prescribes the functions of conciliation officers on complaints made under s 67, the General Notes to the individual sections, s 150 and Sched 12, Pts I and II, which provide for the death of the employer or the employee, and Sched 2, Pt I (particularly para 2 (4)), which contains supplementary provisions relating to maternity and adaptations of these provisions. Note ss 137, 140 particularly subs (2) (*c*), 149 (1) (*b*) and 157.

It should be noted that no minimum period of employment is required for an employee who claims to have been unfairly dismissed on the grounds of trade union membership and activities (see s 58), and that persons in Crown Employment and House of Commons staff are not excluded from these provisions (see ss 138 and 139).

Exclusions:

(i) employees continuously employed for less than twenty-six weeks ending with the effective date of termination (s 64 (1) (*a*));
(ii) employees who have reached the normal retiring age for their particular job or sixty-five (if men) or sixty (if women) (s 64 (1) (*b*));
(iii) employee in employment to which the provisions of a dismissal procedures agreement apply (s 65);
(iv) employment outside Great Britain (s 141 (2) and (5));
(v) certain employees employed under fixed-term contracts (s 142 (1) and (3));
(vi) share fishermen (s 144 (2));
(vii) registered dock workers, except when wholly or mainly engaged in work which is not dock work (s 145 (2) and (5));
(viii) employment by spouse (s 146 (1));
(ix) employment in police service (s 146 (2) and (3));
(x) certain part-timers (Sched 13, paras 5 and 6).

Note the Secretary of State's power to exclude classes or specify additional classes of persons or employment; this is contained in s 149.

Employee and Employer: see note to s 1.

Definitions: 'employment' : see s 153 (1).

Meaning of unfair dismissal

55. Meaning of 'dismissal'

(1) In this Part, except as respects a case to which section 56 applies, "dismissal" and "dismiss" shall be construed in accordance with the following provisions of this section.

(2) Subject to subsection (3), an employee shall be treated as dismissed by his employer if, but only if,—

(*a*) the contract under which he is employed by the employer is terminated by the employer, whether it is so terminated by notice or without notice, or

(*b*) where under that contract he is employed for a fixed term, that term expires without being renewed under the same contract, or

(*c*) the employee terminates that contract, with or without notice, in circumstances such that he is entitled to terminate it without notice by reason of the employer's conduct.

(3) Where an employer gives notice to an employee to terminate his contract of employment and, at a time within the period of that notice, the employee gives notice to the employer to terminate the contract of employment on a date earlier than the date on which the employer's notice is due to expire, the employee shall for the purposes of this Part be taken to be dismissed by his employer, and the reasons for the dismissal shall be taken to be the reasons for which the employer's notice is given.

(4) In this Part " the effective date of termination "—

(*a*) in relation to an employee whose contract of employment is terminated by notice, whether given by his employer or by the employee, means the date on which that notice expires;

(*b*) in relation to an employee whose contract of employment is terminated without notice, means the date on which the termination takes effect; and

(*c*) in relation to an employee who is employed under a contract for a fixed term, where that term expires without being renewed under the same contract, means the date on which that term expires.

(5) Where the notice required to be given by an employer by section 49 would, if duly given when notice of termination was given by the employer, or (where no notice was given) when the contract of employment was terminated by the employer, expire on a date later than the effective date of termination as defined by subsection (4), that later date shall be treated as the effective date of termination in relation to the dismissal for the purposes of sections 53(2), 64(1)(*a*) and 73(3) and paragraph 8(3) of Schedule 14.

NOTES

Derivation: 1974, para 5 (1) to (3), (5), (6); 1975, Sched 16, Pt III, paras 8, 9, 10.

General Note: numerous situations give rise to the question as to whether or not an employee has been dismissed. Apart from those mentioned in subs (2), the most important are: (i) termination by agreement, (ii) employee repudiation/resignation and (iii) frustration. One set of facts may give rise to alternative analyses. So, for example, if an employee resigns, the analysis may be that he has in fact resigned of his own accord, or that he has resigned because of some action by his employer. In the latter situation, the question will arise as to whether subs (2) (*c*) applies, so that the employee may argue that he was 'constructively' dismissed. In another situation, the question may be whether the employer's action in handing the employee his cards is a dismissal within subs (2) (*a*) or an acceptance of the employee's repudiation.

As was mentioned in the General Note to s 54, if an industrial tribunal concludes that the employee was not dismissed, his complaint will fail *in limine*. It should be noted that once a notice terminating the contract has been given, it cannot be withdrawn unilaterally, but only with the agreement of the other party: see *Harris and Russell Ltd* v *Slingsby* [1973] ICR 454. Note also ss 56, 67 (4) and 149 (2) and Sched 12, Pt II, paras 8 and 9.

Subsection (2) (*a*)*: termination by agreement:* if the conclusion is that the contract was terminated by agreement, the employee will be held not to have been dismissed. The courts are reluctant, however, to accept such an analysis (see *McAlwane* v *Boughton Estates Ltd* [1973] ICR 470 and *Lees* v *Arthur Greaves Ltd* [1974] ICR 501), though it can happen: see *British Leyland UK Ltd* v *Ashraf* [1978] IRLR 330.

employee repudiation: if this is accepted as the genuine analysis, then there is no dismissal: see *Dudar* v *Leys Malleable Casting Co Ltd* [1973] IRLR 51; *Gannon* v *J C Firth Ltd* [1976] IRLR 415; and *Trust Houses Forte Hotels Ltd* v *Murphy* [1977] IRLR 186.

frustration: if the event which has happened is a genuine frustrating event, then there will be no dismissal. If the tribunal takes the view that there was no frustration, it may conclude that the employee repudiated the contract (particularly in the case of prison sentences: see *Hare* v *Murphy Brothers Ltd* [1974] ICR 603 and *Waudby* v *HFM* (*Transport*) *Co Ltd* [1976] IRLR 35). The most common problems in this field occur in the case of illness: see *Marshall* v *Harland & Wolff Ltd* [1972] ICR 101; *The Egg Stores*

(Stamford Hill) Ltd v *Leibovici* [1977] ICR 260; and *Hart* v *A R Marshall & Sons (Bulwell) Ltd* [1977] ICR 539.

It may well be that statements on the application form such as 'any misstatement as to date of birth, previous employment, details etc will render this application and any subsequent contract invalid' will probably not enable the employer to argue that the consequent 'termination' of the employee's contract because of the discovery of the misstatements is not a dismissal, because the contract is void *ab initio:* see *Johnson* v *Tesco Stores Ltd* [1976] IRLR 103. *Torr* v *British Railways Board* [1977] ICR 785, however, would tend to suggest the contrary.

Subsection (2) (*b*): it was held by the Court of Appeal in *BBC* v *Ioannou* [1975] ICR 267 that 'a "fixed term" is one which cannot be unfixed by notice', ie that the contract must not be determinable by notice. That case was in fact decided under what is now s 142, but it was thought that its reasoning would apply here also and, if it did, provide a loophole in the legislation. However, in *Dixon* v *BBC* [1978] ICR 357, the EAT, in a decision on *this* provision, distinguished *Ioannou's* case and held that 'fixed term' in this context does not have the same meaning as in s 142, since this provision is concerned with the moment of cessation of employment and with the determination of the question whether that cessation occurred as the result of the dismissal; whereas s 142 is not aimed specifically at the moment of dismissal, but is concerned with the nature of the contract in question. The EAT said that for a contract to come to an end by non-renewal, it must follow that the power to terminate it by notice had not been exercised. 'From the last moment when it ceased to be possible to exercise the power of termination it follows that the contract . . . must . . . continue until it expires by effluxion of time . . . In these circumstances it seems right to say . . . that what has expired without being renewed is a fixed term . . . '

Subsection (2) (*c*): as was mentioned above, a resignation by an employee may be analysed either as a straight resignation by him (in which case there is no dismissal), or a resignation prompted by some action of the employer, in which case it may be a 'constructive dismissal' within this paragraph. The question is what action on the part of the employer will entitle the employee to claim a constructive dismissal, and whether the question should be answered by reference to contractual norms or notions of fairness analogous to those employed when considering a case under s 57 (3) (formerly para 6 (8) of Sched 1 to the 1974 Act). In *Western Excavating (ECC) Ltd* v *Sharp* [1978] ICR 221, the Court of Appeal appeared to re-affirm the 'contractual' test. Lord Denning, MR certainly did, but Lawton, LJ's remarks are somewhat ambiguous and, with their emphasis on common sense and the disavowal of technical language, smack rather of the spurned 'unfairness' test. Nor is his example of 'persistent and unwanted amorous advances' by the employer towards a female employee easy to square with notions of contractual principle. It seems likely, however, that as a result of this case, fuller use will be made of implied terms, particularly the duty of mutual respect suggested by the Court of Appeal in *Wilson* v *Racher* [1974] ICR 428. Perhaps Lawton, LJ's amorous employer would be in breach of such a duty?

See also *Robinson* v *Crompton Parkinson Ltd* [1978] ICR 401; *Warner* v *Barbers Stores* [1978] IRLR 109; and *Simmonds* v *Dowty Seals Ltd* [1978] IRLR 211.

Subsection (3): contrast s 85, in the context of redundancy, which is more restricvely worded. In *Walker* v *Cotswold Chine Home School* (1977) 12 ITR 342, the EAT held that an employee who, after being given seven weeks' notice by her employer, left without giving notice was not protected by this provision. It said that the notice 'must be a notice which, within reason, either specifies the date of termination or specifies sufficient facts from which the employer can reasonably work out the date of termination . . . .' It left open the question whether the notice must be valid (for example should it comply with s 49 (2)?). This case shows that there are pitfalls which have been insufficiently commented upon and hardly ever discussed in decided cases, but they represent a trap for unwary employees. Note s 60 (5).

Subsection (4): problems arise where the employee is given money in lieu of notice, and it is necessary to decide whether the termination is summary in its effect, or one with notice. See *Dixon* v *Stenor Ltd* [1973] ICR 157 and *Leigh* v *James Arnold & Co* (1973) 8 ITR 364. Note Sched 2, Pt I, para 2 (3) and s 47 (8) in relation to maternity.

Subsection (5): in *Fox Maintenance Ltd* v *Jackson* [1978] ICR 110, the EAT said that the expression 'notice required to be given by an employer by section 49' referred to the *statutory* requirement of a minimum period of notice and not the period of notice stated in the contract of employment. One would have thought that, in this sort of provision, it would have been preferable to cater for the possibility that the employee's contract might contain stipulations for a longer notice period than that provided by statute.
Note Sched 13, para 11 (1).

Definitions: 'employee' and 'employer': see note to s 1; 'contract of employment': see s 153 (1).

56. Failure to permit woman to return to work after confinement treated as dismissal

Where an employee is entitled to return to work and has exercised her right to return in accordance with section 47 but is not permitted to return to work, then she shall be treated for the purposes of this Part as if she had been employed until the notified day of return, and, if she would not otherwise be so treated, as having been continuously employed until that day, and as if she had been dismissed with effect from that day for the reason for which she was not permitted to return.

NOTES

Derivation: 1975, s 50 (1).

General Note: the only EAT decision on this provision is *Bovey* v *The Board of Governors of the Hospital for Sick Children* [1978] IRLR 241. See also *McFadden* v *Greater Glasgow Passenger Transport Executive* [1977] IRLR 327 and *Edgell* v *Lloyd's Register of Shipping* [1977] IRLR 463.
See ss 46, 47 (8) and 48, and Sched 2, Pt I, para 2 (2).

Continuously employed: see s 151 and Sched 13, which contains provisions for ascertaining the length of an employee's period of employment and whether it has been continuous. The effect of this provision will be to increase the employment period by nine months (eleven weeks before confinement plus twenty-nine after), or more if any of the extensions in s 47 occur. Note s 47 (8).

Definitions: 'employee': see note to s 1; 'return to work': see s 153 (3); 'notified day of return': see ss 153 (1) and 47 (1) and (8); 'continuously employed': see above.

57. General provisions relating to fairness of dismissal

(1) In determining for the purposes of this Part whether the dismissal of an employee was fair or unfair, it shall be for the employer to show—

(*a*) what was the reason (or, if there was more than one, the principal reason) for the dismissal, and

(*b*) that it was a reason falling within subsection (2) or some other substantial reason of a kind such as to justify the dismissal of an employee holding the position which that employee held.

(2) In subsection (1)(*b*) the reference to a reason falling within this subsection is a reference to a reason which—

(*a*) related to the capability or qualifications of the employee for performing work of the kind which he was employed by the employer to do, or

(*b*) related to the conduct of the employee, or

(*c*) was that the employee was redundant, or

(*d*) was that the employee could not continue to work in the position which he held without contravention (either on his part or on that of his employer) of a duty or restriction imposed by or under an enactment.

(3) Where the employer has fulfilled the requirements of subsection (1), then, subject to sections 58 to 62, the determination of the question whether the dismissal was fair or unfair, having regard to the reason shown by the employer, shall depend on whether the employer can satisfy the tribunal that in the circumstances (having regard to equity and the substantial merits of the case) he acted reasonably in treating it as a sufficient reason for dismissing the employee.

(4) In this section, in relation to an employee,—

(*a*) " capability " means capability assessed by reference to skill, aptitude, health or any other physical or mental quality;

(*b*) " qualifications " means any degree, diploma or other academic, technical or professional qualification relevant to the position which the employee held.

NOTES

Derivation: 1974, para 6 (1) to (3), (8), (9) (*a*), (*b*); 1974, s 30 (1).

General Note: once it has been established that the employee has been dismissed, then his complaint falls to be considered following the next three stages outlined in the General Note to s 54, ie: what was the reason for the dismissal, was it a 'fair' reason, and did the employer act fairly in treating it as sufficient for dismissing the employee? In many cases there is no argument about whether the employee was dismissed, and the employer will therefore start with the burden on him. If the employer fails to show that the dismissal was fair, and the industrial tribunal finds against him, it will pass on to consider what remedy to order under ss 68 to 76. The provisions of s 53 are of importance in the context of this section, since the employer may well be committed to the reasons he has given in the statement, and precluded from bringing forward other reasons at the hearing of the complaint.

See also Sched 2, Pt I, para 2 (1), which contains an adaptation of s 57 (3) in relation to maternity. Note s 149 (2).

Subsection (1) (*a*): it is clear that the reason (or the principal reason) may in fact consist of various elements or 'sub-reasons', all of which the industrial tribunal may need to examine: see *Bates Farms and Dairy Ltd* v *Scott* [1976] IRLR 214 and *Patterson* v *Messrs Bracketts* [1977] IRLR 137. The problem which arises is as to whether the reason must exist *in fact*, or whether the employer's belief that it exists is sufficient. The tribunal is clearly bound to look into the facts and see what the reason was as a matter of substance irrespective of the employer's description of it: see *Trust Houses Forte Leisure Ltd* v *Aquilar* [1976] IRLR 251.

Provided, however, that the employer had reasonable grounds (even if mistaken) for believing that the fact existed at the time of dismissal, it is unnecessary for him to go further and prove that the facts actually did exist: see *St Anne's Board Mill Co Ltd* v *Brien* [1973] ICR 444; *Trust Houses Forte Leisure Ltd* v *Aquilar; Ferodo Ltd* v *Barnes* [1976] ICR 439; *Cook* v *Thomas Linnell & Sons Ltd* [1977] ICR 770; and *Gayle* v *John Wilkinson & Sons* (*Saltley*) [1978] ICR 154. It seems that provided that the facts forming the substance of the reason are sufficiently made known to the employee, a genuine mistake in labelling the reason will not affect the issue: see *Abernethy* v *Mott, Hay and Anderson* [1974] ICR 323. All the foregoing cases should be read in the light of the House of Lords decision in *W Devis & Sons Ltd* v *Atkins* [1977] ICR 662; see particularly the speech of Viscount Dilhorne.

The other problem which arises here concerns what evidence may be adduced to establish the reason. In *Devis* v *Atkins*, the House of Lords said that the determination of whether a dismissal was fair or not depended upon the 'reason' shown by the employer, and the industrial tribunal could not have regard to matters of which the employer was unaware at the time of dismissal and which could not have formed part of his reason or reasons for dismissing the employee. This decision casts doubt upon the earlier decisions of *Da Costa* v *Optolis* [1976] IRLR 178 and *Docherty* v *Reddy* [1977] ICR 365.

Subsection (1) (*b*): 'some other substantial reason': the most common example of this situation is where the employee refuses to accept a contractual change and the proposed change is justifiable: see *Moreton* v *Selby Protective Clothing Ltd* [1974] IRLR 269; *R S Components Ltd* v *Irwin* [1974] 1 All ER 41; and *Mercia Rubber Mouldings Ltd* v *Lingwood* [1974] ICR 256. See, for other examples, *Terry* v *East Sussex County Council* [1976] ICR 536; *Ellis* v *Brighton Co-operative Society Ltd* [1976] IRLR 332; *East African Airways Corporation* v *Foote* [1977] ICR 776; *Wilson* v *Underhill House School Ltd* [1977] IRLR 475; *Priddle* v *Dibble* [1978] ICR 149; *Robinson* v *British Island Airways Ltd* [1978] ICR 304; *Gorman* v *London Computer Training Centre Ltd* [1978] ICR 394; *Hollister* v *National Farmers' Union* [1978] IRLR 161; and *Scott Packing & Warehousing Ltd* v *Paterson* [1978] IRLR 166.

Note s 61, in connection with the dismissal of replacements.

Subsection (2) (*a*): see *A J Dunning* (*Shopfitters*) *Ltd* v *Jacomb* [1973] ICR 448; *Turner* v *Wadham Stringer Commercials* (*Portsmouth*) *Ltd* [1974] ICR 277; *Patterson* v *Barratt Development* (*Aberdeen*) *Ltd* [1977] IRLR 214; and *Cook* v *Thomas Linnell & Sons Ltd* [1977] ICR 770 for cases on capability. For cases on qualifications, see *Blackman* v *PO* [1974] ICR 151 and *Singh* v *London Country Bus Services Ltd* [1976] IRLR 176. Note the definitions of 'capability' and 'qualifications' in subs (4).

Subsection (2) (*b*): 'conduct' has been thought to mean conduct whilst in employment, and not prior to it: see *Johnson* v *Tesco Stores Ltd* [1976] IRLR 103. But *Torr* v *BRB* [1977] ICR 785 suggests the contrary. It was said in *Singh* v *London Country Bus Services Ltd* [1976] IRLR 176 that the definition of conduct does not require something which occurs in the course of the employee's work, or at the actual place of work, or even connected with the work, if in some respect or other it affects the employee, when he is doing his work. Obviously, a conviction for theft (as in *Singh's* case) even if of property not belonging to the employer and committed outside employment hours, is relevant to employment which involves handling money (on a bus). Examples of dismissals for conduct are: *Meridian Ltd* v *Gomersall* [1977] ICR 597 (attendance); *Alidair Ltd* v *Taylor* [1978] ICR 445 (inadequate performance); *James* v *Waltham Holy Cross Urban District Council* [1973] ICR 398 and *Retarded Children's Aid Society Ltd* v *Day* [1978] ICR 437 (refusal to co-operate with management); *Meyer Dunmore International Ltd* v *Rogers* [1978] IRLR 167 (relationship with other employees); *The Council of the City of Cardiff* v *Conde* [1978] IRLR 218 (alleged or proven criminal acts); and *Lees* v *The Orchard* [1978] IRLR 20 (breach of company rules).

Subsection (2) (*c*): redundancy: see s 81 and the notes to that section, and s 59.

Subsection (2) (*d*): see *Sutcliffe & Eaton Ltd* v *Pinney* [1977] IRLR 349 and *Sandhu* v *Department of Education and Science and London Borough of Hillingdon* [1978] IRLR 208, both EAT decisions. Industrial tribunal decisions are: *Appleyard* v *Smith* (*Hull*) *Ltd* [1972] IRLR 19 and *Fearn* v *Tayford Motor Co Ltd* [1975] IRLR 336.

Subsection (3): the number of cases decided under the predecessor of this provision (para 6 (8) of Sched 1 of the Trade Union and Labour Relations Act 1974) is vast, but, since the establishment of the Employment Appeals Tribunal under the Employment Protection Act 1975, certain trends have started to emerge in the decided cases. The *loci classici* remain *Earl* v *Slater and Wheeler* (*Airlyne*) *Ltd* [1972] ICR 508; *A J Dunning & Sons* (*Shopfitters*) *Ltd* v *Jacomb* [1973] ICR 448; and *James* v *Waltham Holy Cross UDC* [1973] ICR 398. It should be noted that the criteria of fairness will tend to vary according to the type of reason advanced for the dismissal. It should also be noted that in deciding the question under this subsection, industrial tribunals will have regard to the provisions of the Code of Practice on Disciplinary Practice and Procedures in Employment, promulgated by the Advisory, Conciliation and Arbitration Service (Code of Practice 1) and the employer's disciplinary procedure.

'The reason shown by the employer' must be a reason which he has taken reasonable steps to establish and which he genuinely believes to be the reason: see *Bates Farms and Dairy Ltd* v *Scott* [1976] IRLR 214; *Trust Houses Forte Leisure Ltd* v *Aquilar* [1976] IRLR 251; *St Anne's Board Mill Co Ltd* v *Brien* [1973] ICR 444; *Ferodo Ltd* v *Barnes* [1976] ICR 439; and *Chrystie* v *Rolls-Royce* (1971) *Ltd* [1976] IRLR 336. See the note to subsection (1) (*a*) for the evidence which can be adduced to establish the reason, and note *Mitchell* v *The Old Hall Exchange and Palatine Club Ltd* [1978] IRLR 160. In situations where the reason for the dismissal is a criminal offence alleged to have been committed by the employee, the employer need not be satisfied beyond reasonable doubt, provided that he conducts a reasonable investigation: see *Ferodo Ltd* v *Barnes* [1976] ICR 439; *Refund Rentals Ltd* v *McDermott* [1977] IRLR 59; *Conway* v *Matthew Wright & Nephew Ltd* [1977] IRLR 89; and *Parkers Bakeries Ltd* v *Palmer* [1977] IRLR 215. The fact that the employee is subsequently acquitted in criminal proceedings does not preclude the tribunal from holding the dismissal to be fair: see *Da Costa* v *Optolis* [1976] IRLR 178. In other situations, the employer should take genuine and reasonable steps to ascertain the facts before taking any action: see *St Anne's Board Mill Co Ltd* v *Brien*; *Chrystie* v *Rolls Royce* (1971) *Ltd*; *City of Edinburgh District Council* v *Stephen* [1977] IRLR 135; and *P O* v *Mughal* [1977] IRLR 178. Finally, it may be noted that a summary (and wrongful) dismissal does not render a dismissal automatically unfair: see *Treganowan* v *Robert Knee & Co Ltd* [1975] ICR 405; nor (probably) does a constructive dismissal.

Capability/Qualifications: see in particular *Spencer* v *Paragon Wallpapers Ltd* [1977] ICR 301; *Williamson* v *Alcan* (*UK*) *Ltd* [1978] ICR 104; *PO* v *Jones* [1977] IRLR 422; and *Liverpool AHA* v *Edwards* [1977] IRLR 471 in relation to health. See also *Dunning* v *Jacomb; The Littlewoods Organisation Ltd* v *Egenti* [1976] IRLR 334; *Lowndes* v *Specialist Heavy Engineering Ltd* [1977] ICR 1; *Cook* v *Thomas Linnell & Sons Ltd* [1977] ICR 770; *Paterson* v *Barratt Developments* (*Aberdeen*) *Ltd* [1977] IRLR 214; *PO* v *Mughal* [1977] ICR 763; and *Brown* v *Hall Advertising Ltd* [1978] IRLR 246.

Conduct: despite one or two decisions to the contrary (eg *Earl*'s case and *Budgen & Co* v *Thomas* [1976] ICR 344), decisions in the EAT and Court of Appeal are tending to suggest that whilst there is a general rule that failure to follow a fair procedure, whether by warnings or by giving an opportunity to be heard before dismissal, will result in the dismissal being held to be unfair, there are exceptions, particularly in cases of serious misconduct or negligence: see *Retarded Children's Aid Society Ltd* v *Day* [1978] ICR 437 and *Alidair Ltd* v *Taylor* [1978] ICR 445 (both Court of Appeal decisions). See also *Lowndes*' case; *Carr* v *Alexander Russell Ltd* [1976] IRLR 220; *Cook*'s case; *C A Parsons & Co Ltd* v *McLoughlin* [1978] IRLR 65; *Meyer Dunmore International Ltd* v *Rogers* [1978] IRLR 167; *Laws Stores Ltd* v *Oliphant* [1978] IRLR 251; and *Wells* v *Derwent Plastics Ltd* [1978] ICR 424.

Redundancy: see notes to s 59.

Contravention of an enactment: see note to subs (2) (*d*).

Other substantial reason: see note to subs (1) (*b*), and the cases cited there. Note s 61, in connection with the dismissal of a replacement and Sched 2, Pt I, para 2 (1), which adapts this subsection in relation to maternity.

Subsection (4) (*b*): the quality of trustworthiness is not a 'qualification': see *Singh* v *London Country Bus Services Ltd* [1976] IRLR 176.

Definitions: 'employee' and 'employer': see note to s 1; 'redundant': see s 81.

58. Dismissal relating to trade union membership

(1) For the purposes of this Part, the dismissal of an employee by an employer shall be regarded as having been unfair if the reason for it (or, if more than one, the principal reason) was that the employee—

(*a*) was, or proposed to become, a member of an independent trade union;

(*b*) had taken, or proposed to take, part at any appropriate time in the activities of an independent trade union; or

(*c*) had refused, or proposed to refuse, to become or remain a member of a trade union which was not an independent trade union.

(2) In subsection (1), " appropriate time " in relation to an employee taking part in the activities of a trade union, means time which either—

(*a*) is outside his working hours, or

(*b*) is a time within his working hours at which, in accordance with arrangements agreed with or consent given by his employer, it is permissible for him to take part in those activities;

and in this subsection " working hours ", in relation to an employee, means any time when, in accordance with his contract of employment, he is required to be at work.

(3) Dismissal of an employee by an employer shall be regarded as fair for the purposes of this Part if—

(*a*) it is the practice, in accordance with a union membership agreement, for employees for the time being of the same class as the dismissed employee to belong to a specified independent trade union, or to one of a number of specified independent trade unions; and

(*b*) the reason for the dismissal was that the employee was not a member of the specified union or one of the specified unions, or had refused or proposed to refuse to become or remain a member of that union or one of those unions;

unless the employee genuinely objects on grounds of religious belief to being a member of any trade union whatsoever, in which case the dismissal shall be regarded as unfair.

(4) For the purposes of subsection (3), a union shall be treated as specified for the purposes of or in relation to a union membership agreement (in a case where it would not otherwise be so treated) if—

(*a*) the Advisory, Conciliation and Arbitration Service has made a recommendation for recognition covering the employee in question which is operative within the meaning of section 15 of the Employment Protection Act 1975; or

(*b*) the union has referred a recognition issue (within the meaning of that Act) covering that employee to the Advisory, Conciliation and Arbitration Service under section 11 of that Act and the Service has not declined to proceed on the reference under section 12 of that Act, the union has not withdrawn the reference, or from the reference, and the issue has not been settled or reported on under that section.

(5) Any reason by virtue of which a dismissal is to be regarded as unfair in consequence of subsection (1) or (3) is in this Part referred to as an inadmissible reason.

(6) In this section, unless the context otherwise requires, references to a trade union include references to a branch or section of a trade union.

NOTES

Derivation: 1974, para 6 (4) to (6), and (9); 1975, Sched 16, Pt III, paras 11 and 12; Trade Union and Labour Relations (Amendment) Act 1976, ss 1 (*e*), 3 (5) and (6).

General Note: the consequences of a dismissal falling within this subsection are:
(i) the dismissal is automatically unfair, unless it falls within subs (3);
(ii) an employee does not have to have been continuously employed for twenty-six weeks (see s 64 (3)); and
(iii) the remedies in ss 77 to 79 are available to him.
See also the notes to s 54. Note s 140, particularly subs (2) (*b*) (ii), and s 149 (2).

Subsection (1) (*b*): in certain circumstances, there may be an overlap between this provision and s 57 (2) (*b*). 'Wholly unreasonable, extraneous or malicious acts done in support of trade union activities' might remove from the employee the protection of this section: see *Lyon* v *St James's Press* [1976] ICR 413. It should be noted that where it is alleged that trade union activities are the reason for the dismissal, the onus of proof lies on the employee: see *H Goodwin Ltd* v *Fitzmaurice* [1977] IRLR 393. It was said in *Dixon* v *West Ella Developments Ltd* [1978] IRLR 151 that 'activities of an independent trade union' should not be given too restricted a meaning, but the EAT in *Chant* v *Aquaboats Ltd* [1978] ICR 643 said that this phrase did not embrace an individual's independent activities as a trade unionist, and held that the organising of a petition against alleged inadequate safety standards, which was vetted by the union before being handed to the employers, did not amount to trade union activities within this paragraph. See also *Brennan and Ging* v *Ellward* (*Lancs*) *Ltd* [1976] IRLR 378; *City of Birmingham District Council* v *Beyer* [1977] IRLR 211; and *The Marley Tile Co Ltd* v *Shaw* [1978] IRLR 238.

Subsection (2): 'appropriate time': see *Brennan and Ging*'s case; *Robb* v *Leon Motor Services Ltd* [1978] ICR 506; and *The Marley Tile Co Ltd* v *Shaw* [1978] IRLR 238.

Subsection (3): 'union membership agreement': see s 153 (1) and *Sarvent* v *Central Electricity Generating Board* [1976] IRLR 66; *Home Counties Dairies Ltd* v *Woods* [1977] ICR 463; *Gayle* v *John Wilkinson and Sons*

(*Saltley*) *Ltd and TGWU* [1978] ICR 154; and *Himpfen* v *Allied Records Ltd* [1978] IRLR 154. Not only must a union membership agreement exist, but it must also be established that there is a practice by which employees are required to join a 'specified' union. In addition, if the agreement contains conditions, the employer must show that he has complied with those conditions before he can avail himself of the provisions of this subsection: see *Jeffrey* v *Laurence Scott & Electromotors Ltd* [1977] IRLR 466.

'employee genuinely objects' . . . : what is important is the employee's religious belief; this exception is not limited to situations where the religious body to which the employee belongs has promulgated written rules which include a prohibition against joining any trade union and a penalty of expulsion for breach of the prohibition: see *Cave* v *BRB* [1976] IRLR 400. The words import a subjective personal test: it is the individual's own belief that has to constitute valid ground for such objection, but the objection must be based on religious considerations and not simply on grounds of conscience which do not possess religious content: see *Goodbody* v *BRB* [1977] IRLR 84 and *Saggers* v *BRB* [1977] ICR 809. Similar considerations will no doubt arise in the context of s 23 (6).

Note Sched 2, Pt I, para 2 (4), and Pt III, para 6 (3), in relation to maternity.

Definitions: 'employee' and 'employer': see note to s 1; 'contract of employment' and 'independent trade union': see s 153 (1); 'specified trade union': note subsection (4); 'trade union': see s 153 (1); 'appropriate time' and 'union membership agreement': see notes to subss (2) and (3); 'recognition issue': see s 11 (3) of the EPA 1975; 'the Advisory, Conciliation and Arbitration Service': see s 1 (1) of the EPA 1975.

59. Dismissal on ground of redundancy

Where the reason or principal reason for the dismissal of an employee was that he was redundant, but it is shown that the circumstances constituting the redundancy applied equally to one or more other employees in the same undertaking who held positions similar to that held by him and who have not been dismissed by the employer, and either—

(*a*) that the reason (or, if more than one, the principal reason) for which he was selected for dismissal was an inadmissible reason; or

(*b*) that he was selected for dismissal in contravention of a customary arrangement or agreed procedure relating to redundancy and there were no special reasons justifying a departure from that arrangement or procedure in his case,

then, for the purposes of this Part, the dismissal shall be regarded as unfair.

NOTES

Derivation: 1974, para 6 (7).

General Note: as has been seen, redundancy (as defined in s 81 (2)) is a fair reason for dismissal. One can say that a dismissal for redundancy may be held to be unfair for two reasons: (i) because the employer acts contrary to s 57 (3); and (ii) because he acts contrary to this section. For the sake of convenience and completeness both are discussed here. The presumption of redundancy in s 91 (2) does not operate in the context of unfair dismissal, so that the burden is on the employer to prove redundancy: see Sched 9, para 5.

See also the General Notes to ss 54, 55, 57 and 58, and note s 149 (2).

Paragraph (*a*): see *Taylor* v *Butler Machine Tool Co* [1976] IRLR 113; *Farmeary* v *Veterinary Drug Co Ltd* [1976] IRLR 322; and *Bristol Channel Ship Repairers Ltd* v *O'Keefe* [1977] IRLR 13.

Paragraph (*b*): 'customary arrangement': see ***Bessenden Properties Ltd*** v ***Corness*** [1974] IRLR 338.

'agreed procedure': for cases on the application of agreed procedures, see *Gargrave* v *Hotel and Catering Industry Training Board* [1974] IRLR 85; *Bygott* v *Woodall-Duckham Ltd* [1976] IRLR 168; and *Jackson* v *General Accident Fire and Life Assurance Co Ltd* [1976] IRLR 338. A common form of agreed procedure, which is sufficiently common to operate as a customary arrangement in the absence of an agreed procedure, is the 'Last In First Out' principle. But the employer is not bound to apply this principle indiscriminately across the board, and is only bound to apply it to departments affected by redundancy; so he may, without contravening paragraph (*b*), select X, the junior member of Department A (which is affected by redundancy), and retain Y, the junior member of Department B (which is not affected by redundancy), although X has served longer than Y: see *Gargrave's* case. See also *Wailes Dove Bitumastic Ltd* v *Woolcocks* [1977] ICR 817.

Dismissal for redundancy contrary to s 57 (3): although redundancy is a fair reason for dismissal, a dismissal for redundancy may still be rendered unfair by the way in which the employer goes about it. A failure to find an employee alternative employment within the group may cause the dismissal to be held unfair: see *Vokes Ltd* v *Bear* [1974] ICR 1; *Modern Injection Moulds Ltd* v *Price* [1976] ICR 370; *British United Shoe Machinery Co Ltd* v *Clarke* [1978] ICR 70; *Barworth Flockton Ltd* v *Kirk* [1978] IRLR 18; *Cox* v *Wildt Mellor Bromley Ltd* [1978] IRLR 157; and *NC Watling Ltd* v *Richardson* [1978] IRLR 255; so will a failure to give as much warning as practicable: *Whyte* v *Burmah Oil Trading Ltd* [1976] IRLR 86 and *Kelly* v *Upholstery and Cabinet Works* (*Amesbury*) *Ltd* [1977] IRLR 91. Failure to engage in consultation with the employee or the appropriate unions may also render the dismissal unfair: see *Clarke*'s case and *Kelly*'s case.

So far as the basis of selection of candidates for redundancy is concerned, the test is whether the employer acted fairly, not whether the tribunal would have reached the same conclusion had it been the employer: see *Grundy* (*Teddington*) *Ltd* v *Willis* [1976] ICR 323; *Vickers Ltd* v *Smith* [1977] IRLR 11; *The Earl of Bradford* v *Jowett* [1978] IRLR 16; *Thomas & Betts Manufacturing Co Ltd* v *Harding* [1978] IRLR 213; and *NC Watling & Co Ltd* v *Richardson* [1978] IRLR 255.

Definitions: 'employee' and 'employer': see note to s 1; 'redundant': see s 81, and the notes to it; 'inadmissible reason': see s 58 (5); 'customary arrangement': see note to para (*b*) above.

60. Dismissal on ground of pregnancy

(1) An employee shall be treated for the purposes of this Part as unfairly dismissed if the reason or principal reason for her dismissal is that she is pregnant or is any other reason connected with her pregnancy, except one of the following reasons—

(*a*) that at the effective date of termination she is or will have become, because of her pregnancy, incapable of adequately doing the work which she is employed to do;

(*b*) that, because of her pregnancy, she cannot or will not be able to continue after that date to do that work without contravention (either by her or her employer) of a duty or restriction imposed by or under any enactment.

(2) An employee shall be treated for the purposes of this Part as unfairly dismissed if her employer dismisses her for a reason mentioned in subsection (1)(*a*) or (*b*), but neither he nor any successor of his, where there

is a suitable available vacancy, makes her an offer before or on the effective date of termination to engage her under a new contract of employment complying with subsection (3).

(3) The new contract of employment must—

(*a*) take effect immediately on the ending of employment under the previous contract, or, where that employment ends on a Friday, Saturday or Sunday, on or before the next Monday after that Friday, Saturday or Sunday;

(*b*) be such that the work to be done under the contract is of a kind which is both suitable in relation to the employee and appropriate for her to do in the circumstances; and

(*c*) be such that the provisions of the new contract as to the capacity and place in which she is to be employed and as to the other terms and conditions of her employment are not substantially less favourable to her than the corresponding provisions of the previous contract.

(4) On a complaint of unfair dismissal on the ground of failure to offer to engage an employee as mentioned in subsection (2), it shall be for the employer to show that he or a successor made an offer to engage her in compliance with subsections (2) and (3) or, as the case may be, that there was no suitable available vacancy for her.

(5) Section 55(3) shall not apply in a case where an employer gives notice to an employee to terminate her contract of employment for a reason mentioned in subsection (1)(*a*) or (*b*).

NOTES

Derivation: 1975, s 34 (1) to (5).

General Note: as with complaints under s 58, the employee's dismissal is treated as unfair. The burden, therefore, lies on the employer to show that the reason for the dismissal falls within subs (1) (*a*) or (*b*). Even if he does succeed in showing this, the dismissal will not be treated as automatically fair, and he will have to show that he has satisfied the requirements of s 57 (3).

As was mentioned in the note to s 33 (4), it is not clear whether the maternity rights referred to in s 33 (1) are intended to be conferred both on employees fairly and unfairly dismissed. When the Employment Protection Act 1975 was in Bill form, only fairly dismissed employees were included; but the word 'fairly' was dropped. This means, in the case of a fairly dismissed employee, that she is to be treated as 'absent from work', despite the fact that she is not temporarily absent because of pregnancy or confinement, but permanently absent because of dismissal. This interpretation is supported by the words 'whether or not a contract of employment subsists during the period of her absence' in s 33 (3). Similarly, if she is unfairly dismissed, presumably she is entitled to her maternity pay and the remedies for unfair dismissal. Such possibilities only arise in the case of employees who have been continuously employed for two years. *Quaere* whether in the case of an unfairly dismissed employee, continuously employed for less than two years, an award of compensation would include a sum to cover loss of potential maternity rights.

See also Sched 2, Pt I, which contains supplementary provisions relating to maternity in the context of unfair dismissal.

Reason connected with . . . pregnancy: see *George* v *Beecham Group* [1977] IRLR 43; *Brear* v *W Wright Hudson Ltd* [1977] IRLR 287; *Elegbede* v *The Wellcome Foundation Ltd* [1977] IRLR 383; and *Martin* v BSC *Footwear Ltd* [1978] IRLR 95.

Suitable available vacancy: quaere to what extent the criteria of suitability are to be evaluated in the same way as they are under s 82 (5), in the case of redundancy. See also s 13 (2).

Definitions: 'employee' and 'employer': see note to s 1; 'effective date of termination': see s 55 (4); 'successor', 'contract of employment': see s 153 (1).

61. Dismissal of replacement

(1) Where an employer—

(*a*) on engaging an employee informs the employee in writing that his employment will be terminated on the return to work of another employee who is, or will be, absent wholly or partly because of pregnancy or confinement; and

(*b*) dismisses the first-mentioned employee in order to make it possible to give work to the other employee;

then, for the purposes of section 57(1)(*b*), but without prejudice to the application of section 57(3), the dismissal shall be regarded as having been for a substantial reason of a kind such as to justify the dismissal of an employee holding the position which that employee held.

(2) Where an employer—

(*a*) on engaging an employee informs the employee in writing that his employment will be terminated on the end of a suspension such as is referred to in section 19 of another employee; and

(*b*) dismisses the first-mentioned employee in order to make it possible to allow the other employee to resume his original work;

then, for the purposes of section 57(1)(*b*), but without prejudice to the application of section 57(3), the dismissal shall be regarded as having been for a substantial reason of a kind such as to justify the dismissal of an employee holding the position which that employee held.

Notes

Derivation: 1975, ss 33, 51.

Definitions: 'employee' and 'employer': see note to s 1; 'confinement' and 'employment': see s 153 (1); 'to return to work': see s 153 (3).

62. Dismissal in connection with a lock-out, strike or other industrial action

(1) The provisions of this section shall have effect in relation to an employee who claims that he has been unfairly dismissed by his employer where at the date of dismissal—

(*a*) the employer was conducting or instituting a lock-out, or

(*b*) the employee was taking part in a strike or other industrial action.

(2) In such a case an industrial tribunal shall not determine whether the dismissal was fair or unfair unless it is shown—

(*a*) that one or more relevant employees of the same employer have not been dismissed, or

(*b*) that one or more such employees have been offered re-engagement, and that the employee concerned has not been offered re-engagement.

(3) Where it is shown that the condition referred to in paragraph (*b*) of subsection (2) is fulfilled, the provisions of sections 57 to 60 shall have effect as if in those sections for any reference to the reason or principal

reason for which the employee was dismissed there were substituted a reference to the reason or principal reason for which he has not been offered re-engagement.

(4) In this section—

(*a*) "date of dismissal" means—

(i) where the employee's contract of employment was terminated by notice, the date on which the employer's notice was given, and

(ii) in any other case, the effective date of termination;

(*b*) "relevant employees" means—

(i) in relation to a lock-out, employees who were directly interested in the trade dispute in contemplation or furtherance of which the lock-out occurred, and

(ii) in relation to a strike or other industrial action, employees who took part in it; and

(*c*) any reference to an offer of re-engagement is a reference to an offer (made either by the original employer or by a successor of that employer or an associated employer) to re-engage an employee, either in the job which he held immediately before the date of dismissal or in a different job which would be reasonably suitable in his case.

NOTES

Derivation: 1974, para 7 (1) to (3), and (5); 1975, Sched 16 Part III, para 13.

General Note: the effect of this provision is to relieve a tribunal of jurisdiction to hear complaints of unfair dismissal from employees where the employer is conducting a lock-out or the employees were taking part in a strike, or other industrial action, at the date of dismissal, unless the dismissals are discriminatory. So an employer can dismiss all the strikers without attracting the provisions of this section, but he cannot be selective. The section is not free from difficulty, however.
Note s 149 (2).

Subsection (1): 'at the date of dismissal': in *Heath* v *J F Longman* (*Meat Salesmen*) *Ltd* [1973] ICR 407 it was decided that the words 'on the date of dismissal' (in s 26 of the Industrial Relations Act 1971) meant 'at the time of dismissal'. So if the strike stops in the morning, and the employer dismisses in the afternoon, he is no longer within s 62. See also subs (4) (*a*).

Subsection (1) (*b*): a strike (or other industrial action) caused or contributed to by the employer is not outside these provisions: see *Thompson* v *Eaton Ltd* [1976] ICR 336, which contains some interesting dicta.

Subsection (2) (*a*): 'relevant employees': see also subs (4) (*b*). If out of a group of strikers two return to work, and the rest are subsequently dismissed, it seems that the employer will not have the protection of this section, since the words 'who took part' means 'who took part at any time during the strike' not 'who were taking part in the strike at the time of the dismissal': see *Stock* v *Frank Jones* (*Tipton*) *Ltd* [1978] ICR 347 and *Gallaher* v *Wragg* [1977] ICR 174. (NB: the other issues in those cases are of marginal relevance now, because of subsequent changes in the law.)

Subsection (2) (*b*): an offer made to an employee whose hearing is deficient does not come within this paragraph, and cannot be regarded as an effective offer: see *Tomczynski* v *J K Miller Ltd* (1976) 11 ITR 127.

Subsection (3): note s 67 (3).

Definitions: 'employee' and 'employer': see note to s 1; 'contract of employment': see s 153 (1); 'effective date of termination': see s 55 (4) and (5);

'trade dispute': see s 153 (1) and note to s 28; 'contemplation or furtherance': see note to s 28; 'successor': see s 153 (1); 'associated employer': see s 153 (4).

63. Pressure on employer to dismiss unfairly

In determining, for the purposes of this Part any question as to the reason, or principal reason, for which an employee was dismissed or any question whether the reason or principal reason for which an employee was dismissed was a reason fulfilling the requirements of section 57(1)(*b*) or whether the employer acted reasonably in treating it as a sufficient reason for dismissing him,—

(*a*) no account shall be taken of any pressure which, by calling, organising, procuring or financing a strike or other industrial action, or threatening to do so, was exercised on the employer to dismiss the employee, and

(*b*) any such question shall be determined as if no such pressure had been exercised.

NOTES

Derivation: 1974, para 15.

General Note: note s 149 (2).

No account shall be taken . . . : see *McColm* v *Agnew & Lithgow Ltd* [1976] IRLR 13; *Trend* v *Chiltern Hunt Ltd* [1977] ICR 612; and *Ford Motor Co Ltd* v *Hudson* [1978] ICR 482.

Definitions: 'employee' and 'employer': see note to s 1.

EXCLUSION OF SECTION 54

64. Qualifying period and upper age limit

(1) Subject to subsection (3), section 54 does not apply to the dismissal of an employee from any employment if the employee—

(*a*) was not continuously employed for a period of not less than twenty-six weeks ending with the effective date of termination, or

(*b*) on or before the effective date of termination attained the age which, in the undertaking in which he was employed, was the normal retiring age for an employee holding the position which he held, or, if a man, attained the age of sixty-five, or, if a woman, attained the age of sixty.

(2) If an employee is dismissed by reason of any such requirement or recommendation as is referred to in section 19(1), subsection (1)(*a*) shall have effect in relation to that dismissal as if for the words " twenty-six weeks " there were substituted the words " four weeks ".

(3) Subsection (1) shall not apply to the dismissal of an employee if it is shown that the reason (or, if more than one, the principal reason) for the dismissal was an inadmissible reason.

NOTES

Derivation: 1974, para 10; 1975, s 29 (4); 1974, para 11 (1); 1975, Sched 16, Pt III, para 15.

General Note: See s 149, particularly subs (1) (*c*) and Sched 2, Pt I, para 2 (4) and Pt III, para 6 (3) (in relation to maternity). See also *IPC Business Press Ltd* v *Gray* [1977] ICR 858.

Continuously employed . . . : see s 151 and Sched 13, which contains provisions for ascertaining the length of an employee's period of employment and whether it has been continuous, and the notes to those provisions. See particularly para 11 (1) of that Schedule.

Effective date of termination: see s 55 (4) and (5) and the note to those subsections.

Subsection (1) (*b*): see *Ord* v *Maidstone and District Hospital Management Committee* [1974] ICR 369; *Post Office* v *Waddell* [1977] IRLR 344; *Randall* v *Post Office* [1977] IRLR 346; *Smith* v *Post Office* [1978] ICR 283; and *Northman* v *Barnet London Borough Council* [1978] ICR 336.

Recommendation . . . referred to in s 19 (1): ie dismissal on medical grounds.

Definitions: 'employee': see note to s 1; 'employment': see s 153 (1); 'inadmissible reason': see s 58 (5).

65. Exclusion in respect of dismissal procedures agreement

(1) An application may be made jointly to the Secretary of State by all the parties to a dismissal procedures agreement to make an order designating that agreement for the purposes of this section.

(2) On any such application the Secretary of State may make such an order if he is satisfied—

(*a*) that every trade union which is a party to the dismissal procedures agreement is an independent trade union;

(*b*) that the agreement provides for procedures to be followed in cases where an employee claims that he has been, or is in the course of being, unfairly dismissed;

(*c*) that those procedures are available without discrimination to all employees falling within any description to which the agreement applies;

(*d*) that the remedies provided by the agreement in respect of unfair dismissal are on the whole as beneficial as (but not necessarily identical with) those provided in respect of unfair dismissal by this Part;

(*e*) that the procedures provided by the agreement include a right to arbitration or adjudication by an independent referee, or by a tribunal or other independent body, in cases where (by reason of an equality of votes or for any other reason) a decision cannot otherwise be reached; and

(*f*) that the provisions of the agreement are such that it can be determined with reasonable certainty whether a particular employee is one to whom the agreement applies or not.

(3) Where a dismissal procedures agreement is designated by an order under this section which is for the time being in force, the provisions of that agreement relating to dismissal shall have effect in substitution for any rights under section 54; and accordingly that section shall not apply to the dismissal of an employee from any employment if it is employment to which, and he is an employee to whom, those provisions of the agreement apply.

(4) Subsection (3) shall not apply to the right not to be unfairly dismissed for any reason mentioned in subsection (1) or (2) of section 60.

NOTES

Derivation: 1974, para 13; 1975, s 34 (7).

General Note: under the Labour Relations (Continuity of Employment) Regulations 1976 (SI 1976 No 660), if a dismissed employee is reinstated or re-engaged under a dismissal procedures agreement, the continuity of his employment will be preserved and will count in the computation of his period of continuous employment. This provision only applies where a *joint* application is made to the Secretary of State. An employer is not prevented from setting up his own dismissal procedure, which would then give the employee an internal procedure in addition to his statutory rights. Note ss 140 (2) (*c*) and 149 (2) and Sched 2, Pt I, para 2 (4), and Pt III, para 6 (3) (in relation to maternity), and Sched 13, para 20 (2).

Definitions: 'dismissal procedures agreement', 'independent trade union' and 'trade union': see s 153 (1); 'employee': see note to s 1.

Orders under this section: none had been made at the time of going to press.

66. Revocation of exclusion order under s 65

(1) At any time when an order under section 65 is in force, any of the parties to the dismissal procedures agreement to which the order relates may apply to the Secretary of State for the order to be revoked.

(2) If on any such application the Secretary of State is satisfied either—

(*a*) that it is the desire of all the parties to the dismissal procedures agreement that the order should be revoked or

(*b*) that the agreement has ceased to fulfil all the conditions specified in section 64(2).

the Secretary of State shall revoke the order by a further order made under this section.

(3) Any order made under this section may contain such transitional provisions as appear to the Secretary of State to be appropriate in the circumstances, and, in particular, may direct—

(*a*) that, notwithstanding section 65(3), an employee shall not be excluded from his rights under section 54 where the effective date of termination falls within a transitional period which is specified in the order and is a period ending with the date on which the order under this section takes effect and shall have an extended time for presenting a complaint under section 67 in respect of a dismissal where the effective date of termination falls within that period, and

(*b*) that in determining any complaint of unfair dismissal presented by an employee to whom the dismissal procedures agreement applies, where the effective date of termination falls within that transitional period, an industrial tribunal shall have regard to such considerations (in addition to those specified in this Part and paragraph 2 of Schedule 9) as may be specified in the order.

NOTES

Derivation: 1974, para 14.

General Note: see s 149 (2) and Sched 2, Pt I, para 2 (4) and Pt III, para 6 (3) (in relation to maternity).

Definitions: 'dismissal procedures agreement': see s 153 (1); 'employee': see note to s 1; 'effective date of termination': see s 55 (4) and (5).

REMEDIES FOR UNFAIR DISMISSAL

67. Complaint to industrial tribunal

(1) A complaint may be presented to an industrial tribunal against an employer by any person (in this Part referred to as the complainant) that he was unfairly dismissed by the employer.

(2) Subject to subsection (4), an industrial tribunal shall not consider a complaint under this section unless it is presented to the tribunal before the end of the period of three months beginning with the effective date of termination or within such further period as the tribunal considers reasonable in a case where it is satisfied that it was not reasonably practicable for the complaint to be presented before the end of the period of three months.

(3) Subsection (2) shall apply in relation to a complaint to which section 62(3) applies as if for the reference to the effective date of termination there were substituted a reference to the first date on which any relevant employee was offered re-engagement (within the meaning of section 62(4)).

(4) An industrial tribunal shall consider a complaint under this section if, where the dismissal is with notice, the complaint is presented after the notice is given notwithstanding that it is presented before the effective date of termination and in relation to such a complaint the provisions of this Act, so far as they relate to unfair dismissal, shall have effect—

(*a*) as if references to a complaint by a person that he was unfairly dismissed by his employer included references to a complaint by a person that his employer has given him notice in such circumstances that he will be unfairly dismissed when the notice expires;

(*b*) as if references to reinstatement included references to the withdrawal of the notice by the employer;

(*c*) as if references to the effective date of termination included references to the date which would be the effective date of termination on the expiry of the notice; and

(*d*) as if references to an employee ceasing to be employed included references to an employee having been given notice of dismissal.

NOTES

Derivation: 1974, paras 17 (1), 21 (4), (4A), 7 (4); 1975, Sched 16, Pt III, paras 13, 16, 20, 21.

General Note: apart from the general rule that an employee must present his complaint within three months of the effective date of termination, it should be noted that an employee who is given his notice may present a complaint before the notice expires. See ss 101 (1) (*d*), 140 (2) (*d*) and (*e*) and 149 (2). Note s 150 and the provisions of Sched 12, Pt I, and Pt II, particularly paras 8 and 9, which deal with with death of the employer or the employee; Sched 9, paras 1 (3) and (4), 2 and 5, and Sched 13, para 20 (2).

Subsection (2): 'reasonable . . . reasonably practicable': see *Porter* v *Bandridge Ltd* [1978] IRLR 271, in which the Court of Appeal discussed this provision. See also *Dedman* v *British Building and Engineering Appliances Ltd* [1974] ICR 53, which the Court of Appeal followed; *Wall's Meat Co* v *Khan* [1978] IRLR 74; *The Open University* v *Triesman* [1978] ICR 524; and *Avon County Council* v *Haywood-Hicks* [1978] ICR 646.

'presented': see *Anglo Continental School of English* (*Bournemouth*) *Ltd* v *Gardiner* [1973] ICR 261. See also *Ruff* v *Smith* [1976] ICR 118.

Definitions: 'employee' and 'employer': see note to s 1; 'effective date of termination': see s 55 (4) and (5); 'reinstatement': see s 69 (2).

68. Remedies for unfair dismissal

(1) Where on a complaint under section 67 an industrial tribunal finds that the grounds of the complaint are well-founded, it shall explain to the complainant what orders for reinstatement or re-engagement may be made under section 69 and in what circumstances they may be made, and shall ask him whether he wishes the tribunal to make such an order, and if he does express such a wish the tribunal may make an order under section 69.

(2) If on a complaint under section 67 the tribunal finds that the grounds of the complaint are well-founded and no order is made under section 69, the tribunal shall make an award of compensation for unfair dismissal, calculated in accordance with sections 72 to 74, to be paid by the employer to the employee.

NOTES

Derivation: 1975, ss 71 (1), 72 (5).

General Note: the primary remedies are orders for reinstatement or re-engagement, and these must be explained to the successful complainant. The tribunal may award compensation where: (*a*) it makes no order for reinstatement or re-engagement; (*b*) an order is not fully complied with (see s 71 (1)); or (*c*) the order is not complied with at all (see s 71 (2) to (5)). Note s 150 and the provisions of Sched 12, particularly Pt II, paras 10 and 11, which provide for the death of the employer or the employee. See the General Note to s 69.

Orders for reinstatement: see s 69 (2), (3), and (5).

Orders for re-engagement: see s 69 (4) and (6).

Definitions: 'employee' and 'employer': see note to s 1.

69. Order for reinstatement or re-engagement

(1) An order under this section may be an order for reinstatement (in accordance with subsections (2) and (3)) or an order for re-engagement (in accordance with subsection (4)), as the industrial tribunal may decide, and in the latter case may be on such terms as the tribunal may decide.

(2) An order for reinstatement is an order that the employer shall treat the complainant in all respects as if he had not been dismissed, and on making such an order the tribunal shall specify—

(*a*) any amount payable by the employer in respect of any benefit which the complainant might reasonably be expected to have had but for the dismissal, including arrears of pay, for the period between the date of termination of employment and the date of reinstatement;

(*b*) any rights and privileges, including seniority and pension rights, which must be restored to the employee; and

(*c*) the date by which the order must be complied with.

(3) Without prejudice to the generality of subsection (2), if the complainant would have benefited from an improvement in his terms and conditions of employment had he not been dismissed, an order for

reinstatement shall require him to be treated as if he had benefited from that improvement from the date on which he would have done so but for being dismissed.

(4) An order for re-engagement is an order that the complainant be engaged by the employer, or by a successor of the employer or by an associated employer, in employment comparable to that from which he was dismissed or other suitable employment, and on making such an order the tribunal shall specify the terms on which re-engagement is to take place including—

(*a*) the identify of the employer;

(*b*) the nature of the employment;

(*c*) the remuneration for the employment;

(*d*) any amount payable by the employer in respect of any benefit which the complainant might reasonably be expected to have had but for the dismissal, including arrears of pay, for the period between the date of termination of employment and the date of re-engagement;

(*e*) any rights and privileges, including seniority and pension rights, which must be restored to the employee; and

(*f*) the date by which the order must be complied with.

(5) In exercising its discretion under this section the tribunal shall first chnsider whether to make an order for reinstatement and in so doing shall take into account the following considerations, that is to say—

(*a*) whether the complainant wishes to be reinstated;

(*b*) whether it is practicable for the employer to comply with an order for reinstatement;

(*c*) where the complainant caused or contributed to some extent to the dismissal, whether it would be just to order his reinstatement.

(6) If the tribunal decides not to make an order for reinstatement it shall then consider whether to make an order for re-engagement and if so on what terms; and in so doing the tribunal shall take into account the following considerations, that is to say—

(*a*) any wish expressed by the complainant as to the nature of the order to be made;

(*b*) whether it is practicable for the employer or, as the case may be, a successor or associated employer to comply with an order for re-engagement;

(*c*) where the complainant caused or contributed to some extent to the dismissal, whether it would be just to order his re-engagement and if so on what terms;

and except in a case where the tribunal takes into account contributory fault under paragraph (*c*) it shall, if it orders re-engagement, do so on terms which are, so far as is reasonably practicable, as favourable as an order for reinstatement.

NOTES

Derivation: 1975, s 71 (2) to (7).

General Note: the only reported EAT case on this provision is *Meridian Ltd* v *Gomersall* [1977] ICR 597.

Further provisions: see s 70, which deals with the situation where the employer has engaged a permanent replacement for the dismissed employee; s 71, which provides for compensation to be awarded when an order for reinstatement or re-engagement is either partially complied with or not complied with at all; and ss 77 to 79, which make provision for interim relief and orders for the continuation of a contract. See also s 150 and Sched 12, particularly Pt II, paras 10 and 11, which deal with the death of the employee or the employer.

Note Sched 13, para 20, and the Labour Relations (Continuity of Employment) Regulations 1976 (SI 1976 No 660), para 4, by which the continuity of the employment of a reinstated or re-engaged employee is preserved, and the interval counts in the computation of his period of continuous employment.

Date of termination: note Sched 2, Pt I, para 2 (3) in relation to maternity.

Definitions: 'employment': see s 153 (1); 'employee' and 'employer': see note to s 1; 'successor': see s 153 (1); 'associated employer': see s 153 (4).

70. Supplementary provisions relating to s 69

(1) Where in any case an employer has engaged a permanent replacement for a dismissed employee, the tribunal shall not take that fact into account in determining, for the purposes of subsection (5)(*b*) or (6)(*b*) of section 69, whether it is practicable to comply with an order for reinstatement or re-engagement unless the employer shows—

(*a*) that it was not practicable for him to arrange for the dismissed employee's work to be done without engaging a permanent replacement; or

(*b*) that he engaged the replacement after the lapse of a reasonable period, without having heard from the dismissed employee that he wished to be reinstated or re-engaged, and that when the employer engaged the replacement it was no longer reasonable for him to arrange for the dismissed employee's work to be done except by a permanent replacement.

(2) In calculating for the purpose of subsection (2)(*a*) or (4)(*d*) of section 69 any amount payable by the employer, the tribunal shall take into account, so as to reduce the employer's liability, any sums received by the complainant in respect of the period between the date of termination of employment and the date of reinstatement or re-engagement by way of—

(*a*) wages in lieu of notice or ex gratia payments paid by the employer;

(*b*) remuneration paid in respect of employment with another employer;

and such other benefits as the tribunal thinks appropriate in the circumstances.

NOTES

Derivation: 1975, s 71 (8), (9).

Date of termination: note Sched 2, Pt I, para 2 (3) in relation to maternity.

Definitions: 'employee' and 'employer': see note to s 1; 'order for reinstatement or re-engagement': see s 69.

71. Enforcement of s 69 order and compensation

(1) If an order under section 69 is made and the complainant is reinstated or, as the case may be, re-engaged but the terms of the order are not fully complied with, then, subject to section 75, an industrial tribunal shall make an award of compensation, to be paid by the employer to the employee, of such amount as the tribunal thinks fit having regard to the loss sustained by the complainant in consequence of the failure to comply fully with the terms of the order.

(2) Subject to subsection (1), if an order under section 69 is made but the complainant is not reinstated or, as the case may be, re-engaged in accordance with the order—

(*a*) the tribunal shall make an award of compensation for unfair dismissal, calculated in accordance with sections 72 to 74, to be paid by the employer to the employee; and

(*b*) unless the employer satisfies the tribunal that it was not practicable to comply with the order, the tribunal shall make an additional award of compensation to be paid by the employer to the employee of an amount—

(i) where the dismissal is of a description referred to in subsection (3), not less than twenty-six nor more than fifty-two weeks' pay, or

(ii) in any other case, not less than thirteen nor more than twenty-six weeks' pay.

(3) The descriptions of dismissal in respect of which an employer may incur a higher additional award in accordance with subsection (2)(*b*)(i) are the following, that is to say,—

(*a*) a dismissal which is unfair by virtue of section 58(1) or (3);

(*b*) a dismissal which is an act of discrimination within the meaning of the Sex Discrimination Act 1975 which is unlawful by virtue of that Act;

(*c*) a dismissal which is an act of discrimination within the meaning of the Race Relations Act 1976 which is unlawful by virtue of that Act.

(4) Where in any case an employer has engaged a permanent replacement for a dismissed employee the tribunal shall not take that fact into account in determining, for the purposes of subsection (2)(*b*) whether it was practicable to comply with the order for reinstatement or re-engagement unless the employer shows that it was not practicable for him to arrange for the dismissed employee's work to be done without engaging a permanent replacement.

(5) Where in any case an industrial tribunal makes an award of compensation for unfair dismissal, calculated in accordance with sections 72 to 74, and the tribunal finds that the complainant has unreasonably prevented an order under section 69 from being complied with, it shall, without prejudice to the generality of section 74(4), take that conduct into account as a failure on the part of the complainant to mitigate his loss.

NOTES

Derivation: 1975, s 72 (1) to (4) and (6); Race Relations Act 1976, Sched 3, para 1 (2).

Further provisions: see s 150 and Sched 12, particularly Pt II, para 11, which deal with the death of the employee or the employer. See also s 122, which deals with the employee's rights on the insolvency of the employer. As the notes to that section point out, an additional award of compensation does not appear to fall within s 122 (3); this situation is anomalous. Note Sched 2, Pt I, para 2 (5) in relation to maternity.

Subsection (2): week's pay: see s 152 and Sched 14, Pt II, and the notes to those provisions, for the calculation of the amount of a week's pay. Note Sched 14, para 7 (1) (*f*), (*g*), (*h*) and (*i*).

Additional award of compensation: see *George* v *Beecham Group* [1977] IRLR 43. Note Sched 14, para 8.

See also s 80 (2) (*a*).

Definitions: 'employee' and 'employer': see note to s 1; 'week's pay': see above; 'order for reinstatement or re-engagement': see s 69.

AMOUNT OF COMPENSATION

72. Compensation for unfair dismissal

Where a tribunal makes an award of compensation for unfair dismissal under section 68(2) or 71(2)(*a*) the award shall consist of a basic award (calculated in accordance with section 73) and a compensatory award (calculated in accordance with section 74).

NOTES

Derivation: 1975, s 73.

Further provisions: see s 122, which deals with the employee's rights on the insolvency of the employer; s 132 which makes provision for the recoupment of certain benefits; s 150 and Sched 12, which deal with the death of the employer or the employee, and Sched 14, para 8.

73. Calculation of basic award

(1) The amount of the basic award shall be the amount calculated in accordance with subsections (3) to (6), subject to—

(*a*) subsection (2) of this section (which provides for an award of two weeks' pay in certain redundancy cases);

(b) subsection (7) (which provides for the amount of the award to be reduced where the employee contributed to the dismissal);

(*c*) subsection (8) (which provides for a minimum award of two weeks' pay in certain cases);

(*d*) subsection (9) (which provides for the amount of the award to be reduced where the employee received a payment in respect of redundancy); and

(*e*) section 76 (which prohibits compensation being awarded under this Part and under the Sex Discrimination Act 1975 or the Race Relations Act 1976 in respect of the same matter).

(2) The amount of the basic award shall be two weeks' pay where the tribunal finds that the reason or principal reason for the dismissal of the employee was that he was redundant and the employee—

(*a*) by virute of section 82(5) or (6) is not, or if he were otherwise entitled would not be, entitled to a redundancy payment; or

(*b*) by virtue of the operation of section 84(1) is not treated as dismissed for the purposes of Part VI.

(3) The amount of the basic award shall be calculated by reference to the period, ending with the effective date of termination, during which the employee has been continuously employed, by starting at the end of that period and reckoning backwards the numbers of years of employment falling within that period, and allowing—

(*a*) one and a half weeks' pay for each such year of employment which consists wholly of weeks in which the employee was not below the age of forty-one;

(*b*) one week's pay for each such year of employment which consists wholly of weeks in which the employee was below the age of forty-one and was not below the age of twenty-two; and

(*c*) half a week's pay for each such year of employment which consists wholly of weeks in which the employee was below the age of twenty-two and was not below the age of eighteen.

(4) Where, in reckoning the number of years of employment in accordance with subsection (3), twenty years of employment have been reckoned no account shall be taken of any year of employment earlier than those twenty years.

(5) Where in the case of an employee the effective date of termination is after the specified anniversary the amount of the basic award calculated in accordance with subsections (3) and (4) shall be reduced by the appropriate fraction.

(6) In subsection (5) "the specified anniversary" in relation to a man means the sixty-fourth anniversary of the day of his birth, and in relation to a woman means the fifty-ninth anniversary of the day of her birth, and "the appropriate fraction" means the fraction of which—

(*a*) the numerator is the number of whole months reckoned from the specified anniversary in the period beginning with that anniversary and ending with the effective date of termination; and

(*b*) the denominator is twelve.

(7) Where the tribunal finds that the dismissal was to any extent caused or contributed to by any action of the complainant it shall, except in a case where the dismissal was by reason of redundancy, reduce the amount of the basic award by such proportion as it considers just and equitable having regard to that finding.

(8) Where the amount calculated in accordance with subsections (3) to (7) is less than the amount of two weeks' pay, the amount of the basic award shall be two weeks' pay.

(9) The amount of the basic award shall be reduced or, as the case may be, be further reduced, by the amount of any redundancy payment awarded by the tribunal under Part VI in respect of the same dismissal or of any payment made by the employer to the employee on the ground that the dismissal was by reason of redundancy, whether in pursuance of Part VI or otherwise.

NOTES

Derivation: 1975, s 74 (1) to (3) and (5) to (7); s 75 (7) and (8).

General Note: in most cases the basic award under this section will be calculated in the same way as a redundancy payment (see Sched 4). The tribunal may only reduce the award in two situations: (1) where the dismissal was to any extent caused or contributed to by any action of the complainant, the tribunal may reduce the amount of the basic award by such an amount as it considers just and equitable (see s 73 (7)); and (ii) where the complainant has already received a redundancy payment, the basic award will be reduced by that amount (see s 73 (9) and *Thomas & Betts Manufacturing Co Ltd* v *Harding* [1978] IRLR 213). If, therefore, an employee is dismissed, and, after the dismissal, evidence of misconduct prior to the dismissal comes to light, as has been seen, that evidence will generally be inadmissible; but, before the provisions of the Employment Protection Act 1975 came into effect, the industrial tribunal had a discretion to award 'such amount as it considers just and equitable in all the circumstances . . .' (see Sched 1, para 19 of the Trade Union and Labour Relations Act 1974) and could, therefore, make a nil award. Now, it appears, it could not, and would have to make a basic award: see *W Devis & Sons Ltd* v *Atkins* [1977] ICR 662, and particularly Lord Diplock's speech, which was followed by the EAT in *D G Moncrieff* (*Farmers*) v *MacDonald* [1978] IRLR 112. The desirability of this position is questionable. See also *Barley* v *Amey Roadstone Corporation Ltd* (*No* 2) [1978] ICR 190 and *Brownson* v *Hire Service Shops Ltd* [1978] ICR 517.

Further provisions: see s 122, which deals with the employee's rights on the insolvency of the employer, and s 150 and Sched 12, which deal with the death of the employer or the employee. See also Sched 2, Pt I, para 2 (5) in relation to maternity.

Week's pay: see s 152 and Sched 14, Pt II, and the notes to those provisions, for the calculation of the amount of a week's pay.

Continuously employed: see s 151 and Sched 13, which contains provisions for ascertaining the length of an employee's period of employment and whether it has been continuous, and the notes to those provisions.

Effective date of termination: see s 55 (4) and (5) and the note to those subsections.

Subsection (3): note Sched 13, para 11 (1).

Subsections (5) *and* (6): note Sched 2, Pt I, para 2 (4) in relation to maternity.

Subsection (7): see the note to s 74 (6).

Definitions: 'week's pay': see above; 'employee': see note to s 1; 'redundancy': see s 81 (2); 'effective date of termination' and 'continuously employed': see above; 'week' and 'employment': see s 153 (1).

74. Calculation of compensatory award

(1) Subject to sections 75 and 76, the amount of the compensatory award shall be such amount as the tribunal considers just and equitable in all the circumstances having regard to the loss sustained by the complainant in consequence of the dismissal in so far as that loss is attributable to action taken by the employer.

(2) The said loss shall be taken to include—

(*a*) any expenses reasonably incurred by the complainant in consequence of the dismissal, and

(*b*) subject to subsection (3), loss of any benefit which he might reasonably be expected to have had but for the dismissal.

(3) The said loss, in respect of any loss of any entitlement or potential entitlement to, or expectation of, a payment on account of dismissal by reason of redundancy, whether in pursuance of Part VI or otherwise, shall include only the loss referable to the amount, if any, by which the amount of that payment would have exceeded the amount of a basic award (apart from any reduction under section 73(7) or (9)) in respect of the same dismissal.

(4) In ascertaining the said loss the tribunal shall apply the same rule concerning the duty of a person to mitigate his loss as applies to damages recoverable under the common law of England and Wales or of Scotland, as the case may be.

(5) In determining, for the purposes of subsection (1), how far any loss sustained by the complainant was attributable to action taken by the employer no account shall be taken of any pressure which, by calling, organising, procuring or financing a strike or other industrial action, or threatening to do so, was exercised on the employer to dismiss the employee, and that question shall be determined as if no such pressure had been exercised.

(6) Where the tribunal finds that the dismissal was to any extent caused or contributed to by any action of the complainant it shall reduce the amount of the compensatory award by such proportion as it considers just and equitable having regard to that finding.

(7) If the amount of any payment made by the employer to the employee on the ground that the dismissal was by reason of redundancy, whether in pursuance of Part VI or otherwise, exceeds the amount of the basic award which would be payable but for section 73(9) that excess shall go to reduce the amount of the compensatory award.

NOTES

Derivation: 1975, s 76.

General Note: the principles applicable to an award of compensation were originally set out in *Norton Tool Co Ltd* v *Tewson* [1972] ICR 501, where it was said that an award of compensation should be considered under four heads: (1) immediate loss of wages; (ii) manner of dismissal; (iii) future loss of wages; and (iv) loss of protection in respect of unfair dismissal or dismissal by reason of redundancy. Head (iv) has been assimilated into the basic award under s 73 (though s 74 (3) seems to envisage a situation in which a loss of potential entitlement to a redundancy payment might exceed the basic award), but to the original four there has been added a fifth head: loss of pension rights. This head is likely to assume increasing importance: see *Tidman* v *Aveling Marshall Ltd* [1977] ICR 506. It should be noted that most of the reported cases have been decided under the pre-Employment Protection Act 1975 law (ie Sched 1, paras 19 and 20 of the Trade Union and Labour Relations Act 1974).

See also s 122, which deals with the employee's rights on the insolvency of the employer, and s 150 and Sched 12, which deal with the death of the employer or the employee. It is not clear, as the notes to s 122 point out, whether a compensatory award falls within s 122 (3) or not; at best, it would fall within s 122 (3) (*a*) and (*c*).

Subsection (1): as had been pointed out in the General Note, a compensatory award should be considered under four heads:

(i) immediate loss of wages: it is not necessary for the tribunal to make a deduction from the award under this head in respect of unemployment benefits received by the employee or any reduction of his income tax liability during the notice period, nor need the employee bring into account any wages paid by his new employers during the notice period: see *Adda International Ltd* v *Curcio* [1976] ICR 407; *Blackwell* v *GEC Elliot Process Automation Ltd* [1976] IRLR 144; *Help the Aged Housing Association (Scotland) Ltd* v *Vidler* [1977] IRLR 104; and *Brownson* v *Hire Service Shops Ltd* [1978] ICR 517.

(ii) manner of dismissal: compensation will only be awarded under this head where the manner of dismissal leads to a financial loss: see *Norton*

Tool Co Ltd v *Tewson; Clarkson Ltd* v *Short* [1973] ICR 191; *Vaughan* v *Weighpack Ltd* [1974] ICR 261; and *Lifeguard Assurance Ltd* v *Zadrozny* [1977] IRLR 56.

(iii) future loss of wages: the restriction on the right of an employee to claim compensation for unfair dismissal after reaching the age of retirement (see s 64 (1) (*b*)) does not affect the assessment of compensation payable to an employee who has been unfairly dismissed before that date: see *Barrel Plating & Phosphating Co Ltd* v *Danks* [1976] ICR 503. In deciding what amount of compensation is just and equitable, the tribunal ought to consider the employee to be in the circumstances and in the state of health in which he was at the date of dismissal: see *Fougère* v *Phoenix Motor Co Ltd* [1976] ICR 495; *Brittains Arborfield Ltd* v *Van Uden* [1977] ICR 211; *Young's of Gosport Ltd* v *Kendell* [1977] ICR 907; and *Barley* v *Amey Roadstone Corporation Ltd* (*No 2*) [1978] ICR 190. See also *Adda International Ltd* v *Curcio* and *Help the Aged Housing Association* (*Scotland*) *Ltd* v *Vidler*.

(iv) loss of pension rights: as has already been stated, this head is likely to assume increasing importance in the future. Apart from *Tidman's* case (mentioned earlier), the most important recent cases dealing with this are *Powrmatic Ltd* v *Bull* [1977] ICR 469 and *Smith, Kline & French Laboratories Ltd* v *Coates* [1977] IRLR 220. Both set out in considerable detail the matters to be considered in assessing the loss under this head. See also *Tesco Stores Ltd* v *Heap* (1978) 13 ITR 17.

'just and equitable . . .': it was said in *Fougère's* case that this formula 'entitles the industrial tribunal, having considered the matter, and all other relevant circumstances, to moderate the figure to which arithmetic alone might lead in arriving at a total which in their view is just and equitable'. This formula also enables the Tribunal to reach the conclusion that despite the fact that he was unfairly dismissed he suffered no loss; examples of this are to be found in *Earl* v *Slater & Wheeler* (*Airlyne*) *Ltd* [1972] ICR 508 and *Carr* v *Alexander Russell Ltd* [1976] IRLR 220.

Subsection (2): 'expenses reasonably incurred': see *Lifeguard Assurance Ltd* v *Zadrozny* [1977] IRLR 56.

Subsection (4): as has already been stated (in the note to subs (1)), the employee need not account for any wages paid by his new employers during the notice period. In addition to the cases cited there, see *Everwear Candlewick Ltd* v *Isaac* [1974] ICR 525. See also *Smith, Kline & French Laboratories Ltd* v *Coates*. Note s 71 (5).

Subsection (5): for the principles to be applied by tribunals when assessing compensation in such cases, see *Morris* v *Gestetner Ltd* [1973] ICR 587. See also *Trend* v *Chiltern Hunt Ltd* [1977] IRLR 66. See also s 80 (2) (*b*).

Subsection (6): the relationship between this subsection and subs (1) has caused considerable discussion: see *Munif* v *Cole & Kirby Ltd* [1973] ICR 486; *Maris* v *Rotherham Corporation* [1974] ICR 435; *Cooper* v *British Steel Corporation* [1975] ICR 454; *Kemp* v *Shipton Automation Ltd* [1976] ICR 514; *Trend* v *Chiltern Hunt Ltd* [1977] ICR 612; and *Nudds* v *W and J B Eastwoods Ltd* [1978] ICR 171. In *Kemp*, the view was expressed that an unfairly dismissed employee is entitled to some compensation in all but very rare circumstances and that the minimum award should be approximately 20 per cent of the sum to which he would have been entitled had he not by his conduct contributed to his own dismissal. Contributions of over 80 per cent might lead to an inconsistency vis-à-vis a finding of unfair dismissal, though in *Trend* and *Nudds* the EAT did not exclude the possibility of a contribution being 90 per cent or 100 per cent without leading to inconsistencies.

See also *Robert Whiting Designs Ltd* v *Lamb* [1978] ICR 89; *Kraft Foods Ltd* v *Fox* [1978] ICR 311; *Brown's Cycles Ltd* v *Brindley* [1978] ICR 467; and *Moncur* v *International Paint Co Ltd* [1978] IRLR 223.

Since compensation now falls to be computed in two parts, it is feasible that greater difficulties will be encountered. One problem has already been thrown up by *Devis* v *Atkins* (see General Note to s 73) in relation to subsequent discoveries of misconduct prior to dismissal (see also *Moncrieff* v *MacDonald* [1978] IRLR 112); another may be the situation where a dismissal is found to be unfair on technical grounds, but might have been fair had the employers gone about it correctly: see, in this context, *Brown's Cycles Ltd* v *Brindley* [1978] ICR 467.

Definitions: 'redundancy': see s 81 (2); 'basic award': see s 73; 'employee' and 'employer': see note to s 1.

75. Limit on compensation

(1) The amount of compensation awarded to a person under section 71(1) or of a compensatory award to a person calculated in accordance with section 74 shall not exceed £5,200.

(2) The Secretary of State may by order increase the said limit of £5,200 or that limit as from time to time increased under this subsection, but no such order shall be made unless a draft of the order has been laid before Parliament and approved by a resolution of each House of Parliament.

(3) It is hereby declared for the avoidance of doubt that the limit imposed by this section applies to the amount which the industrial tribunal would, apart from this section, otherwise award in respect of the subject matter of the complaint after taking into account any payment made by the respondent to the complainant in respect of that matter and any reduction in the amount of the award required by any enactment or rule of law.

NOTES

Derivation: 1974, para 20; 1975 Sched 16, Pt III, para 17.

General Note: note s 149 (2).

Orders under this section: none had been made at the time of going to press.

76. Compensation for act which is both sex or racial discrimination [or both] and unfair dismissal

(1) Where compensation falls to be awarded in respect of any act both under the provisions of this Act relating to unfair dismissal and under one or both of the following Acts, namely the Sex Discrimination Act 1975 and the Race Relations Act 1976, an industrial tribunal shall not award compensation under any one of those two or, as the case may be, three Acts in respect of any loss or other matter which is or has been taken into account under the other or any other of them by the tribunal or another industrial tribunal in awarding compensation on the same or another complaint in respect of that act.

(2) Without prejudice to section 75 (whether as enacted or as applied by section 65 of the Sex Discrimination Act 1975 or section 56 of the Race Relations Act 1976) in a case to which subsection (1) applies, the aggregate of the following amounts of compensation awarded by an industrial tribunal, that is to say—

(*a*) any compensation awarded under the said Act of 1975; and

(*b*) any compensation awarded under the said Act of 1976; and

(*c*) any compensation awarded under section 71(1) or, as the case may be, which is calculated in accordance with section 74,

shall not exceed the limit for the time being imposed by section 75.

NOTES

Derivation: 1975, s 77; Race Relations Act 1976, Sched 3, para 1 (3).

INTERIM RELIEF

77. Interim relief pending determination of complaint of unfair dismissal

(1) An employee who presents a complaint to an industrial tribunal that he has been unfairly dismissed by his employer and that the reason for the dismissal (or, if more than one, the principal reason) was that the employee—

(*a*) was, or proposed to become, a member of a particular independent trade union; or

(*b*) had taken, or proposed to take, part at any appropriate time in the activities of a particular independent trade union of which he was or proposed to become a member;

may, subject to the following provisions of this section, apply to the tribunal for an order under the following provisions of this section.

(2) An industrial tribunal shall not entertain an application under this section unless—

(*a*) it is presented to the tribunal before the end of the period of seven days immediately following the effective date of termination (whether before, on or after that date); and

(*b*) before the end of that period there is also so presented a certificate in writing signed by an authorised official of the independent trade union of which the employee was or had proposed to become a member stating that on the date of the dismissal the employee was or had proposed to become a member of the union and that there appear to be reasonable grounds for supposing that the reason for his dismissal (or, if more than one, the principal reason) was one alleged in the complaint.

(3) An industrial tribunal shall determine an application under this section as soon as practicable after receiving the application and the relevant certificate, but shall, at least seven days before the date of the hearing, give the employer a copy of the application and certificate, together with notice of the date, time and place of the hearing.

(4) An industrial tribunal shall not exercise any power it has of postponing the hearing in the case of an application under this section except where the tribunal is satisfied that special circumstances exist which justify it in doing so.

(5) If on hearing an application under this section it appears to an industrial tribunal that it is likely that on determining the complaint to which the application relates the tribunal will find that the complainant was unfairly dismissed and that the reason for the dismissal (or if more than one, the principal reason) was a reason mentioned in subsection (1), the tribunal shall announce its findings and explain to both parties (if present) what powers the tribunal may exercise on an application under this section and in what circumstances it may exercise them, and shall ask the employer (if present) whether he is willing, pending the determination or settlement of the complaint—

(*a*) to reinstate the employee, that is to say, to treat the employee in all respects as if he had not been dismissed; or (*b*) if not, to re-engage him in another job on terms and conditions not less favourable than those which would have been applicable to him if he had not been dismissed.

(6) In subsection (5) " terms and conditions not less favourable than those which would have been applicable to him if he had not been dismissed " means, as regards seniority, pension rights and other similar rights, that the period prior to the dismissal shall be regarded as continuous with his employment following the dismissal.

(7) If the employer states that he is willing to reinstate the employee, the tribunal shall make an order to that effect.

(8) If the employer states that he is willing to re-engage the employee in another job and specifies the terms and conditions on which he is willing to do so, the tribunal shall ask the employee whether he is willing to accept the job on those terms and conditions, and—

(*a*) if the employee is willing to accept the job on those terms and conditions, the tribunal shall make an order to that effect; and

(*b*) if the employee is unwilling to accept the job on those terms and conditions, then, if the tribunal is of the opinion that the refusal is reasonable, the tribunal shall make an order for the continuation of his contract of employment, but otherwise the tribunal shall make no order under this section.

(9) If, on the hearing of an application under this section, the employer fails to attend before the tribunal or he states that he is unwilling either to reinstate the employee or re-engage him as mentioned in subsection (5), the tribunal shall make an order for the continuation of the employee's contract of employment.

(10) In this section—

" appropriate time " has the same meaning as in section 23;

" authorised official ", in relation to a trade union, means an official of the union authorised by the union to act for the purposes of this section;

and any reference to the date of dismissal is a reference—

(*a*) where the employee's contract of employment was terminated by notice (whether given by his employer or by him), to the date on which the employer's notice was given; and

(*b*) in any other case, to the effective date of termination.

(11) A document purporting to be an authorisation of an official by a trade union to act for the purposes of this section and to be signed on behalf of the union shall be taken to be such an authorisation unless the contrary is proved, and a document purporting to be a certificate signed by such an official shall be taken to be signed by him unless the contrary is proved.

NOTES

Derivation: 1975, s 78.

General Note: the provisions of this section, and sections 78 and 79, apply to employees who are dismissed for reasons connected with trade union membership or activities. By virtue of s 64 (3), there is no minimum period of employment which qualifies the employee. This section makes general provision for interim relief; s 78 makes provision for orders for the continuation of the employee's contract of employment (where the employer either fails to attend the tribunal hearing or states that he is unwilling to reinstate or re-engage the employee); and s 79 contains supplementary provisions relating to interim relief.

See also s 150 and Sched 12, Pts I and II, which make provision for the death of the employer or the employee. Note Sched 9, para 8.

Subsection (2) (*a*): although an application containing no express reference to this section, or to the reason for dismissal, is defective, it is not a nullity, since it is likely to be understood by the staff of the Central Office of Industrial Tribunals to refer to a claim under this section. The defect may be made good by information supplied after the expiry of the time limit: see *Barley* v *Amey Roadstone Corporation Ltd* [1977] ICR 546.

Subsection (2) (*b*): the certificate must fulfil the requirements of this paragraph. If not, it will not constitute a valid certificate, and the industrial tribunal will be correct in refusing the application: see *Stone* v *Charrington & Co Ltd* [1977] ICR 248.

Subsection (5): 'likely': in *Taplin* v *C Shippam Ltd* (unreported at the time of going to press), the EAT said that on a hearing of an application under this section, the tribunal should ask itself whether the applicant had established that he had a 'pretty good' chance of succeeding in the final application to the tribunal. It did not have to be satisfied that he would succeed at the trial.

Order for the continuation of the employee's contract: see ss 78 and 79.

Definitions: 'employee' and 'employer': see note to s 1; 'independent trade union': see s 153 (1); 'effective date of termination': see s 55 (4) and (5); 'contract of employment': see s 153 (1); 'official': see s 153 (1); 'appropriate time', 'authorised official' and 'date of dismissal': note subs (10).

78. Orders for continuation of contract of employment

(1) An order for the continuation of a contract of employment under section 77 shall be an order that the contract of employment, if it has been terminated, shall continue in force as if it had not been terminated and if not, shall on its termination, continue in force, in either case until the determination or settlement of the complaint and only for the purposes of pay or any other benefit derived from the employment, seniority, pension rights and other similar matters and for the purpose of determining for any purpose the period for which the employee has been continuously employed.

(2) Where the tribunal makes any such order it shall specify in the order the amount which is to be paid by the employer to the employee by way of pay in respect of each normal pay period or part of any such period falling between the date of the dismissal and the determination or settlement of the complaint and, subject to subsection (5), the amount so specified shall be that which the employee could reasonably have been expected to earn during that period or part, and shall be paid, in the case of a payment for any such period falling wholly or partly after the order, on the normal pay day for that period and, in the case of a payment for any past period, within a time so specified.

(3) If an amount is payable by way of pay in pursuance of any such order in respect only of part of a normal pay period the amount shall be calculated by reference to the whole period and be reduced proportionately.

(4) Any payment made to an employee by an employer under his contract of employment, or by way of damages for breach of that contract, in respect of any normal pay period or part of any such period shall go towards discharging the employer's liability in respect of that period

under subsection (2), and conversely any payment under subsection (2) in respect of any period shall go towards discharging any liability of the employer under, or in respect of breach of, the contract of employment in respect of that period.

(5) If an employee, on or after being dismissed by his employer, receives a lump sum which, or part of which, is in lieu of wages but is not referable to any normal pay period, the tribunal shall take the payment into account in determining the amount of pay to be payable in pursuance of any such order.

(6) For the purposes of this section the amount which an employee could reasonably have been expected to earn, his normal pay period and the normal pay day for each such period shall be determined as if he had not been dismissed.

NOTES

Derivation: 1975, s 79.

Further provisions: see s 150 and Sched 12, Pts I and II, which make provision for the death of the employer or the employee.

Continuously employed: see s 151 and Sched 13, which contain provisions for ascertaining the length of an employee's period of employment and whether it has been continuous, and the notes to those provisions.

Definitions: 'contract of employment': see s 153 (1); 'employee' and 'employer': see note to s 1.

79. Supplementary provisions relating to interim relief

(1) At any time between the making of an order by an industrial tribunal under section 77 and the determination or settlement of the complaint to which it relates, the employer or the employee may apply to the tribunal for the revocation or variation of the order on the ground of a relevant change of circumstances since the making of the order, and that section shall apply to the application as it applies to an application for an order under that section except that—

(*a*) no certificate need be presented to the tribunal under subsection (2)(*b*), and no copy of the certificate need be given to the employer under subsection (3), of that section; and

(*b*) in the case of an application by an employer, for the reference in the said subsection (3) to the employer there shall be substituted a reference to the employee.

(2) If on the application of an employee an industrial tribunal is satisfied that the employer has not complied with the terms of an order for the reinstatement or re-engagement of the employee under section 77(7) or (8),—

(*a*) the tribunal shall make an order for the continuation of the employee's contract of employment and section 78 shall apply to an order under this subsection as it applies to an order for the continuation of a contract of employment under section 77; and

(*b*) the tribunal shall also order the employer to pay the employee such compensation as the tribunal considers just and equitable in all the circumstances having regard to the infringement of the employee's right to be reinstated or re-engaged in pursuance of the order under section 77(7) or (8) and to any loss suffered by the employee in consequence of the non-compliance.

(3) If on the application of an employee an industrial tribunal is satisfied that the employer has not complied with the terms of an order for the continuation of a contract of employment, then—

(*a*) if the non-compliance consists of a failure to pay an amount by way of pay specified in the order, the tribunal shall determine the amount of pay owed by the employer to the employee on the date of the determination, and, if on that date the tribunal also determines the employee's complaint that he has been unfairly dismissed by his employer, the tribunal shall specify that amount separately from any other sum awarded to the employee; and

(*b*) in any other case, the tribunal shall order the employer to pay the employee such compensation as the tribunal considers just and equitable in all the circumstances having regard to any loss suffered by the employee in consequence of the non-compliance.

NOTES

Derivation: 1975, s 80 (1) to (3).

Further provisions: see similar note to s 78. Note Sched 9, para 8.

Definitions: 'employee' and 'employer': see note to s 1; 'contract of employment': see s 153 (1).

TEACHERS IN AIDED SCHOOLS

80. Teacher in aided school dismissed on requirement of local education authority

(1) Where a teacher in an aided school is dismissed by the governors or managers of the school in pursuance of a requirement of the local education authority under paragraph (*a*) of the proviso to section 24(2) of the Education Act 1944, this Part shall have effect in relation to the dismissal as if—

(*a*) the local education authority had at all material times been the teacher's employer, and

(*b*) the local education authority had dismissed him, and the reason or principal reason for which they did so had been the reason or principal reason for which they required his dismissal.

(2) For the purposes of a complaint under section 67 as applied by this section—

(*a*) section 71(2)(*b*) shall have effect as if for the words "not practicable to comply" there were substituted the words "not practicable for the local education authority to permit compliance"; and

(*b*) section 74(5) shall have effect as if any reference to the employer were a reference to the local education authority.

NOTES

Derivation: 1974, para 27; 1975, Sched 16, Pt III, paras 26 and 27.

General Note: note s 149 (2).

PART VI

REDUNDANCY PAYMENTS

RIGHT TO REDUNDANCY PAYMENTS

81. General provisions as to right to redundancy payment

(1) Where an employee who has been continuously employed for the requisite period—

(*a*) is dismissed by his employer by reason of redundancy, or

(*b*) is laid off or kept on short-time to the extent specified in subsection (1) of section 88 and complies with the requirements of that section,

then, subject to the following provisions of this Act, the employer shall be liable to pay to him a sum (in this Act referred to as a " redundancy payment ") calculated in accordance with Schedules 4, 13 and 14.

(2) For the purposes of this Act an employee who is dismissed shall be taken to be dismissed by reason of redundancy if the dismissal is attributable wholly or mainly to—

(*a*) the fact that his employer has ceased, or intends to cease, to carry on the business for the purposes of which the employee was employed by him, or has ceased, or intends to cease, to carry on that business in the place where the employee was so employed, or

(*b*) the fact that the requirements of that business for employees to carry out work of a particular kind, or for employees to carry out work of a particular kind in the place where he was so employed, have ceased or diminished or are expected to cease or diminish.

For the purposes of this subsection, the business of the employer together with the business or businesses of his associated employers shall be treated as one unless either of the conditions specified in this subsection would be satisfied without so treating those businesses.

(3) In subsection (2), " cease " means cease either permanently or temporarily and from whatsoever cause, and " diminish " has a corresponding meaning.

(4) For the purposes of subsection (1), the requisite period is the period of two years ending with the relevant date, excluding any week which began before the employee attained the age of eighteen.

NOTES

Derivation: 1965, ss 1, 48 (3), 25 (3), 8 (1); 1975, Sched 16, Pt I, paras 1, 5 (1), 18.

General Note: to succeed in a claim for a redundancy payment, an employee needs to show:

(i) that he was dismissed (ss 83, 84, 85 and 86); and (ii) that the dismissal was by reason of redundancy (s 81 (2) and (3)).

He will be excluded if he falls within the exclusionary provisions in s 82 or the other exclusions (see note Exclusions). An employee who is dismissed is presumed to have been dismissed by reason of redundancy (see s 91 (2)). Note, however, that this presumption does not apply where the employee complains of having been unfairly dismissed by reason of redundancy: see Sched 9, para 5.

Apart from the general provisions, an employee may be entitled to a redundancy payment if he is laid off or put on short-time working (ss 87 to 89).

Sections 103 to 109 make provision for the establishment and maintenance of the Redundancy Fund, for the payment of rebates and other payments to employers, and for payments to be made to employees in certain circumstances; they also provide for the making of applications, references and appeals.

The remaining provisions of this Part (ss 110 to 120) contain miscellaneous and supplemental provisions. Note particularly s 110 (7).

Note ss 137, 140, 149, 157 and 158. Note also the provisions of Sched 2, Pts II and III, which contain supplementary provisions relating to maternity and redundancy payments, s 117 and Sched 8, which make provision for employees paid by a person other than the employer and s 150 and Sched 12, Pts I, III and IV which deal with the death of the employer or employee.

Exclusions:

(i) employees continuously employed for less than two years (s 81 (1) and (4));
(ii) employees who have reached sixty-five (if men) or sixty (if women) (s 82 (1));
(iii) employees to whom an exemption order applies (s 96);
(iv) employees with pension rights (s 98);
(v) persons employed in certain public offices (s 99);
(vi) employment as domestic servant, if employee related to employer (s 100);
(vii) persons in Crown employment (s 138);
(viii) House of Commons staff (s 139);
(ix) employee outside Great Britain on relevant date, unless: (a) under his contract he ordinarily works in Great Britain (s 141 (3)); or (b) he is employed as a master or seaman in a British ship and is ordinarily resident in Great Britain (s 144 (3));
(x) employee who ordinarily works outside Great Britain unless: (a) in Great Britain on relevant date in accordance with instructions given him by his employer (s 141 (4)); or (b) he is employed as a master or seaman in a British ship and is ordinarily resident in Great Britain (s 144 (3));
(xi) certain employees employed under fixed-term contracts, unless employed as a master or seaman in a British ship and ordinarily resident in Great Britain (s 142 (2), (3) and (4) and s 144 (3));
(xii) share fishermen (s 144 (2));
(xiii) persons in employment as registered dock workers, unless it is employment by virtue of which they are wholly or mainly engaged in work which is not dock work (s 145 (3), (4) and (5));
(xiv) employment by spouse (s 146 (1)).

Note s 105.

Employee, Employer: see note to s 1.

Continuously employed: see s 151 and Sched 13, which contain provisions for ascertaining the length of an employee's period of employment, and whether that employment has been continuous; see also the notes to Sched 13.

Requisite period: see subs (4).

Dismissed: see ss 83 to 86, and 93 and 94.

Redundancy payment: Sched 4 provides the method of calculating a redundancy payment, which is by reference to the period of continuous employment (calculated in accordance with Sched 13). Schedule 14, Pt II provides the method of calculating a week's pay for the purposes of (inter alia) Sched 4.

Subsection (1) (*b*): note Sched 2, Pt II, para 4 (3), in relation to maternity.

Subsection (2): in deciding whether an employee has been dismissed by reason of redundancy within the meaning of this subsection, the tribunal has in effect to consider the question in two stages: (i) whether a redundancy situation in fact existed; and (ii) whether the dismissal was for that reason, or for some other reason: see *Hindle* v *Percival Boats Ltd* [1969] 1 WLR 174. To satisfy the tribunal that the dismissal was not attributable to the redundancy situation, the employer must show that his reason is genuine and is the main reason for the dismissal (*quaere* even if it is mistaken): see *Hindle*'s case, and *Malton* v *Crystal of Scarborough Ltd* (1971) 6 ITR 106. See also *Chapman* v *Goonvean and Rostowrack China Clay Co Ltd* [1973] ICR 310.

If the employee's action, eg by going on strike, creates a redundancy situation and the employee is dismissed in consequence, the fact that the redundancy is 'self-induced' does not disentitle him to a redundancy payment: see *Sanders* v *Ernest A Neale Ltd* [1974] ICR 565. See, however, the note to s 92 (1): the ghost of self-induced redundancy may not have been so completely exorcised as the NIRC intended.

Subsection (2) (*a*): 'cease': see subsection (3).

'In the place where the employee was . . . employed': this phrase means the place where, under his contract of employment, the employee can be required to work: see *Sutcliffe* v *Hawker Siddeley Aviation Ltd* [1972] ICR 560 and *United Kingdom Atomic Energy Authority* v *Claydon* [1974] ICR 128. In the absence of an express stipulation in the contract, the tribunal may find, on the evidence, that there is an implied term governing the employee's mobility: see *O'Brien* v *Associated Fire Alarms Ltd* (1968) 3 ITR 182; *Stevenson* v *Tees-side Bridge and Engineering Ltd* (1971) 6 ITR 44; *Mumford* v *Boulton and Paul* (*Steel Constructions*) *Ltd* (1971) 6 ITR 76; and the cases already cited in this note. The extent of an employee's mobility obligation varies widely according to the differing facts of different employment situations, but the question of whether an implied term exists is one of law: see *O'Brien*'s case, *supra*. See also *Thomas* v *Jones* [1978] ICR 274.

Note s 93 (3).

Subsection (2) (*b*): 'work of a particular kind': this phrase has probably caused more difficulty than any other in these provisions. Perhaps the requirement (introduced by the Employment Protection Act 1975) that the written particulars of the terms of employment should include the title of the job which the employee is employed to do (see s 1 (3) (*f*)) will assist tribunals in resolving problems under this paragraph.

An employee who is dismissed because he refuses to accept an alteration in existing terms of employment is not dismissed by reason of redundancy, since the phrase 'requirements . . . for employees to carry out work of a particular kind' does not admit of the phrase 'on the existing terms and conditions of employment' being read into it: see *Chapman* v *Goonvean and Rostowrack China Clay Co Ltd* [1973] ICR 310. The employer is entitled to propose to his employees a change in the terms and conditions of their employment, unless the change is due to a redundancy situation: see *Johnson* v *Nottinghamshire Police Authority* [1974] ICR 170; *Kykot* v *Smith Hartley Ltd* [1975] IRLR 372; and *Lesney Products and Co Ltd* v *Nolan* [1977] ICR 235. But if the employer decides to alter his business so that the same work is done by persons possessed of a different status (ie self-employed rather than employed), a dismissal of his employees will be a dismissal by reason of redundancy: see *Bromby and Hoare Ltd* v *Evans* [1972] ICR 113.

An employee who stays in the same kind of work can be expected to adapt to new methods and higher standards of efficiency, unless the nature of the work he is required to do is altered so that no requirement remains for employees to do work of the particular kind which has been superseded; regard should be had to the overall requirements of the business and not to the allocation of duties between individuals: see *North Riding Garages Ltd* v *Butterwick* [1967] 2 QB 56. 'Work of a particular kind' means work which is distinguished from other work of the same general kind by requiring special aptitudes, skill or knowledge: see *Amos* v *Max-arc Ltd* [1973] ICR 46. The tribunal must ask itself what were the terms of the employee's contract: see *O'Neill* v *Merseyside Plumbing Co Ltd* [1973] ICR 96 and *Runnels* v *Richards and Osborne Ltd* [1973] ICR 225. The most difficult problems that have arisen have concerned what work the employee can be required to do, and have led to some surprising decisions, which have tended to turn on the findings of fact made by the tribunals: see *Arnold* v *Thomas Harrington Ltd* [1967] 2 All ER 866; *Vaux and Associated Breweries Ltd* v *Ward* (1970) 5 ITR 62; and *European Chefs (Catering) Ltd* v *Currell* (1971) 6 ITR 37. See also *Scarth* v *Economic Forestry Ltd* [1973] ICR 322 and *Delanair Ltd* v *Mead* [1976] ICR 522. See also *Wilson* v *Underhill House Schools Ltd* [1977] IRLR 475; *Robinson* v *British Island Airways Ltd* [1978] ICR 304; and *North East Coast Shiprepairers Ltd* v *Secretary of State for Employment* [1978] IRLR 149.

'In the place where he was so employed': see corresponding note to subs (2) (a).

'Cease', 'diminish': see subs (3).

Subsection (4) note s 90 (3).

Definitions: 'employee', 'continuously employed', 'requisite period', 'dismissed' and 'employer': see above; 'associated employer': see s 153 (4); 'relevant date': see s 153 (1) and s 90; 'week': see s 153 (1).

82. General exclusions from right to redundancy payment

(1) An employee shall not be entitled to a redundancy payment if immediately before the relevant date the employee—

(*a*) if a man, has attained the age of sixty-five, or

(*b*) if a woman, has attained the age of sixty.

(2) Except as provided by section 92, an employee shall not be entitled to a redundancy payment by reason of dismissal where his employer, being entitled to terminate his contract of employment without notice by reason of the employee's conduct, terminates it either—

(*a*) without notice, or

(*b*) by giving shorter notice than that which, in the absence of such conduct, the employer would be required to give to terminate the contract, or

(*c*) by giving notice (not being such shorter notice as is mentioned in paragraph (*b*)) which includes, or is accompanied by, a statement in writing that the employer would, by reason of the employee's conduct, be entitled to terminate the contract without notice.

(3) If an employer makes an employee an offer (whether in writing or not) before the ending of his employment under the previous contract to renew his contract of employment, or to re-engage him under a new contract of employment, so that the renewal or re-engagement would take effect either immediately on the ending of his employment under the previous contract or after an interval of not more than four weeks thereafter, the provisions of subsections (5) and (6) shall have effect.

(4) For the purposes of the application of subsection (3) to a contract under which the employment ends on a Friday, Saturday or Sunday—

(*a*) the renewal or re-engagement shall be treated as taking effect immediately on the ending of the employment under the previous contract if it takes effect on or before the next Monday after that Friday, Saturday or Sunday; and

(*b*) the interval of four weeks shall be calculated as if the employment had ended on that Monday.

(5) If an employer makes an employee such an offer as is referred to in subsection (3) and either—

(*a*) the provisions of the contract as renewed, or of the new contract, as to the capacity and place in which he would be employed, and as to the other terms and conditions of his employment, would not differ from the corresponding provisions of the previous contract; or

(*b*) the first-mentioned provisions would differ (wholly or in part) from those corresponding provisions, but the offer constitutes an offer of suitable employment in relation to the employee;

and in either case the employee unreasonably refuses that offer, he shall not be entitled to a redundancy payment by reason of his dismissal.

(6) If an employee's contract of employment is renewed, or he is re-engaged under a new contract of employment, in pursuance of such an offer as is referred to in subsection (3), and the provisions of the contract as renewed, or of the new contract, as to the capacity and place in which he is employed, and as to the other terms and conditions of his employment, differ (wholly or in part) from the corresponding provisions of the previous contract but the employment is suitable in relation to the employee, and during the trial period referred to in section 84 the employee unreasonably terminates the contract, or unreasonably gives notice to terminate it and the contract is thereafter, in consequence, terminated, he shall not be entitled to a redundancy payment by reason of his dismissal from employment under the previous contract.

(7) Any reference in this section to re-engagement by the employer shall be construed as including a reference to re-engagement by the employer or by any associated employer, and any reference in this section to an offer made by the employer shall be construed as including a reference to an offer made by an associated employer.

NOTES

Derivation: 1965, ss 2, 48 (1); 1975, Sched 16, Pt I, paras 2 and 18.

General Note: this is an exclusionary section which applies in three situations: (i) where the employee immediately before the relevant date has attained sixty-five (if a man) or sixty (if a woman) (subs (1)); (ii) where the employer is entitled to terminate the employee's contract summarily because of the employee's conduct, and terminates it without notice, by giving short notice, or by giving ordinary notice accompanied by a written statement to the effect that the employer would be entitled to terminate the contract summarily because of the employee's conduct (subs (2)); and (iii) where the employee unreasonably refuses an offer of suitable employment (subss (3) to (7)).

Note the provisions of s 150 and Sched 12, Pts I, III and IV (particularly paras 15, 16, 23 and 24), which deal with the death of the employer or the employee.

Subsection (1): note Sched 2, Pt II, para 4 (3) in relation to maternity.

Subsection (2): this is a provision, distinguished by its opacity, which has caused some surprising and unsatisfactory decisions. It is suggested that it does not apply where the employer dismisses for misconduct, since, if he establishes that he dismissed for that reason, he will rebut the presumption of redundancy in s 91 (2): see *Essen* v *Vanden Plas (England) 1923 Ltd* (1966) 1 ITR 186; *Statham* v *Hadlow's Garage, Ltd* (1967) 2 ITR 656; *X* v *Y Ltd* (1969) 4 ITR 204; and *Sanders* v *Ernest A Neale Ltd* [1974] ICR 565. No case has offered a satisfactory analysis of when the subsection does apply, but it is submitted that the provisions only apply when an employee is dismissed in a redundancy situation, and the employer complies with the requirements of para (*a*), (*b*) or (*c*): see *Harvey on Industrial Relations* (III, 349 to 384). Suggestions in *X* v *Y Ltd* (1969) 4 ITR 204 and *Simmons* v *Hoover Ltd* [1977] ICR 61 that an employer may fall within subs (2) if he dismisses summarily or with short notice but in ignorance of the employee's misconduct are to be treated with caution; the words 'being entitled . . . by . . . conduct' should only enable an employer to take advantage of the provisions if he can adduce evidence that, at the moment of dismissal, he knew of the employee's conduct. Similarly, an employer should not be allowed to plead misconduct in a situation covered by para (*c*) unless he has given a written statement as required, though *Essen* v *Vanden Plas (England) 1923 Ltd* (1966) 1 ITR 186 suggests the contrary.

Note the provisions of s 92 which in certain circumstances protect the employee from the operation of this subsection, and give him the right to the whole or part of a redundancy payment. Section 92 (1) deals with the situation where an employee goes on strike during the currency of the notice given him by his employer or his own notice under s 88 (1); s 92 (3) operates where during the obligatory period of the employer's notice (as defined by s 85(5)) or after the service of the employee's notice under s 88 (1), the employee's contract is terminated by the employer in the circumstances specified in this subsection. See the notes to that section, and note Sched 2, Pt II, para 4 (3) in relation to maternity.

Subsections (3) *to* (6): see s 94, particularly subss (3) to (5), and s 95, particularly, subs (2) (*a*).

Subsection (4): note Sched 2, Pt II, para 4 (1) (*b*) in relation to maternity.

Subsection (5): 'offer of suitable employment' and 'unreasonable refusal': there are two distinct questions here, to be considered consecutively. If the tribunal finds the offer to be unsuitable it need not consider the reasonableness of the refusal, which need only be considered if the offer is found to be suitable. In considering the suitability of the offer, the tribunal should use objective criteria; the reasonableness of the refusal, however, is intended to relate to reasons personal to the employee which in fact induced him to refuse to change his employment: see *Carron Company* v *Robertson* (1967) 2 ITR 484 (*per* the Lord President; Lords Guthrie and Migdale took the view that there was an overlapping and that the questions could be considered using the same factors in each case) and *Taylor* v *Kent County Council* [1969] 2 QB 560. See also *Mitchell* v *NCB* (1970) 5 ITR 88; *Bowman* v *NCB* (1970) 5 ITR 245; *Universal Fisher Engineering Ltd* v *Stratton* (1972) 7 ITR 66; *Morganite Crucible Ltd* v *Street* [1972] ICR 110; *Devonald* v *J D Insulating Co Ltd* [1972] ICR 209; *Harris* v *Turner and Sons (Joinery) Ltd* [1973] ICR 31; *Jones* v *Aston Cabinet Co Ltd* [1973] ICR 292; *Kane* v *Raine & Co Ltd* [1974] ICR 300; *Thomas Wragg and Sons Ltd* v *Wood* [1976] ICR 313; *Wilson-Undy* v *Instrument and Control Ltd* [1976] ICR 508; *Kennedy* v *Werneth Ring Mills Ltd* [1977] ICR 206; and *Fuller* v *Stephanie Bowman (Sales) Ltd* [1977] IRLR 87.

Subsection (7): see s 94 (6).

Definitions: 'employee' and 'employer': see note to s 1; 'redundancy payment': see s 1; 'relevant date': see s 153 (1) and s 90; 'contract of employment': s 153 (1); 'trial period': see s 84; 'associated employer': see s 153 (4).

83. Dismissal by employer

(1) In this Part, except as respects a case to which section 86 applies,

" dismiss " and " dismissal " shall, subject to sections 84, 85 and 93, be construed in accordance with subsection (2).

(2) An employee shall be treated as dismissed by his employer if, but only if,—

(*a*) the contract under which he is employed by the employer is terminated by the employer, whether it is so terminated by notice or without notice, or

(*b*) where under that contract he is employed for a fixed term, that term expires without being renewed under the same contract, or

(*c*) the employee terminates that contract with or without notice in circumstances (not falling within section 92(4)) such that he is entitled to terminate it without notice by reason of the employer's conduct.

NOTES

Derivation: 1965, s 3 (1), (2); 1975, Sched 16, Pt I, para 3.

General Note: as was mentioned in the notes to s 55, numerous situations give rise to the question whether or not an employee has been dismissed. Apart from those mentioned in subs (2), the most important are: termination by agreement; consensual variation of the terms of the contract; employee repudiation/resignation; and frustration. One set of facts may give rise to alternative analyses. So, for example, if the employer reduces the employee's wages and the employee stays on, the analysis may be that the employee has accepted the change or that there has been a wrongful repudiation by the employer and that the employee has been dismissed from his old job and accepted a new one.

It is important to remember that a valid notice of dismissal must contain either a specific date on which the employment is to terminate or contain material from which that date is positively ascertainable: see *Morton Sundour Fabrics Ltd* v *Shaw* (1967) 2 ITR 84 and *The Burton Group Ltd* v *Smith* [1977] IRLR 351. If, therefore, an employee leaves because his employer has indicated that at some future date he will have to be made redundant, he will be held not to have been dismissed.

See also s 84, which makes provision for the renewal of the contract or the re-engagement of the employee; s 85, which deals with the situation where the employee anticipates the expiry of the employer's notice; s 86, which treats a failure to permit a woman to return to work after confinement as a dismissal; s 93, which treats certain acts and events as an implied or constructive termination of the contract by the employer; and s 94, which makes provision for the situation where there is a change of ownership of the business. See s 110, which provides for the situation where the employee takes part in a strike during the currency of the employer's notice, s 116, which provides for the termination of certain employments by statute to be treated as equivalent to a dismissal, and s 119, which makes provisions for the giving of notices by employers and employees. Section 150 and Sched 12 make provision for the death of the employer or the employee. See also Sched 2, Pt II, particularly para 4 (3) in relation to maternity.

Subsection (2) (*a*): *termination by agreement: Steadman* v *Halsales Ltd* (1967) 2 ITR 77 and dicta in *Marriott* v *Oxford and District Co-operative Society Ltd* (*No* 2) [1970] 1 QB 186 suggest that this is a means of terminating the contract the consequence of which will be that the employee will be held not to have been dismissed. *Steadman's* case was, however, held to have been incorrectly decided in *Burton, Allton and Johnson Ltd* v *Peck* [1975] ICR 193.

consensual variation: dicta in *Marriott's* case suggest that if there is a consensual variation of the contract, there will not be a dismissal within subs (2) (*a*). This is an inference which tribunals tend to be reluctant to draw: see the cases mentioned under '*employer repudiation*', below, particularly *Sheet Metal Components Ltd* v *Plumridge* [1974] ICR 373.

employee repudiation/resignation: if the employee is held to have repudiated the contract, there is no dismissal; if he gives in his notice, having been warned of the possibility of redundancy at some indefinite time in the future, that does not amount to a termination by the employer: see *Morton Sundour Fabrics Ltd* v *Shaw* (1967) 2 ITR 84 and *The Burton Group Ltd* v *Smith* [1977] IRLR 351. See also *M S Rose (Heating) Ltd* v *Edgington* [1977] ICR 844.

frustration: if the event which has happened is a genuine frustrating event, then there will be no dismissal. If the tribunal concludes that there was no frustration, it may take the view that the employee repudiated the contract: see *Hare* v *Murphy Bros* [1974] ICR 603 and *Waudby* v *HFM (Transport) Co Ltd* [1976] IRLR 35 (both unfair dismissal cases and cases in which the employee was sentenced to a term of imprisonment). The most common problems in this field occur in the case of illness: see *Marshall* v *Harland and Wolff Ltd* [1972] ICR 101; *Hebden* v *Forsey and Son* [1973] ICR 607; *The Egg Stores (Stamford Hill) Ltd* v *Leibovici* [1977] ICR 260; and *Hart* v *A R Marshall and Sons (Bulwell) Ltd* [1977] ICR 539. Note also the provisions of s 93 by which certain acts or events affecting the employer are treated as a termination by him.

employer repudiation: it is a well-established proposition that a wrongful repudiation of the contract by the employer, which is accepted by the employee when he gives notice, will amount to a dismissal within subs (2) (*a*): see *Marriott* v *Oxford and District Co-operative Society Ltd (No 2)* [1970] 1 QB 186; *G K N (Cwmbran) Ltd* v *Lloyd* [1972] ICR 214; *Shield's Furniture Ltd* v *Goff* [1973] ICR 187; *Sheet Metal Components Ltd* v *Plumridge* [1974] ICR 373; and *Burroughs Machines Ltd* v *Timmoney* [1977] IRLR 404. The reason why these cases were decided under this paragraph and not para (*c*) may be that before amendments were introduced into the appropriate section of the Redundancy Payments Act 1965 by the Employment Protection Act 1975 that section (s 3 (1) (*c*)) was not one which the employee could often use, since it required him to terminate *without* notice. There are, therefore, comparatively few decided cases under what is now subs (2) (*c*).

The cases cited above seem to require some act on the part of the employee accepting the employer's repudiation (ie the giving of notice); but the tribunal case of *Cole* v *Fred Stacey Ltd* (1974) 9 ITR 11 suggests that an employer's wrongful repudiation terminates the contract automatically without the need for any act of acceptance by the employee. If a higher court were to act on this view, the differences of analysis mentioned here could have interesting consequences. See, however, *Thomas Marshall (Exports) Ltd* v *Guinle* [1978] IRLR 174.

If an employee who has already been given notice asks to leave his employment early, that is not a termination by him of the employment; the fact remains that he has been dismissed: see *Tunnel Holdings Ltd* v *Woolf* [1976] ICR 387, and the note to s 85.

Subsection (2) (*b*): for a discussion of para (*b*), see the note to s 55 (2) (*b*). Note s 90 (1) (*c*). See *North East Coast Shiprepairers Ltd* v *Secretary of State for Employment* [1978] IRLR 149.

Subsection (2) (*c*): as was mentioned in the note to subs (2) (*a*), comparatively few cases were decided under the predecessor to this provision, perhaps because s 3 (1) (*c*) of the Redundancy Payments Act 1965 required the employee to terminate *without* notice: any employee who resigned with notice would therefore have to bring himself within para (*a*). Section 3 (1) (*c*) was amended by the Employment Protection Act 1975 to bring it into its present form.

See the note to s 55 (2) (*c*). It is probable that this provision will be interpreted in a manner consistent with the Court of Appeal's interpretation of s 55 (2) (*c*) in *Western Excavating (ECC) Ltd* v *Sharp* [1978] ICR 221:

see *British Leyland UK Ltd* v *McQuilken* [1978] IRLR 245. See also *Devon County Council* v *Cook* [1977] IRLR 188; *Managers (Holborn) Ltd* v *Hohne* [1977] IRLR 230; *Coleman* v *S and W Baldwin (t/a Baldwins)* [1977] IRLR 342; and *G Priestner Ltd* v *Ball* (1977) 12 ITR 451. A failure to provide suitable work for an employee, which leads to his resignation, may amount to a constructive dismissal: see *Breach* v *Epsylon Industries Ltd* [1976] ICR 316 and *Bosworth* v *Angus Jowett & Co Ltd* [1977] IRLR 374 (a case in fact on what is now s 55 (2) (*c*)).

Definitions: 'employee' and 'employer': see note to s 1.

84. Renewal of contract or re-engagement

(1) If an employee's contract of employment is renewed, or he is re-engaged under a new contract of employment in pursuance of an offer (whether in writing or not) made by his employer before the ending of his employment under the previous contract, and the renewal or re-engagement takes effect either immediately on the ending of that employment or after an interval of not more than four weeks thereafter, then, subject to subsections (3) to (6), the employee shall not be regarded as having been dismissed by his employer by reason of the ending of his employment under the previous contract.

(2) For the purposes of the application of subsection (1) to a contract under which the employment ends on a Friday, Saturday or Sunday—

(*a*) the renewal or re-engagement shall be treated as taking effect immediately on the ending of the employment if it takes effect on or before the Monday after that Friday, Saturday or Sunday, and

(*b*) the interval of four weeks referred to in that subsection shall be calculated as if the employment had ended on that Monday.

(3) If, in a case to which subsection (1) applies, the provisions of the contract as renewed, or of the new contract, as to the capacity and place in which the employee is employed, and as to the other terms and conditions of his employment, differ (wholly or in part) from the corresponding provisions of the previous contract, there shall be a trial period in relation to the contract as renewed, or the new contract (whether or not there has been a previous trial period under this section).

(4) The trial period shall begin with the ending of the employee's employment under the previous contract and end with the expiration of the period of four weeks beginning with the date on which the employee starts work under the contract as renewed, or the new contract, or such longer period as may be agreed in accordance with the next following subsection for the purpose of retraining the employee for employment under that contract.

(5) Any such agreement shall—

(*a*) be made between the employer and the employee or his representative before the employee starts work under the contract as renewed or, as the case may be, the new contract;

(*b*) be in writing;

(*c*) specify the date of the end of the trial period; and

(*d*) specify the terms and conditions of employment which will apply in the employee's case after the end of that period.

(6) If during the trial period—

(*a*) the employee, for whatever reason, terminates the contract, or gives notice to terminate it and the contract is thereafter, in consequence, terminated; or

(*b*) the employer, for a reason connected with or arising out of the change to the renewed, or new, employment, terminates the contract, or gives notice to terminate it and the contract is thereafter, in consequence, terminated,

then, unless the employee's contract of employment is again renewed, or he is again re-engaged under a new contract of employment, in circumstances such that subsection (1) again applies, he shall be treated as having been dismissed on the date on which his employment under the previous contract or, if there has been more than one trial period, the original contract ended for the reason for which he was then dismissed or would have been dismissed had the offer (or original offer) of renewed, or new, employment not been made, or, as the case may be, for the reason which resulted in that offer being made.

(7) Any reference in this section to re-engagement by the employer shall be construed as including a reference to re-engagement by the employer or by any associated employer, and any reference in this section to an offer made by the employer shall be construed as including a reference to an offer made by an associated employer.

NOTES

Derivation: 1965, ss 3 (3) to (8) and 48 (1); 1975, Sched 16, Pt I, paras 3, 18.

General Note: if the employee's contract of employment is renewed or he is re-engaged and the other requirements of this section are fulfilled, he will be treated as not having been dismissed, and will therefore not be entitled to claim a redundancy payment. The provisions of s 94 are complementary to this section; they deal with the situation where the employee's contract is renewed or he is re-engaged by an employer who becomes owner by virtue of a change in the ownership of the business. See also s 93 and s 95 particularly subs (2) (*a*).

See s 150 and Sched 12, Pts I, III and IV (particularly paras 14 and 24), which make provision for the death of the employer or the employee, and Sched 13, para 11 (2), which deals with the effect of a renewal or re-engagement after an interval upon the question of continuous employment.

Subsection (1): see *Secretary of State for Employment* v *Rooney* [1977] ICR 440. See also s 93 (2) and (4) and Sched 2, Pt II, para 4 (1) (*b*) (in relation to maternity).

Subsection (3): See Sched 2, Pt II, para 4 (1) (*c*) in relation to maternity.

Subsection (6): note ss 90 (1) (*d*) and 93 (2).

Subsection (7): See s 94 (6).

Definitions: 'employee' and 'employer': see note to s 1; 'contract of employment' and 'renewal': see s 153 (1); 'associated employer': see s 153 (4).

85. Employee anticipating expiry of employer's notice

(1) The provisions of this section shall have effect where—

(*a*) an employer gives notice to an employee to terminate his contract of employment, and

(*b*) at a time within the obligatory period of that notice, the employee gives notice in writing to the employer to terminate the contract of employment on a date earlier than the date on which the employer's notice is due to expire.

(2) Subject to the following provisions of this section, in the circumstances specified in subsection (1) the employee shall, for the purposes of this Part, be taken to be dismissed by his employer.

(3) If, before the employee's notice is due to expire, the employer gives him notice in writing—

(*a*) requiring him to withdraw his notice terminating the contract of employment as mentioned in subsection (1)(*b*) and to continue in the employment until the date on which the employer's notice expires, and

(*b*) stating that, unless he does so, the employer will contest any liability to pay to him a redundancy payment in respect of the termination of his contract of employment,

but the employee does not comply with the requirements of that notice, the employee shall not be entitled to a redundancy payment by virtue of subsection (2) except as provided by subsection (4).

(4) Where, in the circumstances specified in subsection (1), the employer has given notice to the employee under subsection (3), and on a reference to a tribunal it appears to the tribunal, having regard both to the reasons for which the employee seeks to leave the employment and those for which the employer requires him to continue in it, to be just and equitable that the employee should receive the whole or part of any redundancy payment to which he would have been entitled apart from subsection (3), the tribunal may determine that the employer shall be liable to pay to the employee—

(*a*) the whole of the redundancy payment to which the employee would have been so entitled, or

(*b*) such part of that redundancy payment as the tribunal thinks fit.

(5) In this section—

(*a*) if the actual period of the employer's notice (that is to say, the period beginning at the time when the notice is given and ending at the time when it expires) is equal to the minimum period which (whether by virtue of any enactment or otherwise) is required to be given by the employer to terminate the contract of employment, " the obligatory period ", in relation to that notice, means the actual period of the notice;

(*b*) in any other case, " the obligatory period ", in relation to an employer's notice, means that period which, being equal to the minimum period referred to in paragraph (*a*), expires at the time when the employer's notice expires.

NOTES

Derivation: 1965, s 4.

General Note: this section provides for the situation where the employee anticipates the expiry of the employer's notice. Unless he complies with subs (1) (*a*) and (*b*), he will not be taken to be dismissed. The section also provides for the loss of the right to a payment where the employer gives the employee a written notice, before the employee's notice is due to expire, (*a*) requiring him to withdraw his notice and to continue in the employment until the date on which the employer's notice expires, and (*b*) stating that, unless he does so, the employer will contest any liability to pay a redundancy payment, and the employee fails to comply. Subsection (4) gives the Tribunal a discretion to order payment of part or the whole of the redundancy payment, despite the loss of the right under subs (3), where it appears just and equitable to do so.

The corresponding provisions to subss (1) and (2) in Pt V (Unfair Dismissal) (s 55 (3)) are much simpler and less technical. There are comparatively few decided cases on this section, but it seems clear that if the employee cannot bring himself within subs (1), he will be taken not to have been dismissed. In *Tunnel Holdings Ltd* v *Woolf* [1976] ICR 387, one would have thought that this section applied, but the tribunal, for reasons which do not appear in the report, decided that it did not; Phillips, J regarded a request to leave before the expiry of the employer's notice as a request to substitute an earlier date of dismissal rather than a unilateral termination by the employee. The situation where the employee asks to leave early appears to be precisely one for which s 85 is intended to cater. The above case is to be regarded as of doubtful utility.

See ss 98 (3) and 104 (6); and s 150 and Sched 12, Pts I, III and IV, which make provision for the death of the employer or the employee, particularly para 25. See also Sched 2, Pt II, para 4 (3), in relation to maternity, and Sched 6, para 3.

Subsection (2): note s 90 (1) (*e*).

Subsections (3) *and* (4): note s 117 and Sched 8, which make provision for employees paid by a person other than the employer.

Subsection (5): 'obligatory period': this phrase also occurs in s 92; the definition of it here is also adopted there.

'notice . . . required to be given': see s 49.

Definitions: 'contract of employment': see s 153 (1); 'employee' and 'employer': see note to s 1; 'obligatory period': see subs (5) above; 'redundancy payment': see s 153 (1) and s 81 (1); 'notice': see above.

86. Failure to permit woman to return to work after confinement treated as dismissal

Where an employee is entitled to return to work and has exercised her right to return in accordance with section 47 but is not permitted to return to work, then she shall be treated for the purposes of the provisions of this Part as if she had been employed until the notified day of return, and, if she would not otherwise be so treated, as having been continuously employed until that day, and as if she had been dismissed with effect from that day for the reason for which she was not permitted to return.

NOTES

Derivation: 1975, s 50 (1).

General Note: see ss 46, 47 (8) and 48, and Sched 2, Pt II, para 4(2).

Continuously employed: see s 151 and Sched 13, which contains provisions for ascertaining the length of an employee's period of employment and whether it has been continuous. The effect of this provision will be to increase the employment period by nine months (eleven weeks before confinement plus twenty-nine after), or more if any of the extensions in s 47 occur.

Definitions: 'employee': see note to s 1; 'return to work': see s 153 (3); 'notified day of return': see s 153 (1) and s 47 (1) and (8); 'continuously employed': see above. Note s 47 (8).

87. Lay-off and short-time

(1) Where an employee is employed under a contract on such terms and conditions that his remuneration thereunder depends on his being provided by the employer with work of the kind which he is employed to do, he shall, for the purposes of this Part, be taken to be laid off for any

week in respect of which, by reason that the employer does not provide such work for him, he is not entitled to any remuneration under the contract.

(2) Where by reason of a diminution in the work provided for an employee by his employer (being work of a kind which under his contract the employee is employed to do) the employee's remuneration for any week is less than half a week's pay, he shall for the purposes of this Part be taken to be kept on short-time for that week.

NOTES

Derivation: 1965, s 5 (1) and (2); 1975, Sched 16, Pt I, para 4.

General Note: this section defines the terms 'lay-off' and 'short-time'; s 88 prescribes the conditions which have to be fulfilled before an employee who is laid off or put on short-time working is entitled to a redundancy payment; s 89 contains supplementary provisions.

See also the General Note to s 88, and s 150 and Sched 12, Pts I, III and IV (particularly paras 17 to 20), which contain provisions dealing with the death of the employer or employee, and Sched 2, Pt II, para 4 (3) in relation to maternity.

Subsection (1): an employee who is laid off will not come within these provisions (ie ss 87 to 89) if his contract of employment entitles him to a guaranteed weekly wage: see *Puttick* v *John Wright and Sons Ltd* [1972] ICR 457 and *Powell Duffryn Wagon Co Ltd* v *House* [1974] ICR 123. See also *Johnson* v *Cross* [1977] ICR 872.

Subsection (2): 'week's pay': see s 152 and Sched 14, Pt II for the method of calculating a week's pay. Note Sched 14, para 7 (1) (*j*).

Definitions: 'employee' and 'employer': see note to s 1; 'week': see s 153 (1).

88. Right to redundancy payment by reason of lay-off or short-time

(1) An employee shall not be entitled to a redundancy payment by reason of being laid off or kept on short-time unless he gives notice in writing to his employer indicating (in whatsoever terms) his intention to claim a redundancy payment in respect of lay-off or short-time (in this Act referred to as a " notice of intention to claim ") and, before the service of that notice, either—

(*a*) he has been laid off or kept on short-time for four or more consecutive weeks of which the last before the service of the notice ended on the date of service thereof or ended not more than four weeks before that date, or

(*b*) he has been laid off or kept on short-time for a series of six or more weeks (of which not more than three were consecutive) within a period of thirteen weeks, where the last week of the series before the service of the notice ended on the date of service thereof or ended not more than four weeks before that date.

(2) Where an employee has given notice of intention to claim,—

(*a*) he shall not be entitled to a redundancy payment in pursuance of that notice unless he terminates his contract of employment by a week's notice which (whether given before or after or at the same time as the notice of intention to claim) is given before the end of the period allowed for the purposes of this paragraph (as specified in subsection (5) of section 89), and

(*b*) he shall not be entitled to a redundancy payment in pursuance of the notice of intention to claim if he is dismissed by his employer (but without prejudice to any right to a redundancy payment by reason of the dismissal):

Provided that, if the employee is required by his contract of employment to give more than a week's notice to terminate the contract, the reference in paragraph (*a*) to a week's notice shall be construed as a reference to the minimum notice which he is so required to give.

(3) Subject to subsection (4), an employee shall not be entitled to a redundancy payment in pursuance of a notice of intention to claim if, on the date of service of that notice, it was reasonably to be expected that the employee (if he continued to be employed by the same employer) would, not later than four weeks after that date, enter upon a period of employment of not less than thirteen weeks during which he would not be laid off or kept on short-time for any week.

(4) Subsection (3) shall not apply unless, within seven days after the service of the notice of intention to claim, the employer gives to the employee notice in writing that he will contest any liability to pay to him a redundancy payment in pursuance of the notice of intention to claim.

NOTES

Derivations 1965, s 60 (1), (3) to (5).

General Note: this section and s 89 prescribe an elaborate set of conditions which must be fulfilled before the employee is entitled to a redundancy payment. In most cases, it would probably be preferable to claim a guarantee payment under s 12.

Note also Sched 2, Pt II, para 4 (3) in relation to maternity and Sched 12, Pt III, paras 17 to 20 and Pt IV, para 26.

Notice: for provisions relating to the giving of notice by employers and employees, see s 119.

Subsection (1): Late s 90 (2).

Subsection (3): 'period of employment': see *Neepsend Steel and Tool Corporation Ltd* v *Vaughan* [1972] ICR 278.

Subsection (4): note s 117 and Sched 8, which make provision for employees paid by a person other than the employer.

Definitions: 'employee' and 'employer': see note to s 1; 'redundancy payment': see s 81 (1); 'laid off' and 'short-time': see s 87; 'contract of employment' and 'week': see s 153 (1).

89. Supplementary provisions relating to redundancy payments in respect of lay-off or short-time

(1) If, in a case where an employee gives notice of intention to claim and the employer gives notice under section 88(4) (in this section referred to as a "counter-notice"), the employee continues or has continued, during the next four weeks after the date of service of the notice of intention to claim, to be employed by the same employer, and he is or has been laid off or kept on short-time for each of those weeks, it shall be conclusively presumed that the condition specified in subsection (3) of section 88 was not fulfilled.

(2) For the purposes of both subsection (1) of section 88 and subsection (1) of this section, it is immaterial whether a series of weeks (whether it is four weeks, or four or more weeks, or six or more weeks) consists wholly of weeks for which the employee is laid off or wholly of weeks for which he is kept on short-time or partly of the one and partly of the other.

(3) For the purposes mentioned in subsection (2), no account shall be taken of any week for which an employee is laid off or kept on short-time where the lay-off or short-time is wholly or mainly attributable to a strike or a lock-out (within the meaning of paragraph 24 of Schedule 13) whether the strike or lock-out is in the trade or industry in which the employee is employed or not and whether it is in Great Britain or elsewhere.

(4) Where the employer gives a counter-notice within seven days after the service of a notice of intention to claim, and does not withdraw the counter-notice by a subsequent notice in writing, the employee shall not be entitled to a redundancy payment in pursuance of the notice of intention to claim except in accordance with a decision of an industrial tribunal.

(5) The period allowed for the purposes of subsection (2)(*a*) of section 88 is as follows, that is to say,—

- (*a*) if the employer does not give a counter-notice within seven days after the service of the notice of intention to claim, that period is three weeks after the end of those seven days;
- (*b*) if the employer gives a counter-notice within those seven days, but withdraws it by a subsequent notice in writing, that period is three weeks after the service of the notice of withdrawal;
- (*c*) if the employer gives a counter-notice within those seven days and does not so withdraw it, and a question as to the right of the employee to a redundancy payment in pursuance of the notice of intention to claim is referred to a tribunal, that period is three weeks after the tribunal has notified to the employee its decision on that reference.

(6) For the purposes of paragraph (*c*) of subsection (5) no account shall be taken of any appeal against the decision of the tribunal, or of any requirement to the tribunal to state a case for the opinion of the High Court or the Court of Session, or of any proceedings or decision in consequence of such an appeal or requirement.

NOTES

Derivation: 1965, s 7.

General Note: see the General Notes to ss 87 and 88. See also s 119, which makes provision for the giving of notice by employers and employees, s 150 and Sched 12, which provide for the death of the employer or employee, and Sched 2, Pt II, para 4 (3) in relation to maternity.

Subsections (1), (4) *and* (5): note s 117 and Sched 8, which make provision for employees paid by a person other than the employer.

Definitions: 'notice of intention to claim': see s 88 (1); 'employee' and 'employer': see note to s 1; 'laid off' and 'short-time': see s 87; 'week': see s 153 (1); 'redundancy payment': see s 81 (1).

90. The relevant date

(1) Subject to the following provisions of this section, for the purposes of the provisions of this Act so far as they relate to redundancy payments, " the relevant date ", in relation to the dismissal of an employee—

- (*a*) where his contract of employment is terminated by notice, whether given by his employer or by the employee, means the date on which that notice expires;
- (*b*) where his contract of employment is terminated without notice, means the date on which the termination takes effect;

(*c*) where he is employed under a contract for a fixed term and that term expires as mentioned in subsection (2)(*b*) of section 83, means the date on which that term expires;

(*d*) where he is treated, by virtue of subsection (6) of section 84, as having been dismissed on the termination of his employment under a previous contract, means—

(i) for the purposes of section 101, the date which is the relevant date as defined by paragraph (*a*), (*b*) or (*c*) in relation to the renewed, or new, contract, or, where there has been more than one trial period under section 84, the last such contract; and

(ii) for the purposes of any other provision, the date which is the relevant date as defined by paragraph (*a*), (*b*) or (*c*) in relation to the previous contract, or, where there has been more than one trial period under section 84, the original contract; and

(*e*) where he is taken to be dismissed by virtue of section 85(2), means the date on which the employee's notice to terminate his contract of employment expires.

(2) " The relevant date ", in relation to a notice of intention to claim or a right to a redundancy payment in pursuance of such a notice,—

(*a*) in a case falling within paragraph (*a*) of subsection (1) of section 8[8], means the date on which the last of the four or more consecutive weeks before the service of the notice came to an end, and

(*b*) in a case falling within paragraph (*b*) of that subsection means the date on which the last of the series of six or more weeks before the service of the notice came to an end.

(3) Where the notice required to be given by an employer to terminate a contract of employment by section 49(1) would, if duly given when notice of termination was given by the employer, or (where no notice was given) when the contract of employment was terminated by the employer, expire on a date later than the relevant date as defined by subsection (1), then for the purposes of section 81(4) and paragraph 1 of Schedule 4 and paragraph 8(4) of Schedule 14, that later date shall be treated as the relevant date in relation to the dismissal.

NOTES

Derivation: 1965, ss 3 (9), 4 (2), 6 (2) and 3 (10); 1975, Sched 16, Pt I, para 3.

General Note: the equivalent section in the provisions relating to Unfair Dismissal in Pt V (s 55) uses the term 'effective date of termination', although for all general purposes that term and the term 'relevant date' are almost identical in their meaning (contrast subss (1) (*a*), (*b*) and (*c*), and (3) with s 55 (4) and (5)). 'Relevant date', however, has certain additional meanings peculiar to the provisions relating to redundancy payments (see subss (1) (*d*) and (*e*), and (2)). See the notes to s 55 (4) and (5). It is important to ascertain the date on which the dismissal is regarded as having taken effect both for the purposes of deciding whether the employee has been continuously employed long enough to qualify him to make a claim and assessing the amount of redundancy payment. See ss 93, 94 and 95 (2) (*a*) and note Sched II, Pt II, paras 4 (1) (*a*) and 4 (3) in relation to maternity.

Subsection (3): note Sched 12, Pt IV, para 22 (2) and Sched 13, para 11 (3).

Definitions: 'redundancy payments': see s 81 (1); 'employee' and 'employer': see note to s 1; 'contract of employment' and 'week': see s 153 (1).

91. Reference of questions to tribunal

(1) Any question arising under this Part as to the right of an employee to a redundancy payment, or as to the amount of a redundancy payment, shall be referred to and determined by an industrial tribunal.

(2) For the purposes of any such reference, an employee who has been dismissed by his employer shall, unless the contrary is proved, be presumed to have been so dismissed by reason of redundancy.

(3) In relation to lay-off or short-time, the questions which may be referred to and determined by an industrial tribunal, as mentioned in subsection (1), shall include any question whether an employee will become entitled to a redundancy payment if he is not dismissed by his employer and he terminates his contract of employment as mentioned in subsection (2)(*a*) of section 88; and any such question shall for the purposes of this Part be taken to be a question as to the right of the employee to a redundancy payment.

NOTES

Derivation: 1965, s 9 (1), (2) (*b*) and (3).

Subsection (2): it should be noted that where an employee claims a redundancy payment and complains of unfair dismissal, the presumption enacted in this subsection does not apply to the complaint of unfair dismissal: in other words, the employer will have to prove that the reason for the dismissal was redundancy, without being able to rely on the presumption: see Sched 9, para 5. This could have bizarre consequences: see *Midland Foot Comfort Centre* v *Moppett* [1973] ICR 219.

Definitions: 'employee' and 'employer': see note to s 1; 'redundancy payment': see s 81 (1); 'redundancy': see s 81 (2); 'lay-off' and 'short-time': see s 87; 'contract of employment': see s 153 (1).

92. Special provisions as to termination of contract in cases of misconduct or industrial dispute

(1) Where at any such time as is mentioned in subsection (2), an employee who—

(*a*) has been given notice by his employer to terminate his contract of employment, or

(*b*) has given notice to his employer under subsection (1) of section 88,

takes part in a strike, in such circumstances that the employer is entitled, by reason of his taking part in the strike, to treat the contract of employment as terminable without notice, and the employer for that reason terminates the contract as mentioned in subsection (2) of section 82, that subsection shall not apply to that termination of the contract.

(2) The times referred to in subsection (1) are—

(*a*) in a case falling within paragraph (*a*) of that subsection any time within the obligatory period of the employer's notice (as defined by section 85(5)), and

(*b*) in a case falling within paragraph (*b*) of subsection (1), any time after the service of the notice mentioned in that paragraph.

(3) Where at any such time as is mentioned in subsection (2) an employee's contract of employment, otherwise than by reason of his taking part in a strike, is terminated by his employer in the circumstances specified in subsection (2) of section 82, and is so terminated as mentioned

therein, and on a reference to an industrial tribunal it appears to the tribunal, in the circumstances of the case, to be just and equitable that the employee should receive the whole or part of any redundancy payment to which he would have been entitled apart from section 82(2), the tribunal may determine that the employer shall be liable to pay to the employee—

(*a*) the whole of the redundancy payment to which the employee would have been so entitled, or

(*b*) such part of that redundancy payment as the tribunal thinks fit.

(4) Where an employee terminates his contract of employment without notice, being entitled to do so by reason of a lock-out by his employer, section 83(2)(*c*) shall not apply to that termination of the contract.

(5) In this section " strike " and " lock-out " each has the meaning given by paragraph 24 of Schedule 13.

NOTES

Derivation: 1965, ss 10 and 56 (1).

General Note: the relationship between this section and s 82 (2) has caused some difficulty: see *Simmons* v *Hoover Ltd* [1977] ICR 61. As was pointed out in that case, s 82 (2) seems to envisage a single dismissal situation, whereas this section seems to presume the existence of two dismissals. These two provisions should be regarded as being complementary. If the employee is dismissed and the dismissal falls within s 82 (2), he will be completely disentitled from the right to receive a redundancy payment. If, however, he is dismissed for redundancy and *subsequently* dismissed for striking during the obligatory period or the time after the employee has given notice under s 88, he will not lose his entitlement; if the second dismissal is for misconduct, the tribunal has a discretion as to how much of the redundancy payment he should be given. The point is that the employee may still be dismissed for striking or misconduct before the obligatory period or the service of the notice under s 88, and, provided that s 82 (2) is complied with, he will be disentitled. But once he is within the last part of his notice period (ie the obligatory period) the disentitlement is lifted, and the provisions of subss (1) and (3) then operate, as appropriate. See the note to s 82 (2), where it was pointed out that most of the cases decided under these provisions are unsatisfactory. See, however, *Simmons* v *Hoover Ltd* [1977] ICR 61, which has a helpful schedule appended to the judgment which amplifies the above remarks; but the EAT's analysis of these provisions is too brief to clarify the difficulties.

Note also the provisions of s 110, by which the employer, instead of dismissing an employee for taking part in a strike may serve a 'notice of extension', requiring him to make up the time lost as a result of the strike. See also ss 98 (3) and 104 (6) and Scheds 2, Pt II, para 4 (3) (in relation to maternity), and 6, para 3.

Subsection (1): the action of taking part in a strike falls within the words 'employee's conduct' in s 82 (2): see *Simmons* v *Hoover Ltd* [1977] ICR 61 (Mr Blyghton dissenting). If the employee is dismissed and then goes on strike and is dismissed for that reason, this subsection will apply; if, however, he is already on strike and is dismissed for redundancy, the subsection will not apply: see *Simmons* v *Hoover Ltd.* The desirability of this provision operating according to the coincidence of whether the strike precedes the dismissal or *vice versa*, is debatable. But it leads to the reflection that, as the law stands, if a strike leads to a redundancy situation and a striking employee is dismissed for redundancy, he will be disentitled from the right to receive a redundancy payment, according to *Simmons* v *Hoover Ltd;* and that is the 'self-induced' redundancy whose ghost the NIRC thought it had exorcised in *Sanders* v *Ernest A Neale Ltd* [1974] ICR 565.

Subsection (3): see *Simmons* v *Hoover Ltd* [1977] ICR 61, which has a useful schedule appended to the judgment demonstrating the operation of this subsection. Note s 117 and Sched 8, which make provision for employees paid by a person other than the employer.

Definitions: 'employee' and 'employer': see note to s 1; 'contract of employment': see s 153 (1); 'strike' and 'lock-out': note subs (5); 'obligatory period': see s 85 (5); 'redundancy payment': see s 81 (1).

93. Implied or constructive termination of contract

(1) Where in accordance with any enactment or rule of law—

(*a*) any act on the part of an employer, or

(*b*) any event affecting an employer (including, in the case of an individual, his death),

operates so as to terminate a contract under which an employee is employed by him, that act or event shall for the purposes of this Part be treated as a termination of the contract by the employer, if apart from this subsection it would not constitute a termination of the contract by him and, in particular, the provisions of sections 83, 84 and 90 shall apply accordingly.

(2) Where subsection (1) applies, and the employee's contract of employment is not renewed, and he is not re-engaged under a new contract of employment, so as to be treated, by virtue of section 84(1), as not having been dismissed, he shall, without prejudice to section 84(6), be taken for the purposes of this Part to be dismissed by reason of redundancy if the circumstances in which his contract is not so renewed and he is not so re-engaged are wholly or mainly attributable to one or other of the facts specified in paragraphs (*a*) and (*b*) of section 81(2).

(3) For the purposes of subsection (2), section 81(2)(*a*), in so far as it relates to the employer ceasing or intending to cease to carry on the business, shall be construed as if the reference to the employer included a reference to any person to whom, in consequence of the act or event in question, power to dispose of the business has passed.

(4) In this section, any reference to section 84(1) includes a reference to that subsection as applied by section 94(2) or as so applied and (where appropriate) modified by section 95(2), and where section 84(1) applies as so modified the references in subsection (2) of this section to renewal of or re-engagement under a contract of employment shall be construed as including references to renewal of or re-engagement in employment otherwise than under a contract of employment.

NOTES

Derivation: 1965, s 22; 1975, Sched 16, Pt I, para 10.

General Note: the circumstances in which this section is likely to operate are, eg the winding-up of a company or partnership, or the bankruptcy or death of the employer. Although an 'event' terminating the contract of employment under this section may affect an employee as well as an employer, it must so affect the employer that as a result of its effect on him the contract is terminated; a termination requiring the consent of the employee cannot be said to result from an event affecting the employer: see *British Airports Authority* v *Fenerty* [1976] ICR 361.

See also ss 83, 84 and 90; s 150 and Sched 12, Pts I, III and IV (particularly paras 14 and 15), which make provision for the death of the employer or employee; and Sched 2, Pt II, para 4 (3) in relation to maternity.

Definitions: 'act' and 'contract': see s 153 (1); 'employee' and 'employer': see note to s 1; 'renewed' and 're-engaged': see s 84; 'redundancy': see s 81 (2); 'business': see s 153 (1); 'cease': see s 81 (3).

94. Change of ownership of business

(1) The provisions of this section shall have effect where—

(*a*) a change occurs (whether by virtue of a sale or other disposition or by operation of law) in the ownership of a business for the purposes of which a person is employed, or of a part of such a business, and

(*b*) in connection with that change the person by whom the employee is employed immediately before the change occurs (in this section referred to as "the previous owner") terminates the employee's contract of employment, whether by notice or without notice.

(2) If, by agreement with the employee, the person who immediately after the change occurs is the owner of the business, or of the part of the business in question, as the case may be (in this section referred to as "the new owner"), renews the employee's contract of employment (with the substitution of the new owner for the previous owner) or re-engages him under a new contract of employment, sections 84 and 90 shall have effect as if the renewal or re-engagement had been a renewal or re-engagement by the previous owner (without any substitution of the new owner for the previous owner).

(3) If the new owner offers to renew the employee's contract of employment (with the substitution of the new owner for the previous owner) or to re-engage him under a new contract of employment, subsections (3) to (6) of section 82 shall have effect, subject to subsection (4), in relation to that offer as they would have had effect in relation to the like offer made by the previous owner.

(4) For the purposes of the operation, in accordance with subsection (3), of subsections (3) to (6) of section 82 in relation to an offer made by the new owner—

(*a*) the offer shall not be treated as one whereby the provisions of the contract as renewed, or of the new contract, as the case may be, would differ from the corresponding provisions of the contract as in force immediately before the dismissal by reason only that the new owner would be substituted for the previous owner as the employer, and

(*b*) no account shall be taken of that substitution in determining whether the refusal of the offer was unreasonable or, as the case may be, whether the employee acted reasonably in terminating the renewed, or new, employment during the trial period referred to in section 84.

(5) The preceding provisions of this section shall have effect (subject to the necessary modifications) in relation to a case where—

(*a*) the person by whom a business, or part of a business, is owned immediately before a change is one of the persons by whom (whether as partners, trustees or otherwise) it is owned immediately after the change, or (*b*) the persons by whom a business, or part of a business, is owned immediately before a change (whether as partners, trustees or otherwise) include the person by whom, or include one or more of the persons by whom, it is owned immediately after the change,

as those provisions have effect where the previous owner and the new owner are wholly different persons.

(6) Sections 82(7) and 84(7) shall not apply in any case to which this section applies.

(7) Nothing in this section shall be construed as requiring any variation of a contract of employment by agreement between the parties to be treated as constituting a termination of the contract.

NOTES

Derivation: 1965, ss 13 and 48 (2); 1975, Sched 16, Pt I, paras 7, 18.

General Note: this section should be read in conjunction with ss 82, 83 and 84 and Sched 13. See the notes to those provisions. Note also ss 95 and 100 (1), and Sched 12, Pt III, para 13.

Subsection (1) (*a*): 'change . . . in the ownership of the business': for a discussion of what constitutes such a change, see the note to Sched 13, para 17 (2). Note, however, that subs (1) (*a*) refers to a change in the ownership of a part of a business, whereas Sched 13, para 17 (2) does not. Note also Sched 12, Pt III, para 13: if by the death of an employer the ownership of the business passes to his personal representatives, s 94 does not apply. See *Rastill* v *Automatic Refreshment Services Ltd* [1978] ICR 289.

Subsection (2): note s 93 (4).

Subsection (4): note s 95 (2) (*b*).

Definitions: 'change . . . in the ownership of a business': see note to subs (1) (*a*) above; 'business': see s 153 (1); 'employee': see note to s 1; 'contract of employment': see s 153 (1); 'renews' and 're-engages': see s 84 (1).

95. Transfer to Crown employment

(1) Section 94 shall apply to a transfer of functions from a person not acting on behalf of the Crown (in this section referred to as the transferor) to a government department or any other officer or body exercising functions on behalf of the Crown (in this section referred to as the transferee) as that section applies to a transfer of a business, but with the substitution for references to the previous owner and new owner of references to the transferor and transferee respectively.

(2) In so far as the renewal or re-engagement of the employee by the transferee is in employment otherwise than under a contract of employment—

(*a*) references in section 94 (and in sections 82(4) to (6), 84 and 90 as they apply by virtue of that section) to a contract of employment or to the terms of such a contract shall be construed as references to employment otherwise than under such a contract and to the terms of such employment; and

(*b*) references in subsection (4) of section 94, as modified by subsection (1) of this section, to the substitution of the transferee for the transferor shall be construed as references to the substitution of employment by the transferee otherwise than under a contract of employment for employment by the transferor under such a contract.

NOTES

Derivation: 1965, s 13A; 1975, s 120 (2).

Further provisions: note Sched 13, para 19.

Definitions: 'business': see s 153 (1); 'employee': see note to s 1; 'contract of employment': see s 153 (1).

96. Exemption orders

(1) If at any time there is in force an agreement between one or more employers or organisations of employers and one or more trade unions representing employees, whereby employees to whom the agreement applies have a right in certain circumstances to payments on the termination of their contracts of employment, and, on the application of all the parties to the agreement, the Secretary of State, having regard to the provisions of the agreement, is satisfied that section 81 should not apply to those employees, he may make an order under this section in respect of that agreement.

(2) The Secretary of State shall not make an order under this section in respect of an agreement unless the agreement indicates (in whatsoever terms) the willingness of the parties to it to submit to an industrial tribunal such questions as are mentioned in paragraph (*b*) of subsection (3).

(3) Where an order under this section is in force in respect of an agreement—

(*a*) section 81 shall not have effect in relation to any employee who immediately before the relevant date is an employee to whom the agreement applies, but

(*b*) section 91 shall have effect in relation to any question arising under the agreement as to the right of an employee to a payment on the termination of his employment, or as to the amount of such a payment, as if the payment were a redundancy payment and the question arose under this Part.

(4) Any order under this section may be revoked by a subsequent order thereunder, whether in pursuance of an application made by all or any of the parties to the agreement in question or without any such application.

NOTES

Derivation: 1965, s 11.

Further provisions: note ss 104 (1) (*b*), 140 and 154 (4), and Sched 2, Pt II, para 4 (3) (in relation to maternity).

Orders under this section: see the Redundancy Payments (Exemption) (No 1) Order 1969 (SI 1969 No 207), and the Redundancy Payments (Exemption) (No 1) Order 1970 (SI 1970 No 354).

Definitions: 'trade union': see s 153 (1); 'employee' and 'employer': see note to s 1; 'contract of employment': see s 153 (1); 'relevant date': see s 90; 'redundancy payment': see s 81 (1).

97. Claims as to extension of terms and conditions

(1) A claim under paragraph 1 of Schedule 11 to the Employment Protection Act 1975 (claims as to recognised terms and conditions and general level of terms and conditions) may be reported to the Advisory, Conciliation and Arbitration Service in accordance with that Schedule, and may be referred by the Service to the Central Arbitration Committee, and the Committee may make an award under that Schedule, notwith-

standing that the terms and conditions which it is claimed that the employer is not observing consist of or include terms and conditions as to payments to be made to employees in the circumstances specified in paragraph (*a*) or paragraph (*b*) of section 81(1) or in similar circumstances, and that provision for redundancy payments is made by this Act.

(2) Where a claim which is reported to the Advisory, Conciliation and Arbitration Service under the said paragraph 1 is founded upon recognised terms and conditions and relates to an agreement in respect of which an order under section 96 is for the time being in force, and the Central Arbitration Committee makes an award in pursuance of that claim, section 96(3) shall have effect in relation to all persons in respect of whom the employer is required by that award to observe the recognised terms and conditions, whether they are persons to whom section 96(3) would appy apart from this subsection or not.

NOTES

Derivation: 1965, s 12; 1975, Sched 16, Pt I, para 6.

Further provisions: note s 104 (1) (*c*).

Definitions: 'Advisory, Conciliation and Arbitration Service': see s 1 of the Employment Protection Act 1975; 'Central Arbitration Committee': see s 10 of the Employment Protection Act 1975; 'employee' and 'employer': see note to s 1; 'redundancy payment': see s 81 (1).

98. Exclusion or reduction of redundancy payment on account of pension rights

(1) The Secretary of State shall by regulations make provision for excluding the right to a redundancy payment, or reducing the amount of any redundancy payment, in such cases as may be prescribed by the regulations, being cases in which an employee has (whether by virtue of any statutory provision or otherwise) a right or claim (whether legally enforceable or not) to a periodical payment or lump sum by way of pension, gratuity or superannuation allowance which is to be paid by reference to his employment by a particular employer and is to be paid, or to begin to be paid, at the time when he leaves that employment or within such period thereafter as may be prescribed by the regulations.

(2) Provision shall be made by any such regulations for securing that the right to a redundancy payment shall not be excluded, and that the amount of a redundancy payment shall not be reduced, by reason of any right or claim to a periodical payment or lump sum, in so far as that payment or lump sum represents such compensation as is mentioned in section 118(1) and is payable under a statutory provision, whether made or passed before, on or after the passing of this Act.

(3) In relation to any case where, under section 85 or 92 or 110, an industrial tribunal determines that an employer is liable to pay part (but not the whole) of a redundancy payment, any reference in this section to a redundancy payment, or to the amount of a redundancy payment, shall be construed as a reference to that part of the redundancy payment, or to the amount of that part, as the case may be.

NOTES

Derivation: 1965, s 14.

Regulations: see the Redundancy Payments Pensions Regulations 1965 (SI 1965 No 1932) and *Stowe-Woodward BTR Ltd* v *Beynon* [1978] ICR 609. Note Scheds 4, para 6, and 6, para 4.

Subsection (3): note s 117 and Sched 8, which make provision for employees paid by a person other than the employer.

Definitions: 'redundancy payment': see s 81 (1); 'employee' and 'employer': see note to s 1; 'statutory provision', 'employment': see s 153 (1).

99. Public offices etc

(1) Without prejudice to any exemption or immunity of the Crown, section 81 shall not apply to any person in respect of any employment which—

(*a*) is employment in a public office for the purposes of section 38 of the Superannuation Act 1965, or

(*b*) whether by virtue of that Act or otherwise, is treated for the purposes of pensions and other superannuation benefits as service in the civil service of the State, or

(*c*) is employment by any such body as is specified in Schedule 5.

(2) Without prejudice to any exemption or immunity of the Crown, section 81 shall not apply to any person in respect of his employment in any capacity under the Government of an overseas territory (as defined by section 114).

NOTES

Derivation: 1965, s 16 (4), (5); Superannuation Act 1972, Sched 6, para 54.

Further provisions: note ss 111 (1) (*a*) and 149 (1) (*c*).

Subsection (3): see *Bagga* v *Heavy Electricals* (*India*) *Ltd* [1972] ICR 118.

100. Domestic servants

(1) For the purposes of the application of the provisions of this Part to an employee who is employed as a domestic servant in a private household, those provisions (except section 94) shall apply as if the household were a business and the maintenance of the household were the carrying on of that business by the employer.

(2) Without prejudice to section 146(1), section 81 shall not apply to any person in respect of employment as a domestic servant in a private household, where the employer is the father, mother, grandfather, grandmother, stepfather, stepmother, son, daughter, grandson, granddaughter, stepson, stepdaughter, brother, sister, half-brother, or half-sister of the employee.

NOTE;

Derivation: 1965, s. 19.

Further provisions: note Sched 12, Pt III, para 21.

Definitions: 'employee' and 'employer': see note to s 1; 'business', 'employment': see s 153 (1).

101. Claims for redundancy payments

(1) Notwithstanding anything in the preceding provisions of this Part, an employee shall not be entitled to a redundancy payment unless, before the end of the period of six months beginning with the relevant date—

(*a*) the payment has been agreed and paid, or

(*b*) the employee has made a claim for the payment by notice in writing given to the employer, or (*c*) a question as to the right of the employee to the payment, or as to the amount of the payment, has been referred to an industrial tribunal, or

(*d*) a complaint relating to his dismissal has been presented by the employee under section 67.

(2) An employee shall not by virtue of subsection (1) lose his right to a redundancy payment if, during the period of six months immediately following the period mentioned in that subsection, the employee—

(*a*) makes such a claim as is referred to in paragraph (*b*) of that subsection,

(*b*) refers to a tribunal such a question as is referred to in paragraph (*c*) of that subsection, or

(*c*) makes such a complaint as is referred to in paragraph (*d*) of that subsection,

and it appears to the tribunal to be just and equitable that the employee should receive a redundancy payment having regard to the reason shown by the employee for his failure to take any such step as is referred to in paragraph (*a*), (*b*) or (*c*) of this subsection within the period mentioned in subsection (1), and to all the other relevant circumstances.

NOTES

Derivation: 1965, s 21; 1975, Sched 16, Pt I, para 9.

General Note: subs (1) has been criticised as being obscure: see *Bentley Engineering Co Ltd* v *Crown and Miller* [1976] ICR 225. Since that decision, however, what is now subs (2) has been added. Note ss 90 (1) (*d*) (i) and 104 (3) and Sched 12, Pt IV, para 27.

Subsection (1): note s 117 and Sched 12, which make provision for employees paid by a person other than the employer.

Subsection (1) (*a*): see *Bentley Engineering Co Ltd* v *Crown and Miller*. If the employee's entitlement to a payment is agreed within six months, but not the amount of the payment, the requirement in para (*a*) will have been satisfied and his claim will not be statute-barred.

Subsection (1) (*b*): if an employee who has been given notice of dismissal for redundancy gives his employers written notice of his claim for a redundancy payment before the dismissal takes effect, the notice will be premature and the claim invalid: see *Watts* v *Rubery Owen Conveyancer Ltd* [1977] ICR 429. The test of whether there is sufficient written notice of a claim is whether the notice or writing relied on is of such a character that the recipient would reasonably understand in all the circumstances of the case that it was the employee's intention to seek a redundancy payment: see *Price* v *Smithfield and Zwanenberg Group Ltd* [1978] ICR 93. Note also s 119 (2) which provides for the giving of notices by employees.

Subsection (1) (*c*): see *Nash* v *Ryan Plant International Ltd* [1977] ICR 560.

Definitions: 'employee' see note to s 1; 'redundancy payment': see s 81 (1); 'relevant date'': see s 90.

102. Written particulars of redundancy payment

(1) On making any redundancy payment, otherwise than in pursuance of a decision of a tribunal which specifies the amount of the payment to be made, the employer shall give to the employee a written statement indicating how the amount of the payment has been calculated.

(2) Any employer who without reasonable excuse fails to comply with subsection (1) shall be guilty of an offence and liable on summary conviction to a fine not exceeding £20.

(3) If an employer fails to comply with the requirements of subsection (1), then (without prejudice to any proceedings for an offence under subsection (2)) the employee may by notice in writing to the employer require him to give to the employee a written statement complying with those requirements within such period (not being less than one week beginning with the day on which the notice is given) as may be specified in the notice; and if the employer without reasonable excuse fails to comply with the notice he shall be guilty of an offence under this subsection and liable on summary conviction—

(*a*) if it is his first conviction of an offence under this subsection, to a fine not exceeding £20, or

(*b*) in any other case, to a fine not exceeding £100.

NOTES

Derivation: 1965, s 18.

Further provisions: see s 120. Note s 117 and Sched 8, which make provision for employees paid by a person other than the employer.

Definitions: 'redundancy payment': see s 81 (1); 'employee' and 'employer': see note to s 1; 'week': see s 153 (1).

REDUNDANCY FUND

103. Establishment and maintenance of fund

(1) The Secretary of State shall continue to have the control and management of the Redundancy Fund established under section 26 of the Redundancy Payments Act 1965 (in this Part referred to as " the fund "), and payments shall be made out of the fund in accordance with the provisions of sections 104 to 109 and 156 and Part VII.

(2) The Secretary of State shall prepare accounts of the fund in such form as the Treasury may direct, and shall send them to the Comptroller and Auditor General not later than the end of the month of November following the end of the financial year to which the accounts relate; and the Comptroller and Auditor General shall examine and certify the accounts and shall lay copies thereof, together with his report thereon, before Parlaiment.

(3) Any moneys forming part of the fund may from time to time be paid over to the National Debt Commissioners and by them invested, in accordance with such directions as may be given by the Treasury, in such manner as may be specified by an order of the Treasury for the time being in force under section 22(1) of the National Savings Bank Act 1971.

NOTES

Derivation: 1965, s 26; Social Security Act 1973, Sched 27, para 55.

General Note: this section provides for the establishment and maintenance of the Redundancy Fund; s 104 provides for the Secretary of State to pay redundancy rebates in certain circumstances; s 105 enables payments to be made out of the fund to employers in other cases; s 106 enables employees to apply to the Secretary of State for a payment to be made out of the fund in certain circumstances; s 107 contains provisions supplementary to those in s 106; s 108 makes provision for references and appeals to be made to an industrial tribunal on questions arising under ss 104 and 106; and s 109 contains financial provisions relating to the fund. Note also ss 111 (5), 113 (6), 149 (2) and 156 (3).

104. Redundancy rebates

(1) Subject to the provisions of this section, the Secretary of State shall make a payment (in this Part referred to as a " redundancy rebate ") out of the fund to any employer who—

(*a*) is liable under the foregoing provisions of this Part to pay, and has paid, a redundancy payment to an employee, or

(*b*) under an agreement in respect of which an order is in force under section 96, is liable to make, and has made, a payment to an employee on the termination of his contract of employment, or

(*c*) by virtue of any award made by the Central Arbitration Committee as mentioned in section 97(2) in relation to an agreement in respect of which such an order is in force, is liable to make, and has made, a payment to an employee on the termination of his contract of employment.

(2) No redundancy rebate shall be payable by virtue of this section in a case falling within paragraph (*b*) or paragraph (*c*) of subsection (1) if the employee's right to the payment referred to in that paragraph arises by virtue of a period of employment (computed in accordance with the provisions of the agreement in question) which is less than one hundred and four weeks.

(3) The Secretary of State may if he thinks fit pay a redundancy rebate to an employer who has paid an employee a redundancy payment in circumstances in which, owing to section 101, the employee had no right to, and the employer had no liability for, the payment, if the Secretary of State is satisfied that it would be just and equitable to do so having regard to all the relevant circumstances.

(4) The amount of any redundancy rebate shall (subject to subsection (7)) be calculated in accordance with Schedule 6.

(5) The Secretary of State shall make provision by regulations as to the making of claims for redundancy rebates; and any such regulations may in particular—

(*a*) require any claim for a redundancy rebate to be made at or before a time prescribed by the regulations;

(*b*) in such cases as may be so prescribed, require prior notice that such a claim may arise to be given at or before a time so prescribed, so however that, where the claim would relate to an employer's payment in respect of dismissal, the regulations shall not require the notice to be given more than four weeks before the date on which the termination of the contract of employment takes effect; and

(*c*) for the purpose of determining the right of any person to, and the amount of, any redundancy rebate, require a person at any time when he makes a claim or gives prior notice as mentioned in paragraph (*a*) or paragraph (*b*) to provide such evidence and such other information, and to produce for examination on behalf of the Secretary of State documents in his custody or under his control of such descriptions, as may be determined in accordance with the regulations.

(6) In relation to any case where, under section 85 or 92 or 110, an industrial tribunal determines that an employer is liable to pay part

(but not the whole) of a redundancy payment, the reference in subsection (1)(*a*) to a redundancy payment shall be construed as a reference to that part of the redundancy payment.

(7) If any employer who, in accordance with subsection (1), would be entitled to a redundancy rebate fails to give prior notice as required by any such regulations in accordance with paragraph (*b*) of subsection (5) and it appears to the Secretary of State that he has so failed without reasonable excuse, the Secretary of State may, subject to section 108, reduce the amount of the rebate by such proportion (not exceeding one-tenth) as appears to the Secretary of State to be appropriate in the circumstances.

(8) Any person who—

(*a*) in providing any information required by regulations under this section, makes a statement which he knows to be false in a material particular, or recklessly makes a statement which is false in a material particular, or

(*b*) produces for examination in accordance with any such regulations a document which to his knowledge has been wilfully falsified,

shall be guilty of an offence.

(9) A person guilty of an offence under subsection (8) shall be liable on summary conviction to a fine not exceeding the prescribed sum or to imprisonment for a term not exceeding three months or both, or on conviction on indictment to a fine or to imprisonment for a term not exceeding two years or both.

(10) In subsection (9) above " the prescribed sum " means—

(*a*) in England and Wales, the prescribed sum within the meaning of section 28 of the Criminal Law Act 1977 (that is to say, £1,000 or another sum fixed by order under section 61 of that Act to take account of changes in the value of money);

(*b*) in Scotland, the prescribed sum within the meaning of section 289B of the Criminal Procedure (Scotland) Act 1975 (that is to say, £1,000 or another sum fixed by an order made under section 289D of that Act for that purpose).

NOTES

Derivation: 1965, s 30; 1975, Sched 16, Pt I, para 12; Criminal Procedure (Scotland) Act 1975, s 289 B (1); Criminal Law Act 1977, s 28 (2) and Sched 11, para 5.

General Note: see ss 100 and 104 of the Employment Protection Act 1975, which oblige the employer to notify the Secretary of State of certain redundancies and enable the Secretary of State to reduce the rebate for a failure to do so.

Further provisions: ss 106 (particularly subs (4)), 107, 108, 113, 149 (2) and 156 (3) and Scheds 6 and 7. Note s 117 and Sched 8, which make provision for employees paid by a person other than the employer.

Subsection (1) (*a*): the Secretary of State is bound to pay a rebate to the employer, once the employer is made liable for a redundancy payment, however the liability is incurred; it may be because the employer is estopped from denying the continuity of the employee's employment, despite a change in employer, and is therefore liable to make a redundancy payment covering the whole period: see *Secretary of State for Employment* v *Globe Elastic Thread Co Ltd* [1977] ICR 473. This decision of the EAT was affirmed by the Court of Appeal: see The Times, 19 July, 1978. If an employer voluntarily makes a redundancy payment when he is under no legal liability to do so (eg because the employee's claim is time-barred), he is not entitled to a rebate: see *Secretary of State for Employment* v *Atkins Auto Laundries Ltd* [1972] ICR 76 and *North East Coast Shiprepairers Ltd* v *Secretary of State for Employment* [1978] IRLR 149.

Subsection (1) (*c*): s 97 provides for determination by the Central Arbitration Committee of any claim under the Employment Protection Act 1975, Sched 11, which involves an award of a redundancy payment on the basis of a collective agreement falling within s 96.

Subsection (5): Regulations: see the Redundancy Payments Rebates Regulations 1965 (SI 1965 No 1893), amended by the Redundancy Payments Rebates (Amendment) Regulations 1965 (SI 1965 No 2067). See also the Redundancy Rebates Act 1977 and the Redundancy Payments (Variation of Rebates) Order 1977 (SI 1977 No 1321).

'claim': see s 108.

Definitions: 'redundancy payment': see s 153 (1) and s 81 (1); 'employee' and 'employer': see note to s 1; 'contract of employment': see s 153 (1).

105. Payments out of fund to employers in other cases

(1) The Secretary of State may make payments out of the fund to employers in respect of employees to whom this section applies.

(2) This section applies to employees to whom, by virtue of section 144(2), 145 or 149, section 81 does not apply.

(3) The Secretary of State may determine the classes of employees to whom this section applies in respect of whom payments are to be made by virtue of this section, and, with the approval of the Treasury, may determine the amounts of the payments which may be so made in respect of any class of such employees.

(4) The payments made to an employer by virtue of this section shall not, in respect of any period, exceed the amount appearing to the Secretary of State to be equal to the amount paid into the fund from the appropriate employment protection allocation (under section 134 of the Social Security Act 1975) from all secondary Class 1 contributions paid by that employer under Part I of that Act.

NOTES

Derivation: 1965, s 31; Social Security Act 1973, Sched 27, para 56; Social Security (Consequential Provisions) Act 1975, Sched 2, para 21; 1975, Sched 16, Pt I, para 13; Dock Work Regulation Act 1976, s 14 (4).

General Note: share fishermen and registered dock workers are excluded from the provisions of Part VI. This section enables employers to be given payments out of the Redundancy Fund if they are obliged to make an employer's contribution under the Social Security Act 1975 in respect of those employees. The payment will equal the amount paid into the fund from the appropriate employment protection allocation from the employer's contributions. Note also ss 149 (2) and 156 (3).

Subsection (3): see the Redundancy Payments Share Fishermen Regulations 1966 (SI 1966 No 145).

Definitions: 'employee' and 'employer': see note to s 1.

106. Payments out of fund to employees

(1) Where an employee claims that his employer is liable to pay to him an employer's payment, and either—

(*a*) that the employee has taken all reasonable steps (other than legal proceedings) to recover the payment from the employer and that the employer has refused or failed to pay it, or has paid part of it and has refused or failed to pay the balance, or

(*b*) that the employer is insolvent and that the whole or part of the payment remains unpaid,

the employee may apply to the Secretary of State for a payment under this section.

(2) If on an application under this section the Secretary of State is satisfied—

(*a*) that the employee is entitled to the employer's payment;

(*b*) that either of the conditions specified in subsection (1) is fulfilled; and

(*c*) that, in a case where the employer's payment is such a payment as is mentioned in paragraph (*b*) or paragraph (*c*) of section 104(1), the employee's right to the payment arises by virtue of a period of employment (computed in accordance with the provisions of the agreement in question) which is not less than one hundred and four weeks,

the Secretary of State shall pay to the employee out of the fund a sum calculated in accordance with Schedule 7, reduced by so much (if any) of the employer's payment as has been paid.

(3) Where the Secretary of State pays a sum to an employee in respect of an employer's payment—

(*a*) all rights and remedies of the employee with respect to the employer's payment, or (if the Secretary of State has paid only part of it) all his rights and remedies with respect to that part of the employer's payment, shall be transferred to and vest in the Secretary of State; and

(*b*) any decision of an industrial tribunal requiring the employer's payment to be paid to the employee shall have effect as if it required that payment, or, as the case may be, that part of it which the Secretary of State has paid, to be paid to the Secretary of State;

and any moneys recovered by the Secretary of State by virtue of this subsection shall be paid into the fund.

(4) Where the Secretary of State pays a sum under this section in respect of an employer's payment, then (subject to the following provisions of this subsection) section 104 shall apply as if that sum had been paid by the employer to the employee on account of that payment; but if, in a case falling within paragraph (*a*) of subsection (1), it appears to the Secretary of State that the refusal or failure of the employer to pay the employer's payment, or part of it, as the case may be, was without reasonable excuse, the Secretary of State may, subject to section 108, withhold any redundancy rebate to which the employer would otherwise be entitled in respect of the employer's payment, or may reduce the amount of any such rebate to such extent as the Secretary of State considers appropriate.

(5) For the purposes of this section an employer shall be taken to be insolvent if—

(*a*) he has become bankrupt or has made a composition or arrangement with his creditors or a receiving order is made against him;

(*b*) he has died and an order has been made under section 130 of the Bankruptcy Act 1914 for the administration of his estate according to the law of bankruptcy, or by virtue of an order of the court his estate is being administered in accordance with the rules set out in Part I of Schedule 1 to the Administration of Estates Act 1925; or

(*c*) where the employer is a company, a winding-up order has been made with respect to it or a resolution for voluntary winding-up has been passed with respect to it, or a receiver or manager of its undertaking has been duly appointed, or possession has been taken, by or on behalf of the holders of any debentures secured by a floating charge, of any property of the company comprised in or subject to the charge.

(6) In the application of this section to Scotland, for paragraphs (*a*), (*b*) and (*c*) of subsection (5) there shall be substituted the following paragraphs:—

(*a*) an award of sequestration has been made on his estate, or he has executed a trust deed for his creditors or entered into a composition contract;

(*b*) he has died and a judicial factor appointed under section 163 of the Bankruptcy (Scotland) Act 1913 is required by the provisions of that section to divide his insolvent estate among his creditors; or

(*c*) where the employer is a company, a winding-up order has been made or a resolution for voluntary winding-up is passed with respect to it or a receiver of its undertaking is duly appointed.

(7) In this section " legal proceedings " does not include any proceedings before an industrial tribunal, but includes any proceedings to enforce a decision or award of an industrial tribunal.

NOTES

Derivation: 1965, s 32; 1975, Sched 16, Pt I, paras 14, 15.

Further provisions: see ss 107, 108, 149 (2) and 156 (3), and Sched 7. Note s 117 and Sched 8, which make provision for employees paid by a person other than the employer.

Insolvent: see subs (5).

Definitions: 'employee' and 'employer': see note to s 1; 'week': see s 153 (1).

107. Supplementary provisions relating to applications under s 106

(1) Where an employee makes an application to the Secretary of State under section 106, the Secretary of State may, by notice in writing given to the employer, require the employer to provide the Secretary of State with such information, and to produce for examination on behalf of the Secretary of State documents in his custody or under his control of such descriptions, as the Secretary of State may reasonably require for the purpose of determining whether the application is well-founded.

(2) If any person on whom a notice is served under this section fails without reasonable excuse to comply with a requirement imposed by the notice, he shall be guilty of an offence and liable on summary conviction to a fine not exceeding £100.

(3) Any person who—

(*a*) in providing any information required by a notice under this section, makes a statement which he knows to be false in a material particular, or recklessly makes a statement which is false in a material particular, or

(*b*) produces for examination in accordance with any such notice a document which to his knowledge has been wilfully falsified,

shall be guilty of an offence under this subsection.

(4) A person guilty of an offence under subsection (3) shall be liable on summary conviction to a fine not exceeding the prescribed sum or to imprisonment for a term not exceeding three months or both, or on conviction on indictment to a fine or to imprisonment for a term not exceeding two years or both.

(5) In subsection (4) above " the prescribed sum " means—

(*a*) in England and Wales, the prescribed sum within the meaning of section 28 of the Criminal Law Act 1977 (that is to say, £1,000 or another sum fixed by order under section 61 of that Act to take account of changes in the value of money);

(*b*) in Scotland, the prescribed sum within the meaning of section 289B of the Criminal Procedure (Scotland) Act 1975 (that is to say, £1,000 or another sum fixed by an order made under section 289D of that Act for that purpose).

NOTES

Derivation: 1965, s 33; Criminal Procedure (Scotland) Act 1975, s 189 B (1); Criminal Law Act 1977, s 28 (2) and Sched 11, para 5.

Further provisions: note ss 149 (2) and 156 (3).

Subsection (1): note s 117 and Sched 8, which make provision for employees paid by a person other than the employer.

Definitions: 'employee' and 'employer': see note to s 1.

108. References and appeals to tribunal relating to payments out of fund

(1) Subsections (2) and (3) shall have effect where—

(*a*) a claim is made for a redundancy rebate on the grounds that an employer is liable to pay, and has paid, an employer's payment, or prior notice that such a claim may arise is given in accordance with regulations made under section 104(5)(*b*), or

(*b*) an application is made to the Secretary of State for a payment under section 106, where it is claimed that an employer is liable to pay an employer's payment.

(2) Where any such claim or application is made or such prior notice is given, there shall be referred to an industrial tribunal—

(*a*) any question as to the liability of the employer to pay the employer's payment;

(*b*) in a case falling within paragraph (*a*) of subsction (1), any question as to the amount of the rebate payable in accordance with Schedule 6;

(*c*) in a case falling within paragraph (*b*) of subsection (1), any question as to the amount of the sum payable in accordance with Schedule 7.

(3) For the purposes of any reference under subsection (2), an employee who has been dismissed by his employer shall, unless the contrary is proved, be presumed to have been so dismissed by reason of redundancy.

(4) Where, in any case to which section 104(3) applies, the Secretary of State refuses to pay a redundancy rebate, the employer may appeal to an industrial tribunal; and if on any such appeal the tribunal is satisfied that it is just and equitable having regard to all the relevant circumstances that a redundancy rebate should be paid, the tribunal shall determine accordingly, and the Secretary of State shall comply with any such determination of a tribunal.

(5) In any case where the Secretary of State withholds, or reduces the amount of, a redundancy rebate in pursuance of section 104(7) or section 106(4), the employer may appeal to an industrial tribunal; and if on any such appeal the tribunal is satisfied—

(*a*) in a case where the rebate was withheld, that it should be paid in full, or should be reduced instead of being withheld, or

(*b*) in a case where the rebate was reduced, that it should not be reduced, or should be reduced by a smaller or larger proportion than that which the Secretary of State has applied,

the tribunal shall determine accordingly, and the Secretary of State shall comply with any such determination.

NOTES

Derivation: 1965, s 34; 1975, Sched 16, Pt I, para 16.

Further provisions: see ss 149 (2) and 156 (3) and Scheds 6 and 7. Note s 117 and Sched 8 which make provision for employees paid by a person other than the employer.

Definitions: 'redundancy rebate': see s 104 (1); 'employee' and 'employer': see note to s 1.

109. Financial provisions relating to the fund

(1) Subject to the following provisions of this section, the Treasury may from time to time advance out of the National Loans Fund to the Secretary of State for the purposes of the fund such sums as the Secretary of State may request; and any sums advanced to the Secretary of State under this section shall be paid into the fund.

(2) The aggregate amount outstanding by way of principal in respect of sums advanced to the Secretary of State under this section shall not at any time exceed £16 million or such larger sum not exceeding £40 million as the Secretary of State may by order made with the consent of the Treasury determine.

(3) Any sums advanced to the Secretary of State under this section shall be repaid by the Secretary of State out of the fund into the National Loans Fund in such manner and at such times, and with interest thereon at such rate, as the Treasury may direct.

(4) An order shall not be made under this section unless a draft of the order has been laid before Parliament and approved by resolution of each House of Parliament.

NOTES

Derivation: 1965, s 35 (1), (2), (4) and (7); National Loans Act 1968, s 5 (1), Sched 1; 1975, Sched 16, Pt I, para 17.

Further provisions: see ss 149 (2) and 156 (3).

Orders under this section: none had been made at the time of going to press.

MISCELLANEOUS AND SUPPLEMENTAL

110. Strike during currency of employer's notice to terminate contract

(1) The provisions of this section shall have effect where, after an employer has given notice to an employee to terminate his contract of employment (in this section referred to as a " notice of termination ")—

(*a*) the employee begins to take part in a strike of employees of the employer, and

(*b*) the employer serves on him a notice in writing (in this section referred to as a " notice of extension ") requesting him to agree to extend the contract of employment beyond the time of expiry by an additional period comprising as many available days as the number of working days lost by striking (in this section referred to as " the proposed period of extension ").

(2) A notice of extension shall indicate the reasons for which the employer makes the request contained in the notice, and shall state that unless either—

(*a*) the employee complies with the request, or

(*b*) the employer is satisfied that, in consequence of sickness, injury or otherwise, he is unable to comply with it, or that (notwithstanding that he is able to comply with it) in the circumstances it is reasonable for him not to do so,

the employer will contest any liability to pay him a redundancy payment in respect of the dismissal effected by the notice of termination.

(3) For the purposes of this section an employee shall be taken to comply with the request contained in a notice of extension if, but only if, on each available day within the proposed period of extension, he attends at his proper or usual place of work and is ready and willing to work, whether he has signified his agreement to the request in any other way or not.

(4) Where an employee on whom a notice of extension has been served—

(*a*) complies with the request contained in the notice, or

(*b*) does not comply with it, but attends at his proper or usual place of work and is ready and willing to work on one or more (but not all) of the available days within the proposed period of extension,

the notice of termination shall have effect, and shall be deemed at all material times to have had effect, as if the period specified in it had (in a case falling within paragraph (*a*)) been extended beyond the time of expiry by an additional period equal to the proposed period of extension or (in a case falling within paragraph (*b*)) had been extended beyond the time of expiry up to the end of the day (or, if more than one, the last of the days) on which he so attends and is ready and willing to work; and section 50 and Schedule 3 shall apply accordingly as if the period of notice required by section 49 were extended to a corresponding extent.

(5) Subject to subsection (6), if an employee on whom a notice of extension is served in pursuance of subsection (1) does not comply with the request contained in the notice, he shall not be entitled to a redundancy payment by reason of the dismissal effected by the notice of termination,

unless the employer agrees to pay such a payment to him notwithstanding that the request has not been complied with.

(6) Where a notice of extension has been served, and on a reference to an industrial tribunal it appears to the tribunal that the employee has not complied with the request contained in the notice and the employer has not agreed to pay a redundancy payment in respect of the dismissal in question, but that the employee was unable to comply with the request, or it was reasonable for him not to comply with it, as mentioned in subsection (2)(*b*) the tribunal may determine that the employer shall be liable to pay to the employee—

(*a*) the whole of any redundancy payment to which the employee would have been entitled apart from subsection (5), or

(*b*) such part of any such redundancy payment as the tribunal thinks fit.

(7) The service of a notice of extension, and any extension, by virtue of subsection (4) of the period specified in a notice of termination,—

(*a*) shall not affect any right either of the employer or of the employee to terminate the contract of employment (whether before, at or after the time of expiry) by a further notice or without notice, and

(*b*) shall not affect the operation of sections 81 to 102 in relation to any such termination of the contract of employment.

(8) In this section any reference to the number of working days lost by striking is a reference to the number of working days in the period beginning with the date of service of the notice of termination and ending with the time of expiry which are days on which the employee in question takes part in a strike of employees of the employer.

(9) In this section, " strike " has the meaning given by paragraph 24 of Schedule 13, " time of expiry ", in relation to a notice of termination, means the time at which the notice would expire apart from this section, " working day ", in relation to an employee, means a day on which, in accordance with his contract of employment, he is normally required to work, " available day ", in relation to an employee, means a working day beginning at or after the time of expiry which is a day on which he is not taking part in a strike of employees of the employer, and " available day within the proposed period of extension " means an available day which begins before the end of that period.

NOTES

Derivation: 1965, ss 40 and 56 (1).

General Note: the effect of this section is to extend the contract of employment of an employee who has been given notice of termination, and who then goes on strike. If the employer serves a notice of extension, the contract will be extended beyond the time at which it would expire by the number of days the employee was on strike, so that the employee will have to make up the days lost. Failure to comply may cause the employee to lose his entitlement to a redundancy payment (see subs (5)), though if, on a reference to an industrial tribunal, the tribunal finds that the employee was unable to comply, it may award him the whole or part of the redundancy payment he might otherwise claim.

Note also the provisions of ss 92, 98 (3), 104 (6) and 149 (2) and Scheds 2, Pt II, para 4 (3), 6, para 3 and 13, para 15.

Subsections (2), (5) *and* (6)*:* note s 117 and Sched 8, which make provision for employees paid by a person other than the employer.

Definitions: 'contract of employment': see a 153 (1); 'employee' and 'employer': see note to s 1; 'strike', 'time of expiry', 'working day', 'available day' and 'available day with the proposed period of extension': note subs (9); 'redundancy payment': see s 81 (1); 'dismissal': see s 83.

111. Payments equivalent to redundancy rebates in respect of civil servants, etc

(1) The provisions of this section shall have effect with respect to employment of any of the following descriptions, that is to say—

(*a*) any such employment as is mentioned in paragraph (*a*), paragraph (*b*) or paragraph (*c*) of subsection (1) of section 99 (whether as originally enacted or as modified by any order under section 149(1));

(*b*) any employment remunerated out of the revenue of the Duchy of Lancaster or the Duchy of Cornwall;

(*c*) any employment remunerated out of the Queen's Civil List;

(*d*) any employment remunerated out of Her Majesty's Privy Purse.

(2) Where the Secretary of State is satisfied that a payment has been, or will be, made in respect of the termination of any person's employment of any description specified in subsection (1), and that the payment has been, or will be, so made to or in respect of him—

(*a*) in accordance with the Superannuation Act 1965, as that Act continues to have effect by virtue of section 23(1) of the Superannuation Act 1972,

(*b*) in accordance with any provision of a scheme made under section 1 of the Superannuation Act 1972, or

(*c*) in accordance with any such arrangements as are mentioned in subsection (3),

the Secretary of State shall pay the appropriate sum out of the fund to the appropriate fund or authority.

(3) The arrangements referred to in paragraph (*c*) of subsection (2) are any arrangements made with the approval of the Minister for the Civil Service for securing that payments by way of compensation for loss of any such employment as is mentioned in subsection (1) will be made—

(*a*) in circumstances which in the opinion of the Minister for the Civil Service correspond (subject to the appropriate modifications) to those in which a right to a redundancy payment would have accrued if section 81 had applied, and

(*b*) on a scale which in the opinion of the Minister for the Civil Service, taking into account any sums which are payable as mentioned in subsection (2)(*a*) or (*b*) to or in respect of the person losing the employment in question, corresponds (subject to the appropriate modifications) to that on which a redundancy payment would have been payable if section 81 had applied.

(4) For the purposes of subsection (2) the appropriate sum is the sum appearing to the Secretary of State to be equal to the amount of the redundancy rebate which would have been payable under section 104 if such a right as is mentioned in paragraph (*a*) of subsection (3) had

accrued, and such a redundancy payment as is mentioned in paragraph (*b*) of subsection (3) had been payable and had been paid.

(5) Any accounts prepared by the Secretary of State under section 103(2) shall show as a separate item the aggregate amount of sums paid under subsection (2) during the period to which the accounts relate.

(6) In this section " the appropriate fund or authority "—

(*a*) in relation to employment of any description falling within paragraph 7 of subsection (1) of section 39 of the Superannuation Act 1965 (whether as originally enacted or as modified by any order under that section), means the fund out of which, or the body out of whose revenues, the employment is remunerated;

(*b*) in relation to any employment remunerated out of the revenues of the Duchy of Lancaster, means the Chancellor of the Duchy, and, in relation to any employment remunerated out of the revenues of the Duchy of Cornwall, means such person as the Duke of Cornwall, or the possessor for the time being of the Duchy of Cornwall, appoints;

(*c*) in relation to any employment remunerated out of the Queen's Civil List or out of Her Majesty's Privy Purse, means the Civil List or the Privy Purse, as the case may be; and

(*d*) in any other case, means the Consolidated Fund.

NOTES

Derivation: 1965, s 41; Superannuation Act 1972, Sched 6, para 55; Minister for the Civil Service Order 1968 (SI 1968 No 1656).

Further provisions: see ss 112, 115 (1) (*b*), 138 (6) and (7) (*d*), 149 (2) and 156 (3).

Subsection (3): note Sched 13, para 12 (2) (*b*).

Definitions: 'redundancy payment': see s 81 (1); 'redundancy rebate': see s 104.

112. References to tribunal relating to equivalent payments

(1) This section applies to any such payment as is mentioned in subsection (3) of section 111 which is payable in accordance with any such arrangements as are mentioned in that subsection.

(2) Where the terms and conditions (whether constituting a contract of employment or not) on which any person is employed in any such employment as is mentioned in subsection (1) of section 111 include provision—

(*a*) for the making of any payment to which this section applies, and

(*b*) for referring to a tribunal any such question as is mentioned in the following provisions of this subsection,

any question as to the right of any person to such a payment in respect of that employment, or as to the amount of such a payment shall be referred to and determined by an industrial tribunal.

NOTES

Derivation: 1965, s 42.

Further provisions: note s 149 (2).

113. Employment under Government of overseas territory

(1) Where the Secretary of State is satisfied that, in accordance with any such arrangements as are mentioned in subsection (3), a payment

has been, or will be, made in respect of the termination of a person's employment in any capacity under the Government of an overseas territory (in this section referred to as " the relevant Government "), and that in respect of the whole or part of the period during which that person was in that employment, employer's contributions were paid in respect of him, the Secretary of State shall pay the appropriate sum out of the fund to such other fund or authority as may be designated in that behalf by the relevant Government.

(2) The reference in subsection (1) to employer's contributions is a reference to secondary Class 1 contributions paid in respect of the person in question by persons who were in relation to him secondary Class 1 contributors by virtue of section 4(4)(*a*) of the Social Security Act 1975, and in relation to any period before 6th April 1975, to employer's contributions within the meaning of the National Insurance Act 1965.

(3) The arrangements referred to in subsection (1) are any arrangements made by or on behalf of the relevant Government for securing that payments by way of compensation for loss of employment in the capacity in question will be made—

(*a*) in circumstances which in the opinion of the Secretary of State correspond (subject to the appropriate modifications) to those in which a right to a redundancy payment would have accrued if section 81 had applied, and

(*b*) on a scale which in the opinion of the Secretary of State corresponds (subject to the appropriate modifications) to that on which a redundancy payment would have been payable if that section had applied.

(4) For the purposes of subsection (1) the appropriate sum (subject to subsection (5)) is the sum appearing to the Secretary of State to be equal to the amount of the redundancy rebate which would have been payable under section 104 if such a right as is mentioned in paragraph (*a*) of subsection (3) had accrued, and such a redundancy payment as is mentioned in paragraph (*b*) of that subsection had been payable and had been paid.

(5) Where it appears to the Secretary of State that such contributions as are mentioned in subsection (1) were paid in respect of part (but not the whole) of the period of employment in question, the rebate which would have been payable as mentioned in subsection (4) shall be calculated as if the employment had been limited to that part of the period.

(6) Any accounts prepared by the Secretary of State under section 103(2) shall show as a separate item the aggregate amount of sums paid under subsection (1) during the period to which the accounts relate.

NOTES

Derivation: 1965, s 43 (1) to (5); Social Security Act 1973, Sched 27, para 58; Social Security (Consequential Provisions) Act 1975, Sched 2, para 22.

General Note: by virtue of s 99 (2), the provisions of s 81 do not apply to any person in respect of his employment in any capacity with the Government of an overseas territory. The provisions of this section are necessary, therefore, to enable the Secretary of State to make the equivalent of a redundancy rebate to the appropriate authority, in respect of the equivalent to a redundancy payment paid to such a person on the termination of his employment with the overseas Government. But this may only be done where the provisions of this section have been complied with.

Note also ss 114 and 149 (2).

*F**

Definitions: 'Government of an overseas territory': see s 114; 'employer's contributions': note subsection (2); 'redundancy payment': see s 81 (1); 'redundancy rebate': see s 104.

114. Meaning of ' Government of overseas territory '

In this Part " overseas territory " means any territory or country outside the United Kingdom; and any reference to the Government of an overseas territory includes a reference to a Government constituted for two or more overseas territories and to any authority established for the purpose of providing or administering services which are common to, or relate to matters of common interest to, two or more such territories.

NOTES

Derivation: 1965, s 43 (6).

General Note: note ss 99 (2) and 149 (2).

115. Application of Part VI to employment not under contract of employment

(1) This section applies to employment of any description which—

(*a*) is not employment under a contract of service or of apprenticeship, and

(*b*) is not employment of any description falling within paragraphs (*a*) to (*d*) of section 111(1),

but is employment such that secondary Class 1 contributions are payable under Part I of the Social Security Act 1975 in respect of persons engaged therein.

(2) The Secretary of State may by regulations under this section provide that, subject to such exceptions and modifications as may be prescribed by the regulations, this Part and the provisions of this Act supplementary thereto shall have effect in relation to any such employment of a description to which this section applies as may be so prescribed as if—

(*a*) it were employment under a contract of employment, and

(*b*) any person engaged in employment of that description were an employee, and

(*c*) such person as may be determined by or under the regulations were his employer.

(3) Without prejudice to the generality of subsection (2), regulations made under this section may provide that section 105 shall apply to persons engaged in any such employment of a description to which this section applies as may be prescribed by the regulations, as if those persons were employees to whom that section applies.

NOTES

Derivation: 1965, s 49; Social Security Act 1973, Sched 27, para 59; Social Security (Consequential Provisions) Act 1975, Sched 2, para 23.

Further provisions: See s 149 (2).

Regulations: see the Redundancy Payments Office Holders Regulations 1965 (SI 1965 No 2007), the Redundancy Payments Share Fishermen Regulations 1966 (SI 1966 No 145) and the Redundancy Payments Office Holders (Scotland) Regulations 1966 (SI 1966 No 1436).

Definitions: 'contract of employment': see s 153 (1); 'employee' and 'employer': see note to s 1.

116. Provision for treating termination of certain employments by statute as equivalent to dismissal

(1) The Secretary of State may by regulations under this section provide that, subject to such exceptions and modifications as may be prescribed by the regulations, the provisions of this Part shall have effect in relation to any person who, by virtue of any statutory provisions,—

(*a*) is transferred to, and becomes a member of, a body specified in those provisions, but

(*b*) at a time so specified ceases to be a member of that body unless before that time certain conditions so specified have been fulfilled,

as if the cessation of his membership of that body by virtue of those provisions were dismissal by his employer by reason of redundancy.

(2) The power conferred by subsection (1) shall be excercisable whether membership of the body in question constitutes employment within the meaning of section 153 or not; and, where that membership does not constitute such employment, that power may be exercised in addition to any power exercisable by virtue of section 115.

NOTES

Derivation: 1965, s 50.

Further provisions: see s 149 (2).

Regulations: see the Redundancy Payments Termination of Employment Regulations 1965 (SI 1965 No 2022).

Definitions: 'dismissal by reason of redundancy': see s 81 (2); 'statutory provision': see s 153 (1).

117. Employees paid by person other than employer

(1) This section applies to any employee whose remuneration is, by virtue of any statutory provision, payable to him by a person other than his employer.

(2) For the purposes of the operation, in relation to employees to whom this section applies, of the provisions of this Part and Schedule 13 specified in column 1 of Schedule 8, any reference to the employer which is specified in column 2 of Schedule 8 shall be construed as a reference to the person responsible for paying the remuneration.

(3) In relation to employees to whom this section applies, section 119 shall have effect as if—

(*a*) any reference in subsection (1) or subsection (2) of that section to a notice required or authorised to be given by or to an employer included a reference to a notice which, by virtue of subsection (2), is required or authorised to be given by or to the person responsible for paying the remuneration;

(*b*) in relation to a notice required or authorised to be given to that person, any reference to the employer in paragraph (*a*) or paragraph (*b*) of subsection (2) of that section were a reference to that person; and

(*c*) the reference to the employer in subsection (5) of that section included a reference to that person.

(4) In this section and in Schedule 8, " the person responsible for paying the remuneration " means the person by whom the remuneration is payable as mentioned in subsection (1).

NOTES

Derivation: 1965, s 51.

Further provisions: see s 149 (2) and Sched 8.

Definitions: 'employee' and 'employer': see note to s 1; 'statutory provision': see s 153 (1).

118. Statutory compensation schemes

(1) This section applies to any statutory provision which was in force immediately before 6th December 1965, whereby the holders of such situations, places or employments as are specified in that provision are, or may become, entitled to compensation for loss of employment, or for loss or diminution of emoluments or of pension rights, in consequence of the operation of any other statutory provision referred to therein.

(2) The Secretary of State may make provision by regulations for securing that where apart from this section a person is entitled to compensation under a statutory provision to which this section applies, and the circumstances are such that he is also entitled to a redundancy payment, the amount of the redundancy payment shall be set off against the compensation to which he would be entitled apart from this section; and any statutory provision to which any such regulations apply shall have effect subject to the regulations.

NOTES

Derivation: 1965, s 47.

Further provisions: see s 149 (2).

Subsection (1): note s 98 (2).

Regulations: see the Redundancy Payments Statutory Compensation Regulations 1965 (SI 1965 No 1988).

Definitions: 'statutory provision' and 'employment': see s 153 (1); 'redundancy payment': see s 81 (1).

119. Provisions as to notices

(1) Any notice which under this Part is required or authorised to be given by an employer to an employee may be given by being delivered to the employee, or left for him at his usual or last-known place of residence, or sent by post addressed to him at that place.

(2) Any notice which under this Part is required or authorised to be given by an employee to an employer may be given either by the employee himself or by a person authorised by him to act on his behalf, and, whether given by or on behalf of the employee,—

(*a*) may be given by being delivered to the employer, or sent by post addressed to him at the place where the employee is or was employed by him, or

(*b*) if arrangements in that behalf have been made by the employer, may be given by being delivered to a person designated by the employer in pursuance of the arrangements, or left for such a person at a place so designated, or sent by post to such a person at an address so designated.

(3) In the preceding provisions of this section, any reference to the delivery of a notice shall, in relation to a notice which is not required

by this Part to be in writing, be construed as including a reference to the oral communication of the notice.

(4) Any notice which, in accordance with any provision of this section, is left for a person at a place referred to in that provision shall, unless the contrary is proved, be presumed to have been received by him on the day on which it was left there.

(5) Nothing in subsection (1) or subsection (2) shall be construed as affecting the capacity of an employer to act by a servant or agent for the purposes of any provision of this Part, including either of those subsections.

NOTES

Derivation: 1965, s 53.

Further provisions: note ss 117 (3) and 149 (2).

Definitions: 'employee' and 'employer': see note to s 1.

120. Offences

(1) Where an offence under this Part committed by a body corporate is proved to have been committed with the consent or connivance of, or to be attributable to any neglect on the part of, any director, manager, secretary or other similar officer of the body corporate or any person who was purporting to act in any such capacity, he as well as the body corporate shall be guilty of that offence and shall be liable to be proceeded against and punished accordingly.

(2) In this section " director ", in relation to a body corporate established by or under any enactment for the purpose of carrying on under national ownership any industry or part of an industry or undertaking, being a body corporate whose affairs are managed by its members, means a member of that body corporate.

NOTES

Derivation: 1965, s 52.

Further provisions: see s 149 (2).

Definitions: 'director': note subs (2).

PART VII

INSOLVENCY OF EMPLOYER

121. Priority of certain debts on insolvency

(1) An amount to which this section applies shall be treated for the purposes of—

(*a*) section 33 of the Bankruptcy Act 1914;

(*b*) section 118 of the Bankruptcy (Scotland) Act 1913; and

(*c*) section 319 of the Companies Act 1948;

as if it were wages payable by the employer to the employee in respect of the period for which it is payable.

(2) This section applies to any amount owed by an employer to an employee in respect of—

(*a*) a guarantee payment;

(*b*) remuneration on suspension on medical grounds under section 19;

(*c*) any payment for time off under section 27(3) or 31(3);

(*d*) remuneration under a protective award made under section 101 of the Employment Protection Act 1975.

NOTES

Derivation: 1975, s 63.

General Note: s 121 provides for certain debts to be given priority on the insolvency of the employer; s 122 enables the Secretary of State to pay out of the Redundancy Fund certain debts owed by an insolvent employer to his employee; s 123 empowers the Secretary of State to pay out of the Redundancy Fund into an occupational pension scheme, contributions which fall to be paid by an employer who has become insolvent; s 124 provides remedies for a failure to pay under s 122 and s 123; s 125 provides for the Secretary of State, on making payments under s 122 and s 123, to have transferred to him the rights and remedies of the persons otherwise entitled under those sections; s 126 gives the Secretary of State power to obtain information in connection with applications under ss 122 and 123; s 127 is an interpretation section relating to ss 122 to 126. See also s 150 and Sched 12, Pt I, which provide for the death of the employer or the employee. Note ss 137, 140, 149 and 157.

Exclusions:

(i) certain types of Crown Employment (s 138 (1) and (5) and Sched 5);
(ii) House of Commons staff (s 139);
(iii) employment outside Great Britain (s 141 (2) and (5));
(iv) share fishermen (s 144 (2));
(v) (ss 122 and 123 only) merchant seamen (s 144 (4), and (5));
(vi) (ss 122 and 123 only) registered dock workers except when wholly or mainly engaged in work which is not dock work (s 145 (2) and (5)):
(vii) (ss 122 and 123 only) employment by spouse (s 146 (1));
(viii) employment in police service (s 146 (2) and (3)).

Guarantee payment: see ss 12 to 18 and s 122 (3) (*a*) and (4).

Remuneration on suspension on medical grounds: see ss 19 to 22 and s 122 (3) (*a*) and (4).

Payment for time off under section 27 (3) *or* 31 (3): see ss 27 to 32 and s 122 (3) (*a*) and (4).

Remuneration under a protective award . . . : see ss 99 and 101 to 3 of the Employment Protection Act 1975, and s 122 (3) (*a*) and (4).

Definitions: 'employee' and 'employer': see note to s 1.

122. Employee's rights on insolvency of employer

(1) If on an application made to him in writing by an employee the Secretary of State is satisfied—

(*a*) that the employer of that employee has become insolvent; and

(*b*) that on the relevant date the employee was entitled to be paid the whole or part of any debt to which this section applies,

the Secretary of State shall, subject to the provisions of this section, pay the employee out of the Redundancy Fund the amount to which in the opinion of the Secretary of State the employee is entitled in respect of that debt.

(2) In this section the " relevant date " in relation to a debt means the date on which the employer became insolvent or the date of the termination of the employee's employment, whichever is the later.

(3) This section applies to the following debts:—

(*a*) any arrears of pay in respect of a period or periods not exceeding in the aggregate eight weeks;

(*b*) any amount which the employer is liable to pay the employee for the period of notice required by section 49(1) or (2) or for any failure of the employer to give the period of notice required by section 49(1);

(*c*) any holiday pay in respect of a period or periods of holiday, not exceeding six weeks in all, to which the employee became entitled during the twelve months immediately preceding the relevant date;

(*d*) any basic award of compensation for unfair dismissal (within the meaning of section 72);

(*e*) any reasonable sum by way of reimbursement of the whole or part of any fee or premium paid by an apprentice or articled clerk.

(4) For the purposes of subsection (3)(*a*), any such amount as is referred to in section 121(2) shall be treated as if it were arrears of pay.

(5) The total amount payable to an employee in respect of any debt mentioned in subsection (3), where the amount of that debt is referable to a period of time, shall not exceed £100 in respect of any one week or, in respect of a shorter period, an amount bearing the same proportion to £100 as that shorter period bears to a week.

(6) The Secretary of State may vary the limit referred to in subsection (5) after a review under section 148, by order made in accordance with that section.

(7) A sum shall be taken to be reasonable for the purposes of subsection (3)(*e*) in a case where a trustee in bankruptcy or liquidator has been or is required to be appointed if it is admitted to be reasonable by the trustee in bankruptcy or liquidator under section 34 of the Bankruptcy Act 1914 (preferential claims of apprentices and articled clerks), whether as originally enacted or as applied to the winding up of a company by section 317 of the Companies Act 1948.

(8) Subsection (7) shall not apply to Scotland, but in Scotland a sum shall be taken to be reasonable for the purposes of subsection (3)(*e*) in a case where a trustee in bankruptcy or liquidator has been or is required to be appointed if it is admitted by the trustee in bankruptcy or the liquidator for the purposes of the bankruptcy or winding up.

(9) The provisions of subsections (10) and (11) shall apply in a case where one of the following officers (hereafter in this section referred to as the " relevant officer ") has been or is required to be appointed in connection with the employer's insolvency, that is to say, a trustee in bankruptcy, a liquidator, a receiver or manager, or a trustee under a composition or arrangement between the employer and his creditors or under a trust deed for his creditors executed by the employer; and in this subsection " liquidator " and " receiver " include the Official Receiver in his capacity as a provisional liquidator or interim receiver.

(10) Subject to subsection (11), the Secretary of State shall not in such a case make any payment under this section in respect of any debt until he has received a statement from the relevant officer of the amount of that debt which appears to have been owed to the employee on the relevant date and to remain unpaid; and the relevant officer shall, on request by the Secretary of State, provide him, as soon as reasonably practicable, with such a statement.

(11) Where—

(*a*) a period of six months has elapsed since the application for a payment under this section was received by the Secretary of State, but no such payment has been made;

(*b*) the Secretary of State is satisfied that a payment under this section should be made; and

(*c*) it appears to the Secretary of State that there is likely to be further delay before he receives a statement about the debt in question,

then, the Secretary of State may, if the applicant so requests or, if the Secretary of State thinks fit, without such a request, make a payment under this section, notwithstanding that no such statement has been received.

NOTES

Derivation: 1975, s 64; 1977 Order (No 2), Art 2.

Applicability: see Sched 15, para 13. Note ss 144 (4) and 145 (2).

General Note: note s 125, under which the employee's rights and remedies are transferred to the Secretary of State, where he makes a payment to the employee in respect of a debt to which this section applies; and if the Secretary of State has paid such a debt and an industrial tribunal requires an employer to pay it to an employee, it becomes payable instead to the Secretary of State. See *Secretary of State for Employment* v *Wilson* [1978] ICR 200. Note ss 126, 156 (2) and 157.

Insolvent: see s 127 (1) for the circumstances in which an employer is taken to be insolvent.

Redundancy Fund: see ss 103 to 109.

Subsection (3): it is unclear whether a compensatory award for unfair dismissal will fall within this subsection; at best, it could only fall within paras (*a*) and (*c*), and therefore only partially within the subsection. An additional award, made under s 71, appears to fall outside it. This is anomalous.

Subsections (5) *and* (6): note s 148.

Basic award of compensation for unfair dismissal: this is calculated in accordance with s 73.

Definitions: 'employee' and 'employer': see note to s 1; 'holiday pay': see s 127 (3); 'insolvent': see above; 'relevant date': note subs (2).

123. Payment of unpaid contributions to occupational pension scheme

(1) If, on application made to him in writing by the persons competent to act in respect of an occupational pension scheme, the Secretary of State is satisfied that an employer has become insolvent and that at the time that he did so there remained unpaid relevant contributions falling to be paid by him to the scheme, the Secretary of State shall, subject to the provisions of this section, pay into the resources of the scheme out of the Redundancy Fund the sum which in his opinion is payable in respect of the unpaid relevant contributions.

(2) In this section "relevant contributions" means contributions falling to be paid by an employer in accordance with an occupational pension scheme, either on his own account or on behalf of an employee; and for the purposes of this section a contribution of any amount shall not be treated as falling to be paid on behalf of an employee unless a sum equal to that amount has been deducted from the pay of the employee by way of a contribution from him.

(3) The sum payable under this section in respect of unpaid contributions of an employer on his own account to an occupational pension scheme shall be the least of the following amounts—

(*a*) the balance of relevant contributions remaining unpaid on the date when he became insolvent and payable by the employer on his own account to the scheme in respect of the twelve months immediately preceding that date;

(*b*) the amount certified by an actuary to be necessary for the purpose of meeting the liability of the scheme on dissolution to pay the benefits provided by the scheme to or in respect of the employees of the employer;

(*c*) an amount equal to ten per cent. of the total amount of remuneration paid or payable to those employees in respect of the twelve months immediately preceding the date on which the employer became insolvent.

(4) For the purposes of subsection (3)(*c*), "remuneration" includes holiday pay, maternity pay and any such payment as is referred to in section 121(2).

(5) Any sum payable under this section in respect of unpaid contributions on behalf of an employee shall not exceed the amount deducted from the pay of the employee in respect of the employee's contributions to the occupational pension scheme during the twelve months immediately preceding the date on which the employer became insolvent.

(6) The provisions of subsections (7) to (9) shall apply in a case where one of the following officers (hereafter in this section referred to as the "relevant officer") has been or is required to be appointed in connection with the employer's insolvency, that is to say, a trustee in bankruptcy, a liquidator, a receiver or manager, or a trustee under a composition or arrangement between the employer and his creditors or under a trust deed for his creditors executed by the employer; and in this subsection "liquidator" and "receiver" include the Official Receiver in his capacity as a provisional liquidator or interim receiver.

(7) Subject to subsection (9), the Secretary of State shall not in such a case make any payment under this section in respect of unpaid relevant contributions until he has received a statement from the relevant officer of the amount of relevant contributions which appear to have been unpaid on the date on which the employer became insolvent and to remain unpaid; and the relevant officer shall, on request by the Secretary of State provide him, as soon as reasonably practicable, with such a statement.

(8) Subject to subsection (9), an amount shall be taken to be payable, paid or deducted as mentioned in subsection (3)(*a*) or (*c*) or subsection (5), only if it is so certified by the relevant officer.

(9) Where—

(*a*) a period of six months has elapsed since the application for a payment under this section was received by the Secretary of State, but no such payment has been made;

(*b*) the Secretary of State is satisfied that a payment under this section should be made; and

(*c*) it appears to the Secretary of State that there is likely to be further delay before he receives a statement or certificate about the contributions in question,

then, the Secretary of State may, if the applicants so request or, if the Secretary of State thinks fit, without such a request, make a payment under this section, notwithstanding that no such statement or certificate has been received.

NOTES

Derivation: 1975, s 65.

Applicability: see Sched 15, para 13. Note s 144 (4) and 145 (2).

General Note: if the Secretary of State makes a payment under this section, the rights and remedies belonging to the persons competent to act in respect of the scheme, are transferred to him under s 125 (3) and (4). Note also ss 125, 156 (2) and 157.

Insolvent: see s 127 (1) for the circumstances in which an employer is taken to be insolvent.

Redundancy Fund: see ss 103 to 109.

Definitions: 'employee' and 'employer': see note to s 1; 'occupational pension scheme' and 'holiday pay': see s 127 (3); 'insolvent': see above; 'maternity pay': see s 33 and 34; 'relevant contributions': note subs (2); 'remuneration': note subs (4); 'liquidator' and 'receiver': note subs (6).

124. Complaint to industrial tribunal

(1) A person who has applied for a payment under section 122 may, within the period of three months beginning with the date on which the decision of the Secretary of State on that application was communicated to him or, if that is not reasonably practicable, within such further period as is reasonable, present a complaint to an industrial tribunal that—

(*a*) the Secretary of State has failed to make any such payment; or

(*b*) any such payment made by the Secretary of State is less than the amount which should have been paid.

(2) Any persons who are competent to act in respect of an occupational pension scheme and who have applied for a payment to be made under section 123 into the resources of the scheme may, within the period of three months beginning with the date on which the decision of the Secretary of State on that application was communicated to them, or, if that is not reasonably practicable, within such further period as is reasonable, present a complaint to an industrial tribunal that—

(*a*) the Secretary of State has failed to make any such payment; or

(*b*) any such payment made by him is less than the amount which should have been paid.

(3) Where an industrial tribunal finds that the Secretary of State ought to make a payment under section 122 or 123, it shall make a declaration

to that effect and shall also declare the amount of any such payment which it finds the Secretary of State ought to make.

NOTES

Derivation: 1975, s 66.

Further provisions: note ss 156 (2) and 157.

Complaint: a complaint to an industrial tribunal is to be made in accordance with regulations under s 128 and Sched 9.

Appeals: these lie to the Employment Appeal Tribunal, and thence to the Court of Appeal: see ss 135 and 136.

Reasonably practicable . . . reasonable: see note to s 67 (2).

Definitions: 'occupational pension scheme': see s 127 (3).

125. Transfer to Secretary of State of rights and remedies

(1) Where, in pursuance of section 122, the Secretary of State makes any payment to an employee in respect of any debt to which that section applies—

(*a*) any rights and remedies of the employee in respect of that debt (or, if the Secretary of State has paid only part of it, in respect of that part) shall, on the making of the payment, become rights and remedies of the Secretary of State; and

(*b*) any decision of an industrial tribunal requiring an employer to pay that debt to the employee shall have the effect that the debt or, as the case may be, that part of it which the Secretary of State has paid, is to be paid to the Secretary of State.

(2) There shall be included among the rights and remedies which become rights and remedies of the Secretary of State in accordance with subsection (1)(*a*) any right to be paid in priority to other creditors of the employer in accordance with—

(*a*) section 33 of the Bankruptcy Act 1914;

(*b*) section 118 of the Bankruptcy (Scotland) Act 1913; and

(*c*) section 319 of the Companies Act 1948,

and the Secretary of State shall be entitled to be so paid in priority to any other unsatisfied claim of the employee; and in computing for the purposes of any of those provisions any limit on the amount of sums to be so paid any sums paid to the Secretary of State shall be treated as if they had been paid to the employee.

(3) Where in pursuance of section 123 the Secretary of State makes any payment into the resources of an occupational pension scheme in respect of any contributions to the scheme, any rights and remedies in respect of those contributions belonging to the persons competent to act in respect of the scheme shall, on the making of the payment, become rights and remedies of the Secretary of State.

(4) Any sum recovered by the Secretary of State in exercising any right or pursuing any remedy which is his by virtue of this section shall be paid into the Redundancy Fund.

NOTES

Derivation: 1975, s 67.

Further provisions: note ss 156 (2) and 157.

Redundancy Fund: see ss 103 to 109.

Definitions: 'employee' and 'employer': see note to s 1; 'occupational pension scheme': see s 127 (3).

126. Power of Secretary of State to obtain information in connection with applications

(1) Where an application is made to the Secretary of State under section 122 or 123 in respect of a debt owed, or contributions to an occupational pension scheme falling to be made, by an employer, the Secretary of State may require—

(*a*) the employer to provide him with such information as the Secretary of State may reasonably require for the purpose of determining whether the application is well-founded; and

(*b*) any person having the custody or control of any relevant records or other documents to produce for examination on behalf of the Secretary of State any such document in that person's custody or under his control which is of such a description as the Secretary of State may require.

(2) Any such requirement shall be made by notice in writing given to the person on whom the requirement is imposed and may be varied or revoked by a subsequent notice so given.

(3) If a person refuses or wilfully neglects to furnish any information or produce any document which he has been required to furnish or produce by a notice under this section he shall be liable on summary conviction to a fine not exceeding £100.

(4) If a person, in purporting to comply with a requirement of a notice under this section, knowingly or recklessly makes any false statement he shall be liable on summary conviction to a fine not exceeding £400.

NOTES

Derivation: 1975, s 68

Further provisions: note ss 138 (5), 155, 156 (2), and 157.

Definitions: 'employer': see note to s 1; 'occupational pension scheme': see s 127 (3).

127. Interpretation of ss 122 to 126

(1) For the purposes of sections 122 to 126, an employer shall be taken to be insolvent if, but only if, in England and Wales,—

(*a*) he becomes bankrupt or makes a composition or arrangement with his creditors or a receiving order is made against him;

(*b*) he has died and an order is made under section 130 of the Bankruptcy Act 1914 for the administration of his estate according to the law of bankruptcy, or by virtue of an order of the court his estate is being administered in accordance with rules set out in Part I of Schedule 1 to the Administration of Estates Act 1925; or

(*c*) where the employer is a company, a winding up order is made or a resolution for voluntary winding up is passed with respect to it, or a receiver or manager of its undertaking is duly appointed, or possession is taken, by or on behalf of the holders of any debentures secured by a floating charge, of any property of the company comprised in or subject to the charge.

(2) For the purposes of sections 122 to 126, an employer shall be taken to be insolvent if, but only if, in Scotland,—

(*a*) an award of sequestration is made on his estate or he executes a trust deed for his creditors or enters into a composition contract;

(*b*) he has died and a judicial factor appointed under section 163 of the Bankruptcy (Scotland) Act 1913 is required by that section to divide his insolvent estate among his creditors; or

(*c*) where the employer is a company, a winding-up order is made or a resolution for voluntary winding up is passed with respect to it or a receiver of its undertaking is duly appointed.

(3) In sections 122 to 126—

" holiday pay " means—

(*a*) pay in respect of a holiday actually taken; or

(*b*) any accrued holiday pay which under the employee's contract of employment would in the ordinary course have become payable to him in respect of the period of a holiday if his employment with the employer had continued until he became entitled to a holiday;

" occupational pension scheme " means any scheme or arrangement which provides or is capable of providing, in relation to employees in any description of employment, benefits (in the form of pensions or otherwise) payable to or in respect of any such employees on the termination of their employment or on their death or retirement;

and any reference in those sections to the resources of such a scheme is a reference to the funds out of which the benefits provided by the scheme are from time to time payable.

NOTES

Derivation: 1975, s 69.

Definitions: 'employee' and 'employer': see note to s 1; 'contract of employment': see s 153 (1).

PART VIII

RESOLUTION OF DISPUTES RELATING TO EMPLOYMENT

INDUSTRIAL TRIBUNALS

128. Industrial tribunals

(1) The Secretary of State may by regulations make provision for the establishment of tribunals, to be known as industrial tribunals, to exercise the jurisdiction conferred on them by or under this Act or any other Act, whether passed before or after this Act.

(2) Regulations made wholly or partly under section 12 of the Industrial Training Act 1964 and in force immediately before the date on which this section comes into force shall, so far as so made, continue to have effect as if they had been made under subsection (1), and tribunals established in accordance with such regulations shall continue to be known as industrial tribunals.

(3) Schedule 9, which makes provision, among other things, with respect to proceedings before industrial tribunals, shall have effect.

(4) Complaints, references and appeals to industrial tribunals shall be made in accordance with regulations made under paragraph 1 of Schedule 9.

NOTES

Derivation: 1974, para 16; Industrial Training Act 1964, s 12 (1); 1965, ss 9 (1), 34 (2); 1972, s 8 (7), (8); 1975, s 108 (1).

Further provisions: note ss 137, 140, 149 particularly subs (2) and 157, and Sched 9, paras 9, 10 and 11.

Subsection (1): regulations: none had been made at the time of going to press.

Subsection (2): regulations under the Industrial Training Act 1964: see the Industrial Tribunals (England and Wales) Regulations 1965 (SI 1965 No 1101), as amended by the Industrial Tribunals (Amendment) Regulations 1977 (SI 1977 No 1473) and the Industrial Tribunals (Scotland) Regulations 1965 (SI 1965 No 1157), as amended by the Industrial Tribunal (Scotland) (Amendment) Regulations 1977 (SI 1977 No 1474).

Subsection (4): regulations made under para 1 of Sched 9: These are at present the Industrial Tribunals (Labour Relations) Regulations 1974 (SI 1974 No 1386), as amended by the Industrial Tribunals (Labour Relations) (Amendment) Regulations 1976 (SI 1976 No 661) and the Industrial Tribunals (Labour Relations) (Amendment) Regulations 1977 (SI 1977 No 911), and the Industrial Tribunals (Labour Relations) (Scotland) Regulations 1974 (SI 1974 No 1387), as amended by the Industrial Tribunals (Labour Relations) (Scotland) (Amendment) Regulations 1976 (SI 1976 No 662) and the Industrial Tribunals (Labour Relations) (Scotland) (Amendment) Regulations 1977 (SI 1977 No 912).

Appeals from Industrial tribunals: these lie to the Employment Appeal Tribunal and thence to the Court of Appeal: see ss 135 and 136.

129. Remedy for infringement of certain rights under this Act

The remedy of an employee for infringement of any of the rights conferred on him by sections 8 and 53 and Parts II, III, V and VII shall, if provision is made for a complaint or for the reference of a question to an industrial tribunal, be by way of such complaint or reference and not otherwise.

NOTES

Derivation: 1975, s 108 (1); 1974, para 4 (1).

Complaint or reference: for the regulations governing complaints and references, and appeals from the decision of an industrial tribunal, see the notes to s 128.

Employee: see the note to s 1.

130. Jurisdiction of referees to be exercised by tribunals

(1) There shall be referred to and determined by an industrial tribunal any question which by any statutory provision is directed (in whatsoever

terms) to be determined by a referee or board of referees constituted under any of the statutory provisions specified in Schedule 10 or which is so directed to be determined in the absence of agreement to the contrary.

(2) The transfer of any jurisdiction by this section shall not affect the principles on which any question is to be determined or the persons on whom the determination is binding, or any provision which requires particular matters to be expressly dealt with or embodied in the determination, or which relates to evidence.

NOTES

Derivation: 1965, s 44.

131. Power to confer jurisdiction on industrial tribunals in respect of damages etc for breach of contract of employment

(1) The appropriate Minister may by order provide that on any claim to which this section applies or any such claim of a description specified in the order, being in either case a claim satisfying the relevant condition or conditions mentioned in subsection (3), proceedings for the recovery of damages or any other sum, except damages or a sum due in respect of personal injuries, may be brought before an industrial tribunal.

(2) Subject to subsection (3), this section applies to any of the following claims, that is to say—

(*a*) a claim for damages for breach of a contract of employment or any other contract connected with employment;

(*b*) a claim for a sum due under such a contract;

(*c*) a claim for the recovery of a sum in pursuance of any enactment relating to the terms or performance of such a contract;

being in each case a claim such that a court in England and Wales or Scotland, as the case may be, would under the law for the time being in force have jurisdiction to hear and determine an action in respect of the claim.

(3) An order under this section may make provision with respect to any such claim only if it satisfies either of the following conditions, that is to say—

(*a*) it arises or is outstanding on the termination of the employee's employment; or

(*b*) it arises in circumstances which also give rise to proceedings already or simultaneously brought before an industrial tribunal otherwise than by virtue of this section;

or, if the order so provides, it satisfies both those conditions.

(4) Where on proceedings under this section an industrial tribunal finds that the whole or part of a sum claimed in the proceedings is due, the tribunal shall order the respondent to the proceedings to pay the amount which it finds due.

(5) Without prejudice to section 154(3), an order under this section may include provisions—

(*a*) as to the manner in which and time within which proceedings are to be brought by virtue of this section; and

(*b*) modifying any other enactment.

(6) Any jurisdiction conferred on an industrial tribunal by virtue of this section in respect of any claim shall be exercisable concurrently with any court in England and Wales or in Scotland, as the case may be, which has jurisdiction to hear and determine an action in respect of the claim.

(7) In this section—

"appropriate Minister", as respects a claim in respect of which an action could be heard and determined in England and Wales, means the Lord Chancellor and, as respects a claim in respect of which an action could be heard and determined by a court in Scotland, means the Secretary of State;

"personal injuries" includes any disease and any impairment of a person's physical or mental condition;

and any reference to breach of a contract includes a reference to breach of—

(*a*) a term implied in a contract by or under any enactment or otherwise;

(*b*) a term of a contract as modified by or under any enactment or otherwise; and

(*c*) a term which, although not contained in a contract, is incorporated in the contract by another term of the contract.

(8) No order shall be made under this section unless a draft of the order has been laid before Parliament and approved by resolution of each House of Parliament.

NOTES

Derivation: 1975, s 109 (1) to (5) and (7) to (9).

Further provisions: see s 131 (1) (*c*) and (2) to (7).

Definitions: 'employee': see note to s 1; 'contract of employment': see s 153 (1); 'appropriate minister' and 'personal injuries': note subs (7).

Orders under this section: none had been made at the time of going to press.

RECOUPMENT OF CERTAIN BENEFITS

132. Recoupment of unemployment benefit and supplementary benefit

(1) This section applies to payments which are the subject of proceedings before industrial tribunals, and which are—

(*a*) payments of wages or compensation for loss of wages; or

(*b*) payments, by employers to employees, under Part II, III or V or section 53 or in pursuance of an award under section 103 of the Employment Protection Act 1975; or

(*c*) payments, by employers to employees, of a nature similar to, or for a purpose corresponding to the purpose of, such payments as are mentioned in paragraph (*b*);

and to payments of remuneration in pursuance of a protective award under section 101 of the said Act of 1975.

(2) The Secretary of State may by regulations make provision with respect to payments to which this section applies for all or any of the following purposes—

(*a*) enabling the Secretary of State to recover from an employer, by way of total or partial recoupment of unemployment benefit or supplementary benefit, a sum not exceeding the amount of the prescribed element of the monetary award or, in the case of a protective award, the amount of the remuneration;

(*b*) requiring or authorising the tribunal to order the payment of such a sum, by way of total or partial recoupment of either benefit, to the Secretary of State instead of to the employee;

(*c*) requiring the tribunal to order the payment to the employee of only the excess of the prescribed element of the monetary award over the amount of any unemployment benefit or supplementary benefit shown to the tribunal to have been paid to the employee, and enabling the Secretary of State to recover from the employer, by way of total or partial recoupment of the benefit, a sum not exceeding that amount.

(3) Without prejudice to subsection (2), regulations under that subsection may—

(*a*) be so framed as to apply to all payments to which this section applies or one or more classes of those payments, and so as to apply both to unemployment benefit and supplementary benefit or only to one of those benefits;

(*b*) confer powers and impose duties on industrial tribunals, on the Supplementary Benefits Commission and on insurance officers and other persons;

(*c*) impose, on an employer to whom a monetary award or protective award relates, a duty to furnish particulars connected with the award and to suspend payments in pursuance of the award during any period prescribed by the regulations;

(*d*) provide for an employer who pays a sum to the Secretary of State in pursuance of this section to be relieved from any liability to pay the sum to another person;

(*e*) confer on an employee who is aggrieved by any decision of the Commission as to the total or partial recoupment of supplementary benefit in pursuance of the regulations (including any decision as to the amount of benefit) a right to appeal against the decision to an Appeal Tribunal constituted in accordance with the Supplementary Benefits Act 1976 and for that purpose apply section 15(2) and (3) of that Act (appeals) with or without modifications;

(*f*) provide for the proof in proceedings before industrial tribunals (whether by certificate or in any other manner) of any amount of unemployment benefit or supplementary benefit paid to an employee; and

(*g*) make different provision for different cases.

(4) Where in pursuance of any regulations under subsection (2) a sum has been recovered by or paid to the Secretary of State by way of total or partial recoupment of unemployment benefit or supplementary benefit—

(*a*) section 119(1) and (2) of the Social Security Act 1975 (repayment of benefit revised on review) shall not apply to the unemployment benefit recouped; and (*b*) sections 18 and 20 of the Supplementary Benefits Act 1976 (recovery of expenditure on supplementary benefits from persons liable for maintenance and recovery in cases of misrepresentation or non-disclosure) shall not apply to the supplementary benefit recouped.

(5) Any amount found to have been duly recovered by or paid to the Secretary of State in pursuance of regulations under subsection (2) by way of total or partial recoupment of unemployment benefit shall be paid into the National Insurance Fund.

(6) In this section—

" monetary award " means the amount which is awarded, or ordered to be paid, to the employee by the tribunal or would be so awarded or ordered apart from any provision or regulations under this section;

" the prescribed element ", in relation to any monetary award, means so much of that award as is attributable to such matters as may be prescribed by regulations under subsection (2);

" supplementary benefit " has the same meaning as in the Supplementary Benefits Act 1976; and

" unemployment benefit " means unemployment benefit under the Social Security Act 1975.

NOTES

Derivations: 1975, s 112 (2), (3), (5) to (8); Supplementary Benefits Act 1976, Sched 7, para 40; Social Security (Miscellaneous Provisions) Act 1977, s 16.

Further provisions: note ss 137, 149 and 157.

Supplementary Benefits Commission: see the Supplementary Benefits Act 1976, s 27 and Sched 3.

National Insurance Fund: see the Social Security Act 1975, s 133.

Insurance Officers: see the Social Security Act 1975, s 97.

Definitions: 'employee' and 'employer': see note to s 1.

Regulations under this section: see the Employment Protection (Recoupment of Unemployment Benefit and Supplementary Benefit) Regulations 1977 (SI 1977 No 674).

CONCILIATION OFFICERS

133. General provisions as to conciliation officers

(1) The provisions of subsections (2) to (6) shall have effect in relation to industrial tribunal proceedings, or claims which could be the subject of tribunal proceedings,—

(*a*) arising out of a contravention, or alleged contravention, of any of the following provisions of this Act, that is to say, sections 8, 12, 19, 23, 27, 28, 29, 31, 33 and 53; or

(*b*) arising out of a contravention, or alleged contravention, of section 99 or 102 of the Employment Protection Act 1975 or of a provision of any other Act specified by an order under subsection (7) as one to which this paragraph applies; or

(*c*) which are proceedings or claims in respect of which an industrial tribunal has jurisdiction by virtue of an order under section 131.

(2) Where a complaint has been presented to an industrial tribunal, and a copy of it has been sent to a conciliation officer, it shall be the duty of the conciliation officer—

(*a*) if he is requested to so so by the complainant and by the person against whom the complaint is presented, or

(*b*) if, in the absence of any such request, the conciliation officer considers that he could act under this subsection with a reasonable prospect of success,

to endeavour to promote a settlement of the complaint without its being determined by an industrial tribunal.

(3) Where at any time—

(*a*) a person claims that action has been taken in respect of which a complaint could be presented by him to an industrial tribunal, but

(*b*) before any complaint relating to that action has been presented by him,

a request is made to a conciliation officer (whether by that person or by the person against whom the complaint could be made) to make his services available to them, the conciliation officer shall act in accordance with subsection (2) as if a complaint has been presented to an industrial tribunal.

(4) Subsections (2) and (3) shall apply, with appropriate modifications, to the presentation of a claim and the reference of a question to an industrial tribunal as they apply to the presentation of a complaint.

(5) In proceeding under subsection (2) or (3) a conciliation officer shall, where appropriate, have regard to the desirability of encouraging the use of other procedures available for the settlement of grievances.

(6) Anything communicated to a conciliation officer in connection with the performance of his functions under this section shall not be admissible in evidence in any proceedings before an industrial tribunal, except with the consent of the person who communicated it to that officer.

(7) The Secretary of State may by order—

(*a*) direct that further provisions of this Act be added to the list in subsection (1)(*a*);

(*b*) specify a provision of any other Act as one to which subsection (1)(*b*) applies.

NOTES

Derivation: 1975, s 108 (2) to (8).

Further provisions: note ss 137, 140 (2) (*g*), 149 and 157.

Conciliation Officer: an officer designated by the Advisory, Conciliation and Arbitration Service under s 2 (4) Employment Protection Act 1975.

Orders under this section: none had been made at the time of going to press.

134. Functions of conciliation officers on complaint under s 67

(1) Where a complaint has been presented to an industrial tribunal under section 67 by a person (in this section referred to as the complainant) and a copy of it has been sent to a conciliation officer, it shall be the duty of the conciliation officer—

(*a*) if he is requested to do so by the complainant and by the employer against whom it was presented, or

(*b*) if, in the absence of any such request, the conciliation officer considers that he could act under this section with a reasonable prospect of success,

to endeavour to promote a settlement of the complaint without its being determined by an industrial tribunal.

(2) For the purpose of promoting such a settlement, in a case where the complainant has ceased to be employed by the employer against whom the complaint was made,—

(*a*) the conciliation officer shall in particular seek to promote the reinstatement or re-engagement of the complainant by the employer, or by a successor of the employer or by an associated employer, on terms appearing to the conciliation officer to be equitable; but

(*b*) where the complainant does not wish to be reinstated or re-engaged, or where reinstatement or re-engagement is not practicable, and the parties desire the conciliation officer to act under this section, he shall seek to promote agreement between them as to a sum by way of compensation to be paid by the employer to the complainant.

(3) Where at any time—

(*a*) after the complainant has ceased to be employed by an employer, in circumstances where the employee claims that he was unfairly dismissed, but

(*b*) before any complaint relating to that claim has been presented by the claimant under section 67,

a request is made to a conciliation officer (whether by the employer or by the employee) to make his services available to them, the conciliation officer shall act in accordance with subsections (1) and (2) as if a complaint had been presented in pursuance of that claim.

(4) In proceeding under subsections (1) to (3), a conciliation officer shall where appropriate have regard to the desirability of encouraging the use of other procedures available for the settlement of grievances.

(5) Anything communicated to a conciliation officer in connection with the performance of his functions under this section shall not be admissible in evidence in any proceedings before an industrial tribunal, except with the consent of the person who communicated it to that officer.

NOTES

Derivation: 1974, para 26 (2), (3), (4), (4A), (5); 1975 Sched 16, Pt III, paras 24, 25.

Further provisions: note ss 137, 140 (2) (*d*) and (*e*), 149 (2) and 157, and Sched 13, para 20 (2).

Complaint . . . under section 67 . . . : ie a complaint of unfair dismissal.

Reinstatement: see ss 68 and 69, particularly s 69 (2) and (3).

Re-engagement: see ss 68 and 69, particularly s 69 (4).

Compensation: failing agreement, compensation is calculated in accordance with ss 72 to 74. Note the limits on compensation set by s 75.

Definitions: 'employee': see note to s 1; 'conciliation officer': see notes to s 133; 'reinstatement', 're-engagement' and 'compensation': see above; 'successor': see s 153 (1); 'associated employer': see s 153 (4).

EMPLOYMENT APPEAL TRIBUNAL

135. Employment Appeal Tribunal

(1) The Employment Appeal Tribunal established under section 87 of the Employment Protection Act 1975 shall continue in existence by that name for the purpose of hearing appeals under section 136.

(2) The Employment Appeal Tribunal (in this Act referred to as " the Appeal Tribunal ") shall consist of—

(*a*) such number of judges as may be nominated from time to time by the Lord Chancellor from among the judges (other than the Lord Chancellor) of the High Court and the Court of Appeal;

(*b*) at least one judge of the Court of Session nominated from time to time by the Lord President of that Court; and

(*c*) such number of other members as may be appointed from time to time by Her Majesty on the joint recommendation of the Lord Chancellor and the Secretary of State.

(3) The members of the Appeal Tribunal appointed under subsection (2)(*c*) shall be persons who appear to the Lord Chancellor and the Secretary of State to have special knowledge or experience of industrial relations, either as representatives of employers or as representatives of workers (within the meaning of the Trade Union and Labour Relations Act 1974).

(4) The Lord Chancellor shall, after consultation with the Lord President of the Court of Session, appoint one of the judges nominated under subsection (2) to be President of the Appeal Tribunal.

(5) No judge shall be nominated a member of the Appeal Tribunal except with his consent.

(6) The provisions of Schedule 11 shall have effect with respect to the Appeal Tribunal and proceedings before the Tribunal.

NOTES

Derivation: 1975, s 87.

Definitions: 'employer': see note to s 1; 'worker': see s 30 (1) of the Trade Union and Labour Relations Act 1974.

136. Appeals to Tribunal from industrial tribunals and Certification Officer

(1) An Appeal shall lie to the Appeal Tribunal on a question of law arising from any decision of, or arising in any proceedings before, an industrial tribunal under, or by virtue of, the following Acts—

(*a*) the Equal Pay Act 1970;

(*b*) the Sex Discrimination Act 1975;

(*c*) the Employment Protection Act 1975;

(*d*) the Race Relations Act 1976;

(*e*) this Act.

(2) The Appeal Tribunal shall hear appeals on questions of law arising in any proceedings before, or arising from any decision of, the Certification Officer under the following enactments—

(*a*) sections 3, 4 and 5 of the Trade Union Act 1913;

(*b*) section 4 of the Trade Union (Amalgamations, etc.) Act 1964.

(3) The Appeal Tribunal shall hear appeals on questions of fact or law arising in any proceedings before, or arising from any decision of, the Certification Officer under the following enactments—

(*a*) section 8 of the Trade Union and Labour Relations Act 1974;

(*b*) section 8 of the Employment Protection Act 1975.

(4) Without prejudice to section 13 of the Administration of Justice Act 1960 (appeal in case of contempt of court), an appeal shall lie on any question of law from any decision or order of the Appeal Tribunal with the leave of the Tribunal or of the Court of Appeal or, as the case may be, the Court of Session,—

(*a*) in the case of proceedings in England and Wales, to the Court of Appeal;

(*b*) in the case of proceedings in Scotland, to the Court of Session.

(5) No appeal shall lie except to the Appeal Tribunal from any decision of an industrial tribunal under the Acts listed in subsection (1) or from any decision under the enactments listed in subsections (2) and (3) of the Certification Officer appointed under section 7 of the Employment Protection Act 1975.

NOTES

Derivation: 1975, s 88; Race Relations Act 1976, Sched 3, para 1 (4).

Certification Officer: see s 7 Employment Protection Act 1975, which provides for his appointment and prescribes his functions. See *Blue Circle Staff Association* v *Certification Officer* [1977] ICR 224, which discusses the procedure to be followed by the EAT when hearing appeals from the Certification Officer. See also *General and Municipal Workers' Union* v *Certification Officer* [1977] ICR 183; *Association of HSD (Hatfield) Employees* v *Certification Officer* [1978] ICR 21; and *Squibb United Kingdom Staff Association* v *Certification Officer* [1978] ICR 115.

PART IX

MISCELLANEOUS AND SUPPLEMENTAL

EXTENSION OF EMPLOYMENT PROTECTION LEGISLATION

137. Power to extend employment protection legislation

(1) Her Majesty may by Order in Council provide that—

(*a*) the provisions of this Act; and

(*b*) any legislation (that is to say any enactment of the Parliament of Northern Ireland and any provision made by or under a Measure of the Northern Ireland Assembly) for the time being in force in Northern Ireland which makes provision for purposes corresponding to any of the purposes of this Act,

shall, to such extent and for such purposes as may be specified in the Order, apply (with or without modification) to or in relation to any person in employment to which this section applies.

(2) This section applies to employment for the purposes of any activities—

(*a*) in the territorial waters of the United Kingdom; or

(*b*) connected with the exploration of the sea bed or subsoil or the exploitation of their natural resources in any area designated by order under section 1(7) of the Continental Shelf Act 1964; or

(*c*) connected with the exploration or exploitation, in a foreign sector of the continental shelf, of a cross-boundary petroleum field.

(3) An Order in Council under subsection (1)—

(*a*) may make different provision for different cases;

(*b*) may provide that all or any of the enactments referred to in subsection (1), as applied by such an Order, shall apply to individuals whether or not they are British subjects and to bodies corporate whether or not they are incorporated under the law of any part of the United Kingdom (notwithstanding that the application may affect their activities outside the United Kingdom);

(*c*) may make provision for conferring jurisdiction on any court or class of court specified in the Order, or on industrial tribunals, in respect of offences, causes of action or other matters arising in connection with employment to which this section applies;

(*d*) without prejudice to the generality of subsection (1) or of paragraph (*a*), may provide that the enactments referred to in subsection (1), as applied by the Order, shall apply in relation to any person in employment for the purposes of such activities as are referred to in subsection (2) in any part of the areas specified in paragraphs (*a*) and (*b*) of that subsection;

(*e*) may exclude from the operation of section 3 of the Territorial Waters Jurisdiction Act 1878 (consents required for prosecutions) proceedings for offences under the enactments referred to in subsection (1) in connection with employment to which this section applies;

(*f*) may provide that such proceedings shall not be brought without such consent as may be required by the Order;

(*g*) may, without prejudice to the generality of the power under subsection (1) to modify the enactments referred to in that subsection in their application for the purposes of this section, modify or exclude the operation of sections 141 and 144 or paragraph 14 of Schedule 13 or of any corresponding provision in any such Northern Irish legislation as is referred to in subsection (1)(*b*).

(4) Any jurisdiction conferred on any court or tribunal under this section shall be without prejudice to jurisdiction exercisable apart from this section by that or any other court or tribunal.

(5) In subsection (2) above—

"cross-boundary petroleum field" means a petroleum field that extends across the boundary between a designated area and a foreign sector of the continental shelf;

"foreign sector of the continental shelf" means an area which is outside the territorial waters of any State and within which rights are exercisable by a State other than the United Kingdom with respect to the sea bed and subsoil and their natural resources;

"petroleum field" means a geological structure identified as an oil or gas field by the Order in Council concerned.

NOTES

Derivation: 1975, s 127 (1) (*c*) to (*g*), (2) to (4).

General Note: see the Employment (Continental Shelf) Act 1978.

Orders under this section: see the Employment Protection (Offshore Employment) Order 1976 (SI 1976 No 766) and the Employment Protection (Offshore Employment) (Amendment) Order 1977 (SI 1977 No 588).

CROWN EMPLOYMENT

138. Application of Act to Crown employment

(1) Subject to the following provisions of this section, Parts I (so far as it relates to itemised pay statements), II, III (except section 44), V, VIII and this Part and section 53 shall have effect in relation to Crown employment and to persons in Crown employment as they have effect in relation to other employment and to other employees.

(2) In this section, subject to subsections (3) to (5), "Crown employment" means employment under or for the purposes of a government department or any officer or body exercising on behalf of the Crown functions conferred by any enactment.

(3) This section does not apply to service as a member of the naval, military or air forces of the Crown, or of any women's service administered by the Defence Council, but does apply to employment by any association established for the purposes of the Auxiliary Forces Act 1953.

(4) For the purposes of this section, Crown employment does not include any employment in respect of which there is in force a certificate issued by or on behalf of a Minister of the Crown certifying that employment of a description specified in the certificate, or the employment of a particular person so specified, is (or, at a time specified in the certificate, was) required to be excepted from this section for the purpose of safeguarding national security; and any document purporting to be a certificate so issued shall be received in evidence and shall, unless the contrary is proved, be deemed to be such a certificate.

(5) For the purposes of Parts I (so far as it relates to itemised pay statements), II, III (except section 44(3) and (4)), V, VII (except section 126(3) and (4)), VIII and this Part and section 53, none of the bodies referred to in Schedule 5 shall be regarded as performing functions on behalf of the Crown and accordingly employment by any such body shall not be Crown employment within the meaning of this section.

(6) For the purposes of the application of the provisions of this Act in relation to employment by any such body as is referred to in subsection (5), any reference to redundancy shall be construed as a reference to the existence of such circumstances as, in accordance with any arrangements for the time being in force as mentioned in section 111(3), are treated as equivalent to redundancy in relation to such employment.

(7) For the purposes of the application of the provisions of this Act in relation to Crown employment in accordance with subsection (1)—

(*a*) any reference to an employee shall be construed as a reference to a person in Crown employment;

(*b*) any reference to a contract of employment shall be construed as a reference to the terms of employment of a person in Crown employment;

(*c*) any reference to dismissal shall be construed as a reference to the termination of Crown employment;

(*d*) any reference to redundancy shall be construed as a reference to the existence of such circumstances as, in accordance with any arrangements for the time being in force as mentioned in section 111(3), are treated as equivalent to redundancy in relation to Crown employment;

(*e*) the reference in paragraph 1(5)(*c*) of Schedule 9 to a person's undertaking or any undertaking in which he works shall be construed as a reference to the national interest; and

(*f*) any other reference to an undertaking shall be construed, in relation to a Minister of the Crown, as a reference to his functions or (as the context may require) to the department of which he is in charge and, in relation to a government department, officer or body, shall be construed as a reference to the functions of the department, officer or body or (as the context may require) to the department, officer or body.

(8) Where the terms of employment of a person in Crown employment restrict his right to take part in—

(*a*) certain political activities; or

(*b*) activities which may conflict with his official functions,

nothing in section 29 shall require him to be allowed time off work for public duties connected with any such activities.

NOTES

Derivation: 1974, para 33; 1975 s 121, Sched 16, Pt III, paras 33 and 34.

Further provisions: note Sched 13, para 19.

Definitions: 'redundancy': see s 81 (2); 'employee': see note to s 1; 'contract of employment': see s 153 (1); 'Crown employment': note subss (2) and (4).

HOUSE OF COMMONS STAFF

139. Provisions as to House of Commons staff

(1) The provisions of Parts I (so far as it relates to itemised pay statements), II, III (except section 44), V and VIII, and this Part and section 53 shall apply to relevant members of House of Commons staff as they apply to persons in Crown employment within the meaning of section 138 and accordingly for the purposes of the application of those provisions in relation to any such members—

(*a*) any reference to an employee shall be construed as a reference to any such member;

(*b*) any reference to a contract of employment shall be construed as including a reference to the terms of employment of any such member;

(*c*) any reference to dismissal shall be construed as including a reference to the termination of any such member's employment;

(*d*) the reference in paragraph 1(5)(*c*) of Schedule 9 to a person's undertaking or any undertaking in which he works shall be construed as a reference to the national interest or, if the case so requires, the interests of the House of Commons; and

(*e*) any other reference to an undertaking shall be construed as a reference to the House of Commons.

(2) Nothing in any rule of law or the law or practice of Parliament shall prevent a relevant member of the House of Commons staff from bringing a civil employment claim before the court or from bringing before an industrial tribunal proceedings of any description which could be brought before such a tribunal by any person who is not such a member.

(3) In this section—

" relevant member of the House of Commons staff " means—

(*a*) any person appointed by the House of Commons Commission (in this section referred to as the Commission) or employed in the refreshment department; and

(*b*) any member of Mr. Speaker's personal staff;

" civil employment claim " means a claim arising out of or relating to a contract of employment or any other contract connected with employment, or a claim in tort arising in connection with a person's employment; and

" the court " means the High Court or the county court.

(4) It is hereby declared that for the purposes of the enactments applied by subsection (1) and of Part VI (where applicable to relevant members of House of Commons staff) and for the purposes of any civil employment claim—

(*a*) the Commission is the employer of staff appointed by the Commission; and

(*b*) Mr. Speaker is the employer of his personal staff and of any person employed in the refreshment department and not falling within paragraph (*a*);

but the foregoing provision shall have effect subject to subsection (5).

(5) The Commission or, as the case may be, Mr. Speaker may designate for all or any of the purposes mentioned in subsection (4)—

(*a*) any description of staff other than Mr. Speaker's personal staff; and

(*b*) in relation to staff so designated, any person;

and where a person is so designated he, instead of the Commission or Mr. Speaker, shall be deemed for the purposes to which the designation relates to be the employer of the persons in relation to whom he is so designated.

(6) Where any proceedings are brought by virtue of this section against the Commission or Mr. Speaker or any person designated under subsection (5), the person against whom the proceedings are brought may apply to the court or the industrial tribunal, as the case may be, to have

some other person against whom the proceedings could at the time of the application be properly brought substituted for him as a party to those proceedings.

(7) For the purposes mentioned in subsection (4) a person's employment in or for the purposes of the House of Commons shall not, provided he continues to be employed in such employment, be treated as terminated by reason only of a change (whether effected before or after the passing of the House of Commons (Administration) Act 1978, and whether effected by virtue of that Act or otherwise) in his employer and (provided he so continues) his first appointment to such employment shall be deemed after the change to have been made by his employer for the time being, and accordingly—

(*a*) he shall be treated for the purposes so mentioned as being continuously employed by that employer from the commencement of such employment until its termination; and

(*b*) anything done by or in relation to his employer for the time being in respect of such employment before the change shall be so treated as having been done by or in relation to the person who is his employer for the time being after the change.

(8) In subsection (7) " employer for the time being ", in relation to a person who has ceased to be employed in or for the purposes of the House of Commons, means the person who was his employer immediately before he ceased to be so employed, except that where some other person would have been his employer for the time being if he had not ceased to be so employed, it means that other person.

(9) If the House of Commons resolves at any time that any provision of subsections (3) to (6) should be amended in its application to any member of the staff of that House, Her Majesty may by Order in Council amend that provision accordingly.

NOTES

Derivation: 1975, s 122 (1), (3) to (8); House of Commons (Administration) Act 1978, Sched 2, para 5.

Definitions: 'employee' and 'employer': see note to s 1; 'contract of employment'; see s 153 (1).

Orders in Council: none had been made at the time of going to press.

CONTRACTING OUT OF PROVISIONS OF ACT

140. Restrictions on contracting out

(1) Except as provided by the following provisions of this section, any provision in an agreement (whether a contract of employment or not) shall be void in so far as it purports—

(*a*) to exclude or limit the operation of any provision of this Act; or

(*b*) to preclude any person from presenting a complaint to, or bringing any proceedings under this Act before, an industrial tribunal.

(2) Subsection (1) shall not apply—

(*a*) to any provision in a collective agreement excluding rights under section 12 if an order under section 18 is for the time being in force in respect of it;

(*b*) to any union membership agreement so far as it affects the rights of an employee—

(i) under section 23 in accordance with subsection (4) of that section;

(ii) under section 58 in accordance with subsection (3) of that section;

(*c*) to any provision in a dismissal procedures agreement excluding rights under section 54 if that provision is not to have effect unless an order under section 65 is for the time being in force in respect of it;

(*d*) to any agreement to refrain from presenting a complaint under section 67, where in complaince with a request under section 134(3) a conciliation officer has taken action in accordance with that subsection;

(*e*) to any agreement to refrain from proceeding with a complaint presented under section 67 where a conciliation officer has taken action in accordance with section 134(1) and (2);

(*f*) to any provision in an agreement if an order under section 96 is for the time being in force in respect of it;

(*g*) to any agreement to refrain from instituting or continuing any proceedings before an industrial tribunal where a conciliation officer has taken action in accordance with section 133(2) or (3);

(*h*) to any provision of an agreement relating to dismissal from employment such as is mentioned in section 142(1) or (2).

NOTES

Derivation: 1965, s 25 (4), (5); 1972, s 2 (4); 1974, para 32; 1975, s 118.

General Note: see *Council of Engineering Institutions* v *Maddison* [1977] ICR 30 and *Naqvi* v *Stephens Jewellers Ltd* [1978] ICR 631, both cases on para 32 of the 1974 Act.

Definitions: 'collective agreement' and 'union membership agreement': see s 153 (1); 'dismissal procedures agreement': see s 153 (1); 'Conciliation Officer': see note to s 133; 'contract of employment': see s 153 (1).

EXCLUDED CLASSES OF EMPLOYMENT

141. Employment outside Great Britain

(1) Sections 1 to 4 and 49 to 51 do not apply in relation to employment during any period when the employee is engaged in work wholly or mainly outside Great Britain unless the employee ordinarily works in Great Britain and the work outside Great Britain is for the same employer.

(2) Sections 8 and 53 and Parts II, III, V and VII do not apply to employment where under his contract of employment the employee ordinarily works outside Great Britain.

(3) An employee shall not be entitled to a redundancy payment if on the relevant date he is outside Great Britain, unless under his contract of employment he ordinarily worked in Great Britain.

(4) An employee who under his contract of employment ordinarily works outside Great Britain shall not be entitled to a redundancy payment unless on the relevant date he is in Great Britain in accordance with instructions given to him by his employer.

(5) For the purpose of subsection (2), a person employed to work on board a ship registered in the United Kingdom (not being a ship registered at a port outside Great Britain) shall, unless—

(*a*) the employment is wholly outside Great Britain, or

(*b*) he is not ordinarily resident in Great Britain,

be regarded as a person who under his contract ordinarily works in Great Britain.

NOTES

Derivation: 1972, s 12 (1); 1974, para 9 (2), (3); 1975, s 119 (5), (6); 1965, s 17 (1), (2).

Further provisions: note s 137 (3) (*g*).

Subsection (*1*): note s 149 (2).

Subsection (*2*): in *Wilson* v *Maynard Shipbuilding Consultants A B* [1978] ICR 376, the Court of Appeal said that in order to decide whether an employee 'ordinarily works' inside or outside Great Britain, an industrial tribunal should look at the relevant terms of the contract, express or implied, over the whole period of the contract, and not at what has happened during the period of employment before termination took place; but where the times and places of work are left to the employer's discretion, the correct approach is to ascertain from the terms of the contract where the employee's base was to be, and, in the absence of special factors leading to a contrary conclusion, the country where his base was to be is likely to be the place where the employee is to be treated as ordinarily working. This case was followed in *Todd* v *British Midland Airways Ltd* [1978] IRLR 370, in which the Court of Appeal held that an airline pilot, based in Great Britain, who flew on international routes, was 'ordinarily working' in Great Britain. It declared to be incorrectly decided the EAT case of *Claisse* v *Hostetter, Stewart & Keydril Ltd* [1978] IRLR 205, in which the EAT had held that a man working on an oil rig in the North Sea was not 'ordinarily working' in Great Britain.

Note Sched 2, Pt I, para 2 (4) and Pt III, para 6 (3) in relation to maternity and s 149 (1) (*c*).

Subsections (3) *and* (4): see *Roux International Ltd* v *Licudi* [1975] ICR 424 and *Costain Civil Engineering Ltd* v *Draycott* [1977] ICR 335; see also the note to subs (2) above. Note s 144 (3).

Subsection (5): see *Royle* v *Globtik Management Ltd* [1977] ICR 552 and *Wilson's* case. Note s 149 (1) (*c*).

Ordinarily resident: see *Levene* v *IRC* [1928] AC 271; *IRC* v *Lysaght* [1928] AC 234; and *Langford Property Ltd* v *Tureman* [1949] 1 KB 29.

Definitions: 'employee' and 'employer': see note to s 1.

142. Contracts for a fixed term

(1) Section 54 does not apply to dismissal from employment under a contract for a fixed term of two years or more, where the dismissal consists only of the expiry of that term without its being renewed, if before the term so expires the employee has agreed in writing to exclude any claim in respect of rights under that section in relation to that contract.

(2) An employee employed under a contract of employment for a fixed term of two years or more entered into after 5th December 1965 shall not be entitled to a redundancy payment in respect of the expiry of that term without its being renewed (whether by the employer or by an associated employer of his), if before the term so expires he has agreed in writing to exclude any right to a redundancy payment in that event.

(3) Such an agreement as is mentioned in subsection (1) or (2) may be contained either in the contract itself or in a separate agreement.

(4) Where an agreement under subsection (2) is made during the currency of a fixed term, and that term is renewed, the agreement under that subsection shall not be construed as applying to the term as renewed, but without prejudice to the making of a further agreement under that subsection in relation to the term so renewed.

NOTES

Derivation: 1974, para 12 (*b*); 1965, s 15 (2) to (4).

Further provisions: note s 140 (2) (*h*).

Subsection (1): in *BBC* v *Ioannou* [1975] ICR 267, the Court of Appeal held that a 'fixed term' is one which cannot be unfixed by notice. Contrast the different interpretation put upon the phrase by the EAT in *Dixon* v *BBC* [1978] ICR 357 in the context of s 55 (2) (*b*), in which *Ioannou's* case was distinguished. See Sched 2, Pt I, para 2 (4) in relation to maternity. Note s 149 (2). See also notes to s 55 (2) (*b*), and *Open University* v *Triesman* [1978] ICR 524.

Subsection (2): see notes to s 55 (2) (*b*) and subs (1) above. See also *Open University* v *Triesman* [1978] ICR 524. Note s 144 (3).

Definitions: 'employee' and 'employer': see note to s 1; 'associated employer': see s 153 (4); 'redundancy payment': see ss 153 (1) and 81 (1).

143. Minimum periods of employment

(1) An employee shall not be entitled to a guarantee payment in respect of any day unless he has been continuously employed for a period of four weeks ending with the last complete week before that day.

(2) An employee shall not be entitled to remuneration under section 19 unless he has been continuously employed for a period of four weeks ending with the last complete week before the day on which the suspension begins.

(3) Subject to subsection (4)—

(*a*) sections 12 and 19 do not apply to employment under a contract for a fixed term of twelve weeks or less; and

(*b*) sections 12, 19 and 49 do not apply to employment under a contract made in contemplation of the performance of a specific task which is not expected to last for more than twelve weeks.

(4) Subsection (3) does not apply where the employee has been continuously employed for a period of more than twelve weeks.

NOTES

Derivation: 1975, ss 22 (3), 30 (1), 119 (7); 1972, s 9 (2A); 1975 Sched 16, Pt II, para 10 (*a*).

Further provisions: note ss 147 and 149 (1) (*c*) and (2).

Subsection (1): see *Mailway (Southern) Ltd* v *Willsher* [1978] ICR 511.

Guarantee payment: see s 12.

Continuously employed: see s 151 and Sched 13, and the notes to those provisions.

Contract for a fixed term: see notes to s 55.

Definitions: 'employee': see note to s 1.

144. Mariners

(1) Sections 1 to 6 and 49 to 51 do not apply to—

(*a*) a person employed as a master of or a seaman on a sea-going British ship having a gross registered tonnage of eighty tons or more, including a person ordinarily employed as a seaman who is employed in or about such a ship in port by the owner or charterer of the ship to do work of a kind ordinarily done by a seaman on such a ship while it is in port, or

(*b*) a person employed as a skipper of or a seaman on a fishing boat for the time being required to be registered under section 373 of the Merchant Shipping Act 1894.

(2) Sections 8 and 53 and Parts II, III and V to VII do not apply to employment as master or as a member of the crew of a fishing vessel where the employee is remunerated only by a share in the profits or gross earnings of the vessel.

(3) Section 141(3) and (4) do not apply to an employee, and section 142(2) does not apply to a contract of employment, if the employee is employed as a master or seaman in a British ship and is ordinarily resident in Great Britain.

(4) Sections 8, 29, 31, 122 and 123 do not apply to employment as a merchant seaman.

(5) Employment as a merchant seaman does not include employment in the fishing industry or employment on board a ship otherwise than by the owner, manager or charterer of that ship except employment as a radio officer, but, save as aforesaid, it includes employment as master or a member of the crew of any ship and as a trainee undergoing training for the sea service, and employment in or about a ship in port by the owner, manager or charterer of the ship to do work of the kind ordinarily done by a merchant seaman on a ship while it is in port.

NOTES

Derivation: 1972, s 9 (2); 1975, s 119 (4); 1974, para 9 (1) (*d*); 1965, ss 16 (2), 20; 1975, s 119 (12), (13).

Subsections (1) *and* (2): note Sched 2, Pt I, para 2 (4), Pt II, para 4 (3) and Pt III, para 6 (3) in relation to maternity.

Ordinarily resident: see note to s 141.

Further provisions: note ss 137 (3) (*g*), 147 and 149 (1) (*c*).

Definitions: 'employee': see note to s 1; 'contract of employment' and 'employment': see s 153 (1).

145. Dock workers

(1) Sections 1 to 6 and 49 to 51 do not apply to any registered dock worker except when engaged in work which is not dock work.

(2) Sections 12, 19, 31, 53, 54, 122 and 123 do not apply to employment as a registered dock worker other than employment by virtue of which the employee is wholly or mainly engaged in work which is not dock work.

(3) Subject to subsection (4), section 81 does not apply to any person in respect of his employment as a registered dock worker, unless it is employment by virtue of which he is wholly or mainly engaged in work which is not dock work.

(4) Subsection (3) does not apply where—

(*a*) the person became a registered dock worker in consequence of having been employed on work which became classified;

(*b*) at the date of the termination of his employment he has been continuously employed since a time before that work was classified; and

(*c*) as a result of the termination he ceases to be a registered dock worker,

and, for the purposes of this subsection, Schedule 13 shall have effect subject to the provisions of the new Scheme.

(5) In this section—

" classified " means classified as dock work for the purposes of the new Scheme by an order under section 11 of the Dock Work Regulation Act 1976;

" dock work ", in relation to a dock worker registered under the 1967 Scheme, means the same as in that Scheme and in relation to one registered under the new Scheme means any work which, by reference to what it is or where it is done, is classified;

" registered " means registered under the 1967 Scheme or under the new Scheme, and in relation to a worker who is registered under the new Scheme, means registered in a main register thereunder, and not in an extension register;

" the 1967 Scheme " means the Scheme made under the Dock Workers (Regulation of Employment) Act 1946 and set out, as varied, in Schedule 2 to the Dock Workers (Regulation of Employment) (Amendment) Order 1967;

" the new Scheme " means the Scheme made and in force under section 4 of the Dock Work Regulation Act 1976.

NOTES

Derivation: Dock Work Regulation Act 1976, ss 14 (1) to (6), (8), 15 (1).

Further provisions: note ss 147 and 149 (1) (*c*).

Subsection (2): note Sched 2, Pt I, para 2 (4) and Pt III, para 6 (3) in relation to maternity.

Continuously employed: see note to s 143.

Definitions: 'employee': see note to s 1.

146. Miscellaneous classes of employment

(1) The following provisions of this Act do not apply to employment where the employer is the husband or wife of the employee, that is to say, sections 1, 4, 8, 53, 122 and 123 and Parts II, III, V and VI.

(2) Parts II, III, V and VII and sections 8, 9, 53 and 86 do not apply to employment under a contract of employment in police service or to persons engaged in such employment.

(3) In subsection (2), " police service " means service—

(*a*) as a member of any constabulary maintained by virtue of any enactment, or

(*b*) in any other capacity by virtue of which a person has the powers or privileges of a constable.

(4) Subject to subsections (5), (6) and (7), the following provisions of this Act (which confer rights which do not depend upon an employee having a qualifying period of continuous employment) do not apply to employment under a contract which normally involves employment for less than sixteen hours weekly, that is to say, sections 8, 27, 28 and 29.

(5) If the employee's relations with his employer cease to be governed by a contract which normally involves work for sixteen hours or more weekly and become governed by a contract which normally involves employment for eight hours or more, but less than sixteen hours, weekly, the employee shall nevertheless for a period of twenty-six weeks, computed in accordance with subsection (6), be treated for the purposes of subsection (4) as if his contract normally involved employment for sixteen hours or more weekly.

(6) In computing the said period of twenty-six weeks no account shall be taken of any week—

(*a*) during which the employee is in fact employed for sixteen hours or more;

(*b*) during which the employee takes part in a strike (as defined by paragraph 24 of Schedule 13) or is absent from work because of a lock-out (as so defined) by his employer; or

(*c*) during which there is no contract of employment but which, by virtue of paragraph 9(1) of Schedule 13, counts in computing a period of continuous employment.

(7) An employee whose relations with his employer are governed by a contract of employment which normally involves employment for eight hours or more, but less than sixteen hours, weekly shall nevertheless, if he has been continuously employed for a period of five years or more be treated for the purposes of subsection (4) as if his contract normally involved employment for sixteen hours or more weekly.

NOTES

Derivation: Subsection (1): 1972, s 9 (3); 1975, s 119 (2), Sched 16, Pt II, para 10 (*b*), Pt III, para 14 (*b*); 1974, para 9 (1) (*b*); 1965, s 16 (3). Subsections (2), (3): 1974, s 30 (1); 1975, s 126 (1). Subsections (4) to (7): 1975, s 119 (8) to (11).

Further provisions: note ss 147 and 149 (1) (*c*).

Subsection (1): note Sched 2, Pt I, para 2 (4), Pt II, para 4 (3) and Pt III, para 6 (3) in relation to maternity. See also s 100 (2) in relation to Pt VI.

Continuously employed: see note to s 143.

Definitions: 'employee' and 'employer': see note to s 1; 'contract of employment': see s 153 (1).

147. Application of ss 1 to 4 to excluded employment

Sections 1 to 4 shall apply to an employee who at any time comes or ceases to come within the exceptions from those sections provided for by or under sections 3(1), 143 to 146 and 149 as if a period of employment terminated or began at that time.

NOTES

Derivation: 1972, s 4 (7), 9 (4).

Definitions: 'employee': see note to s 1.

SUPPLEMENTARY PROVISIONS

148. Review of limits

(1) The Secretary of State shall in each calendar year review—

(*a*) the limits referred to in section 15;

(*b*) the limit referred to in section 122(5); and

(*c*) the limits imposed by paragraph 8(1) of Schedule 14 on the amount of a week's pay for the purposes of those provisions;

and shall determine whether any of those limits should be varied.

(2) In making a review under this section the Secretary of State shall consider—

(*a*) the general level of earnings obtaining in Great Britain at the time of the review;

(*b*) the national economic situation as a whole; and

(*c*) such other matters as he thinks relevant.

(3) If on a review under this section the Secretary of State determines that, having regard to the considerations mentioned in subsection (2), any of those limits should be varied, he shall prepare and lay before each House of Parliament the draft of an order giving effect to his decision.

(4) Where a draft of an order under this section is approved by resolution of each House of Parliament the Secretary of State shall make an order in the form of the draft.

(5) If, following the completion of an annual review under this section, the Secretary of State determines that any of the limits referred to in subsection (1) shall not be varied, he shall lay before each House of Parliament a report containing a statement of his reasons for that determination.

(6) The Secretary of State may at any time, in addition to the annual review provided for in subsection (1), conduct a further review of the limits mentioned in subsection (1) so as to determine whether any of those limits should be varied, and subsections (2) to (4) shall apply to such a review as if it were a review under subsection (1).

NOTES

Derivation: 1975, s 86.

Orders under this section: none had been made at the time of going to press.

149. General power to amend Act

(1) Subject to the following provisions of this section, the Secretary of State may by order—

(*a*) provide that any enactment contained in this Act which is specified in the order shall not apply to persons or to employments of such classes as may be prescribed in the order;

(*b*) provide that any such enactment shall apply to persons or employments of such classes as may be prescribed in the order subject, except in relation to section 54 (but without prejudice to paragraph (*a*)), to such exceptions and modifications as may be so prescribed;

(*c*) vary, or exclude the operation of, any of the following provisions of this Act, that is to say, sections 64(1), 99, 141(2) and (5), 143(3) and (4), 144(1), (2), (4) and (5), 145(1), (2) and (3) and 146(1) and (4) to (7);

(*d*) add to, vary or delete any of the provisions of Schedule 5.

(2) Subsection (1) does not apply to the following provisions of this Act, namely, sections 7, 52, 55, 57, 58, 59, 62, 63, 65, 66, 67, 75, 80, 103 to 120, 128, 134, 141(1) and 142(1) and Schedules 3, 9 and 13, and, in addition, paragraph (*b*) of subsection (1) does not apply to sections 1 to 6 and 49 to 51 and paragraph (*c*) of subsection (1) does not apply to section 143 as that section applies in relation to section 49.

(3) The provisions of this section are without prejudice to any other power of the Secretary of State to amend, vary or repeal any provision of this Act or to extend or restrict its operation in relation to any person or employment.

(4) No order under subsection (1) shall be made unless a draft of the order has been laid before Parliament and approved by a resolution of each House of Parliament.

NOTES

Derivation: 1965, ss 16 (6), (8); 1972, s 9 (5), (7); 1974, para 11 (2), (3); 1975, s 119 (15), (16); Dock Work Regulation Act 1976, s 14 (7).

Further provisions: note s 147.

Orders under this section: none had been made at the time of going to press.

150. Death of employee or employer

Schedule 12 shall have effect for the purpose of supplementing and modifying the provisions of Part I (so far as it relates to itemised pay statements), section 53 and Parts II, III, and V to VII as respects the death of an employee or employer.

NOTES

Derivation: 1965, s 23; 1975, s 110.

General Note: see Sched 2, Pt II, para 4 (3) in relation to maternity.

Definitions: 'employee' and 'employer': see note to s 1.

151. Continuous employment

(1) Subject to sections 104(2) and 106(2), Schedule 13 shall have effect for the purposes of this Act for ascertaining the length of an employee's period of employment and whether that employment has been continuous, and references in this Act to a period of employment shall be construed accordingly.

(2) For the purposes of any proceedings under this Act, other than proceedings for a breach of section 1, 2, 4 or 49, a person's employment during any period shall, unless the contrary is shown, be presumed to have been continuous.

NOTES

Derivation: 1965, ss 8 (2), 9 (2) (*a*); 1972, s 1 (5); 1974, para 30 (1), (2); 1975, s 126 (5); Dock Work Regulation Act 1976, s 14 (3).

General Note: see *Wood* v *York City Council* [1978] IRLR 228.

Definitions: 'employee': see note to s 1.

152. Calculation of normal working hours and a week's pay

Schedule 14 shall have effect for the purposes of this Act for calculating the normal working hours and the amount of a week's pay of any employee.

NOTES

Derivation: 1972, Sched 2, para 1 (1) (*b*); 1975, ss 62 (*c*), 85, Sched 5, para 1 (1) (*b*).

Definitions: 'employee': see note to s 1.

153. Interpretation

(1) In this Act, except so far as the context otherwise requires—

" act " and " action " each includes omission and references to doing an act or taking action shall be construed accordingly;

" business " includes a trade or profession and includes any activity carried on by a body of persons, whether corporate or unincorporate;

" certified midwife " means a midwife certified under the Midwives Act 1951 or the Midwives (Scotland) Act 1951;

" collective agreement " has the meaning given by section 30(1) of the Trade Union and Labour Relations Act 1974;

" confinement " means the birth of a living child or the birth of a child whether living or dead after twenty-eight weeks of pregnancy;

" contract of employment " means a contract of service or apprenticeship, whether express or implied, and (if it is express) whether it is oral or in writing;

" dismissal procedures agreement " means an agreement in writing with respect to procedures relating to dismissal made by or on behalf of one or more independent trade unions and one or more employers or employers' associations;

" effective date of termination " has the meaning given by section 55(4) and (5);

" employee " means an individual who has entered into or works under (or, where the employment has ceased, worked under) a contract of employment;

" employer ", in relation to an employee, means the person by whom the employee is (or, in a case where the employment has ceased, was) employed;

" employers' association " has the same meaning as it has for the purposes of the Trade Union and Labour Relations Act 1974;

" employer's payment " means a payment falling within paragraph (*a*), (*b*) or (*c*) of section 104(1);

" employment ", except for the purposes of sections 111 to 115, means employment under a contract of employment;

" expected week of confinement " means the week, beginning with midnight between Saturday and Sunday, in which it is expected that confinement will take place;

" government department ", except in section 138 and paragraph 19 of Schedule 13, includes a Minister of the Crown;

" guarantee payment " has the meaning given by section 12(1);

" inadmissible reason " has the meaning given by section 58(5);

" independent trade union " means a trade union which—

(*a*) is not under the domination or control of an employer or a group of employers or of one or more employers' associations; and

(*b*) is not liable to interference by an employer or any such group or association (arising out of the provision of financial or material support or by any other means whatsoever) tending towards such control;

and, in relation to a trade union, " independent " and " independence " shall be construed accordingly;

" job ", in relation to an employee, means the nature of the work which he is employed to do in accordance with his contract and the capacity and place in which he is so employed;

" maternity pay " has the meaning given by section 33(1);

" Maternity Pay Fund " means the fund referred to in section 37;

" maternity pay rebate " has the meaning given by section 39;

" notice of intention to claim " has the meaning given by section 88;

" notified day of return " has the meaning given by section 47(1) and (8);

" official ", in relation to a trade union, has the meaning given by section 30(1) of the Trade Union and Labour Relations Act 1974;

" original contract of employment ", in relation to an employee who is absent from work wholly or partly because of pregnancy or confinement, means the contract under which she worked immediately before the beginning of her absence or, if she entered into that contract during her pregnancy by virtue of section 60(2) or otherwise by reason of her pregnancy, the contract under which she was employed immediately before she entered into the later contract or, if there was more than one later contract, the first of the later contracts;

" position ", in relation to an employee, means the following matters taken as a whole, that is to say, his status as an employee, the nature of his work and his terms and conditions of employment;

" Redundancy Fund " means the fund referred to in section 103;

" redundancy payment " has the meaning given by section 81(1);

" redundancy rebate " has the meaning given by section 104;

" relevant date ", for the purposes of the provisions of this Act which relate to redundancy payments, has the meaning given by section 90;

" renewal " includes extension, and any reference to renewing a contract or a fixed term shall be construed accordingly;

" statutory provision " means a provision, whether of a general or a special nature, contained in, or in any document made or issued under, any Act, whether of a general or special nature;

" successor " has the meaning given by section 30(3) and (4) of the Trade Union and Labour Relations Act 1974;

" trade dispute " has the meaning given by section 29 of the said Act of 1974;

" trade union " has the meaning given by section 28 of the said Act of 1974;

"union membership agreement" has the meaning given by section 30(1) of the said Act of 1974 and "employees", in relation thereto, has the meaning given by section 30(5A) of that Act;

"week" means, in relation to an employee whose remuneration is calculated weekly by a week ending with a day other than Saturday, a week ending with that other day, and in relation to any other employee, a week ending with Saturday.

(2) References in this Act to dismissal by reason of redundancy, and to cognate expressions, shall be construed in accordance with section 81.

(3) In sections 33, 47, 56, 61 and 86 and Schedule 2, except where the context otherwise requires, "to return to work" means to return to work in accordance with section 45(1), and cognate expressions shall be construed accordingly.

(4) For the purposes of this Act, any two employers are to be treated as associated if one is a company of which the other (directly or indirectly) has control, or if both are companies of which a third person (directly or indirectly) has control; and the expression "associated employer" shall be construed accordingly.

(5) For the purposes of this Act it is immaterial whether the law which (apart from this Act) governs any person's employment is the law of the United Kingdom, or of a part of the United Kingdom, or not.

(6) In this Act, except where otherwise indicated—

(*a*) a reference to a numbered Part, section or Schedule is a reference to the Part or section of, or the Schedule to, this Act so numbered, and

(*b*) a reference in a section to a numbered subsection is a reference to the subsection of that section so numbered, and

(*c*) a reference in a section, subsection or Schedule to a numbered paragraph is a reference to the paragraph of that section, subsection or Schedule so numbered, and

(*d*) a reference to any provision of an Act (including this Act) includes a Schedule incorporated in the Act by that provision.

(7) Except so far as the context otherwise requires, any reference in this Act to an enactment shall be construed as a reference to that enactment as amended or extended by or under any other enactment, including this Act.

NOTES

Derivation: 1965, ss 5 (3), 25 (1), (2), 36 (5), (6), 48 (4), 56, Sched 1, para 9, Sched 4, para 11, Sched 6, para 3; 1972, ss 11 (1), 12 (2), Sched 1, para 10 (2); 1974, s 30, Sched 1, para 6 (9) (*c*); 1975, ss 24 (5), 31 (5), 48 (2), (3), 52, 61 (6), 126, Sched 4, para 8 (*b*), Sched 16, Pt I, para 18, Pt II, para 19, Pt III, para 7 (2), (3), (4); Trade Union and Labour Relations (Amendment) Act 1976, s 3 (3), (4).

154. Orders, rules and regulations

(1) Any power conferred by any provision of this Act to make an order (other than an Order in Council or an order under section 65 or 66) or to make rules or regulations shall be exercisable by statutory instrument.

(2) Any statutory instrument made under any power conferred by this Act to make an Order in Council or other order or to make rules or regulations, except—

(*a*) an instrument required to be laid before Parliament in draft; and

(*b*) an order under section 18,

shall be subject to annulment in pursuance of a resolution of either House of Parliament.

(3) Any power conferred by this Act which is exercisable by statutory instrument shall include power to make such incidental, supplementary or transitional provisions as appear to the authority exercising the power to be necessary or expedient.

(4) An order made by statutory instrument under any provision of this Act may be revoked or varied by a subsequent order made under that provision.

This subsection does not apply to an order under section 96 but is without prejudice to subsection (4) of that section.

NOTES

Derivation: 1965, ss 11 (4), 16 (7), (8), 35 (6), (7), Sched 1, para 5 (5), (6), Sched 4, para 21A (3); Superannuation (Miscellaneous Provisions) Act 1967, s 9 (4); 1972, ss 7 (2), (3), 9 (6), (7), 10 (3), (4); 1974, s 26, Sched 1, para 20 (4); 1975, s 123, Sched 16, Pt I, paras 21, 34, Pt II, para 11; Redundancy Rebates Act 1977, s 1 (3).

Sections 65 *and* 66: these relate to dismissal procedures agreements.

Section 18: this relates to exemption orders where there is an agreement covering guaranteed remuneration.

Section 96: an exemption order may be made under this section excluding employees to whom it relates from the operation of s 81 (right to redundancy payments) where an agreement providing for payments to those employees on termination of their contracts is in force.

Subsection (4): note s 18 (5).

155. Offences by bodies corporate

(1) Where an offence under section 44 or 126 committed by a body corporate is proved to have been committed with the consent or connivance of, or to be attributable to any neglect on the part of, any director, manager, secretary or other similar officer of the body corporate, or any person who was purporting to act in any such capacity, he as well as the body corporate shall be guilty of that offence and shall be liable to be proceeded against and punished accordingly.

(2) Where the affairs of a body corporate are managed by its members, subsection (1) shall apply in relation to the acts and defaults of a member in connection with his functions of management as if he were a director of the body corporate.

NOTES

Derivation: 1975, s 117.

156. Payments into the Consolidated Fund

(1) There shall be paid out of the Maternity Pay Fund into the Consolidated Fund sums equal to the amount of any expenses incurred

by the Secretary of State in exercising his functions under this Act relating to maternity pay.

(2) There shall be paid out of the Redundancy Fund into the Consolidated Fund sums equal to the amount of any expenses incurred—

(*a*) by the Secretary of State in consequence of Part VI, except expenses incurred in the payment of sums in accordance with any such arrangements as are mentioned in section 111(3);

(*b*) by the Secretary of State (or by persons acting on his behalf) in exercising his functions under sections 122 to 126.

(3) There shall be paid out of the Redundancy Fund into the Consolidated Fund such sums as the Secretary of State may estimate in accordance with directions given by the Treasury to be the amount of any expenses incurred by any government department other than the Secretary of State in consequence of the provisions of sections 103 to 109.

NOTES

Derivation: 1975, s 124 (3), (4); 1965, s 55 (5), (6); National Loans Act 1968, Sched 1.

Maternity Pay Fund: see s 37.

Redundancy Fund: see s 103.

157. Northern Ireland

(1) If provision is made by Northern Irish legislation (that is to say by or under a Measure of the Northern Ireland Assembly) for purposes corresponding to any of the purposes of this Act, except sections 1 to 7 and 49 to 51, the Secretary of State may, with the consent of the Treasury, make reciprocal arrangements with the appropriate Northern Irish authority for co-ordinating the relevant provisions of this Act with the corresponding provisions of the Northern Irish legislation, so as to secure that they operate, to such extent as may be provided by the arrangements, as a single system.

(2) For the purpose of giving effect to any such arrangements, the Secretary of State shall have power, in conjunction with the appropriate Northern Irish authority—

(*a*) where the arrangements relate to the provisions of this Act relating to maternity pay, to make any necessary financial adjustments between the Maternity Pay Fund and any fund established under Northern Irish legislation; and

(*b*) where the arrangements relate to Part VI or to sections 122 to 126, to make any necessary financial adjustments between the Redundancy Fund and the Northern Ireland Redundancy Fund.

(3) The Secretary of State may make regulations for giving effect in Great Britain to any such arrangements, and any such regulations may make different provision for different cases, and may provide that the relevant provisions of this Act shall have effect in relation to persons affected by the arrangements subject to such modifications and adaptations as may be specified in the regulations, including provision—

(*a*) for securing that acts, omissions and events having any effect for the purposes of the Northern Irish legislation shall have a corresponding effect for the purposes of this Act (but not so as to confer a right to double payment in respect of the same act, omission or event); and

(*b*) for determining, in cases where rights accrue both under this Act and under the Northern Irish legislation, which of those rights shall be available to the person concerned.

(4) In this section " the appropriate Northern Irish authority " means such authority as may be specified in that behalf in the Northern Irish legislation.

NOTES

Derivation: 1975, s 128; 1965, s 58.

Maternity Pay Fund, Redundancy Fund: see note to s 156.

Regulations under this section: see the Redundancy Payments Northern Ireland Reciprocal Arrangements Regulations 1965 (SI 1965 No 2027).

158. The Isle of Man

(1) If an Act of Tynwald is passed for purposes similar to the purposes of Part VI, the Secretary of State may, with the consent of the Treasury, make reciprocal arrangements with the appropriate Isle of Man authority for co-ordinating the provisions of Part VI with the corresponding provisions of the Act of Tynwald so as to secure that they operate, to such extent as may be provided by the arrangements, as a single system.

(2) For the purpose of giving effect to any such arrangements, the Secretary of State shall have power, in conjunction with the appropriate Isle of Man authority, to make any necessary financial adjustments between the Redundancy Fund and any fund established under the Act of Tynwald.

(3) The Secretary of State may make regulations for giving effect in Great Britain to any such arrangements, and any such regulations may provide that Part VI shall have effect in relation to persons affected by the arrangements subject to such modifications and adaptations as may be specified in the regulations, including provision—

(*a*) for securing that acts, omissions and events having any effect for the purposes of the Act of Tynwald shall have a corresponding effect for the purposes of Part VI (but not so as to confer a right to double payment in respect of the same act, omission or event); and

(*b*) for determining, in cases where rights accrue both under this Act and under the Act of Tynwald, which of those rights shall be available to the person concerned.

(4) In this section " the appropriate Isle of Man authority " means such authority as may be specified in that behalf in an Act of Tynwald.

NOTES

Derivation: 1965, s 57.

Redundancy Fund: see notes to s 156.

Regulations under this section: none had been made at the time of going to press.

159. Transitional provisions, savings, consequential amendments and repeals

(1) The transitional provisions and savings in Schedule 15 shall have effect but nothing in that Schedule shall be construed as prejudicing section 38 of the Interpretation Act 1889 (effect of repeals).

(2) The enactments specified in Schedule 16 shall have effect subject to the amendments specified in that Schedule.

(3) The enactments specified in the first column of Schedule 17 are hereby repealed to the extent specified in column 3 of that Schedule.

160. Citation, commencement and extent

(1) This Act may be cited as the Employment Protection (Consolidation) Act 1978.

(2) This Act, except section 139(2) to (9) and the repeals in section 122 of the Employment Protection Act 1975 provided for in Schedule 17 to this Act, shall come into force on 1st November 1978, and section 139(2) to (9) and those repeals shall come into force on 1st January 1979.

(3) This Act, except sections 137 and 157 and paragraphs 12 and 28 of Schedule 16, shall not extend to Northern Ireland.

SCHEDULES

SCHEDULE 1

Provisions Leading to Suspension on Medical Grounds

1. The Paints and Colours Manufacture Regulations 1907.	S.R. & O. 1907 No. 17 ...	Reg. 5.
2. The Yarn (Dyed by Lead Compounds) Heading Regulations 1907.	S.R. & O. 1907 No. 616	Reg. 4.
3. The Vitreous Enamelling Regulations 1908.	S.R. & O. 1908 No. 1258	Reg. 10.
4. The Tinning of Metal Hollow-ware, Iron Drums and Harness Furniture Regulations 1909.	S.R. & O. 1909 No. 720	Reg. 6.
5. The Lead Smelting and Manufacture Regulations 1911.	S.R. & O. 1911 No. 752	Reg. 13.
6. The Lead Compounds Manufacture Regulations 1921.	S.R. & O. 1921 No. 1443	Reg. 11.
7. The Indiarubber Regulations 1922.	S.R. & O. 1922 No. 329	Reg. 12.
8. The Chemical Works Regulations 1922.	S.R. & O. 1922 No. 731	Reg. 30.
9. The Electric Accumulator Regulations 1925.	S.R. & O. 1925 No. 28 ...	Reg. 13.
10. The Lead Paint Regulations 1927.	S.R. & O. 1927 No. 847	Reg. 6.
11. The Pottery (Health and Welfare) Special Regulations 1950.	S.I. 1950 No. 65 ...	Reg. 7.
12. The Factories Act 1961. ...	1961 c. 34	(Section 75(2) including that section as extended by section 128).
13. The Ionising Radiations (Unsealed Radioactive Substances) Regulations 1968.	S.I. 1968 No. 780 ...	Regs. 12 and 33.
14. The Ionising Radiations (Sealed Sources) Regulations 1969.	S.I. 1969 No. 808 ...	Regs. 11 and 30.
15. The Radioactive Substances (Road Transport Workers) (Great Britain) Regulations 1970.	S.I. 1970 No. 1827 ...	Reg. 14.

Notes

Derivation: 1975, Sched 2.

General Note: note the power given to the Secretary of State by section 19 (3) to add provisions to or remove provisions from the list in this Schedule.

SCHEDULE 2

Supplementary Provisions Relating to Maternity

Part I

Unfair Dismissal

Introductory

1. References in this Part to provisions of this Act relating to unfair dismissal are references to those provisions as they apply by virtue of section 56.

Adaptation of unfair dismissal provisions

2.—(1) Section 57 shall have effect as if for subsection (3) there were substituted the following subsection:—

"(3) Where the employer has fulfilled the requirements of subsection (1), then, subject to sections 58(1), 59, 60 and 62, the determination of the question whether the dismissal was fair or unfair, having regard to the reason shown by the employer, shall depend on whether the employer can satisfy the tribunal that in the circumstances (having regard to equity and the substantial merits of the case) he would have been acting reasonably in treating it as a sufficient reason for dismissing the employee if she had not been absent from work.".

(2) If in the circumstances described in section 45(3) no offer is made of such alternative employment as is referred to in that subsection, then the dismissal which by virtue of section 56 is treated as taking place shall, notwithstanding anything in section 57 or 58, be treated as an unfair dismissal for the purposes of Part V of this Act.

(3) The following references shall be construed as references to the notified day of return, that is to say—

(*a*) references in Part V of this Act to the effective date of termination;

(*b*) references in sections 69 and 70 to the date of termination of employment.

(4) The following provisions of this Act shall not apply, that is to say, sections 55, 58(3), 64(1), 65, 66, 73(5) and (6), 141(2), 142(1), 144(2), 145(2) and 146(1), paragraph 11(1) of Schedule 13, paragraphs 7(1)(*f*) to (*i*) and (2) and 8(3) of Schedule 14 and paragraph 10 of Schedule 15.

(5) For the purposes of Part II of Schedule 14 as it applies for the calculation of a week's pay for the purposes of section 71 or 73, the calculation date is the last day on which the employee worked under the original contract of employment.

Part II

Redundancy Payments

Introductory

3. References in this Part to provisions of this Act relating to redundancy are references to those provisions as they apply by virtue of section 86.

Adaptation of redundancy payments provisions

4.—(1) References in Part VI of this Act shall be adapted as follows, that is to say—

(*a*) references to the relevant date, wherever they occur, shall be construed, except where the context otherwise requires, as references to the notified day of return;

(*b*) references in sections 82(4) and 84(1) to a renewal or re-engagement taking effect immediately on the ending of employment under the previous contract or after an interval of not more than four weeks thereafter, shall be construed as references to a renewal or re-engagement taking effect on the notified day of return or not more than four weeks after that day; and

(*c*) references in section 84(3) to the provisions of the previous contract shall be construed as references to the provisions of the original contract of employment.

(2) Nothing in section 86 shall prevent an employee from being treated, by reason of the operation of section 84(1), as not having been dismissed for the purposes of Part VI of this Act.

(3) The following provisions of this Act shall not apply, that is to say, sections 81(1)(*b*), 82(1) and (2), 83(1) and (2), 85, 87 to 89, 90(3), 92, 93, 96, 110, 144(2), 146(1) and 150, paragraph 4 of Schedule 4, Schedule 12 and paragraphs 7(1)(*j*) and (*k*) and 8(4) of Schedule 14.

(4) For the purposes of Part II of Schedule 14 as it applies for the calculation of a week's pay for the purposes of Schedule 4, the calculation date is the last day on which the employee worked under the original contract of employment.

Prior redundancy

5. If, in proceedings arising out of a failure to permit an employee to return to work, the employer shows—

(*a*) that the reason for the failure is that the employee is redundant; and

(*b*) that the employee was dismissed or, had she continued to be employed by him, would have been dismissed, by reason of redundancy during her absence on a day earlier than the notified day of return and falling after the beginning of the eleventh week before the expected week of confinement,

then, for the purposes of Part VI of this Act the employee—

(i) shall not be treated as having been dismissed with effect from the notified day of return; but

(ii) shall, if she would not otherwise be so treated, be treated as having been continuously employed until that earlier day and having been dismissed by reason of redundancy with effect from that day.

Part III

General

Dismissal during period of absence

6.—(1) This paragraph applies to the dismissal of an employee who is under this Act entitled to return to work and whose contract of employment continues to subsist during the period of her absence but who is dismissed by her employer during that period after the beginning of the eleventh week before the expected week of confinement.

(2) For the purposes of sub-paragraph (1), an employee shall not be taken to be dismissed during the period of her absence if the dismissal occurs in the course of the employee's attempting to return to work in accordance with her contract in circumstances in which section 48 applies.

(3) In the application of Part V of this Act to a dismissal to which this paragraph applies, the following provisions shall not apply, that is to say, sections 58(3), 64, 65, 66, 141(2), 144(2), 145 and 146(1).

(4) Any such dismissal shall not affect the employee's right to return to work, but—

(*a*) compensation in any unfair dismissal proceedings arising out of that dismissal shall be assessed without regard to the employee's right to return; and

(*b*) that right shall be exercisable only on her repaying any redundancy payment or compensation for unfair dismissal paid in respect of that dismissal, if the employer requests such repayment.

Power to amend or modify

7.—(1) The Secretary of State may by order amend the provisions of this Schedule and section 48 or modify the application of those provisions to any description of case.

(2) No order under this paragraph shall be made unless a draft of the order has been laid before Parliament and approved by a resolution of each House of Parliament.

NOTES

Derivation: 1975, Sched 3, paras 1 to 4, 6, 7.

Paragraphs 1 *to* 4: note s 48.

Paragraph 2 (3): 'notified day of return': note s 47 (8).

Paragraph 5: 'proceedings arising out of a failure to permit . . . to return to work': ie proceedings taken under s 86.

Paragraph 6: note s 48.

Paragraph 6 (4): 'compensation . . . shall be assessed': see ss 72 to 76.

Definitions: 'employee' and 'employer': see note to s 1; 'notified day of return': see s 153 (1) and s 47 (1) and (8); 'effective date of termination': see s 55 (4); 'original contract of employment': see s 153 (1); 'relevant date': see s 153 (1) and s 90; 'to return to work': see s 153 (3); 'redundant': see s 81 (2); 'expected week of confinement': see s 153 (1); 'continuously employed': see s 151 and Schedule 13; 'contract of employment': see s 153 (1).

Orders under this schedule: none had been made at the time of going to press.

SCHEDULE 3

Rights of Employee in Period of Notice

Preliminary

1. In this Schedule the " period of notice " means the period of notice required by section 49(1) or, as the case may be, section 49(2).

Employments for which there are normal working hours

2.—(1) If an employee has normal working hours under the contract of employment in force during the period of notice, and if during any part of those normal working hours—

(*a*) the employee is ready and willing to work but no work is provided for him by his employer; or

(*b*) the employee is incapable of work because of sickness or injury; or

(*c*) the employee is absent from work in accordance with the terms of his employment relating to holidays,

then the employer shall be liable to pay the employee for the part of normal working hours covered by paragraphs (*a*), (*b*) and (*c*) a sum not less than the amount of remuneration for that part of normal working hours calculated at the average hourly rate of remuneration produced by dividing a week's pay by the number of normal working hours.

(2) Any payments made to the employee by his employer in respect of the relevant part of the period of notice whether by way of sick pay,holiday pay or otherwise, shall go towards meeting the employer's liability under this paragraph.

(3) Where notice was given by the employee, the employer's liability under this paragraph shall not arise unless and until the employee leaves the service of the employer in pursuance of the notice.

Employments for which there are no normal working hours

3.—(1) If an employee does not have normal working hours under the contract of employment in force in the period of notice the employer shall be liable to pay the employee for each week of the period of notice a sum not less than a week's pay.

(2) Subject to sub-paragraph (3), the employer's obligation under this paragraph shall be conditional on the employee being ready and willing to do work of a reasonable nature and amount to earn a week's pay.

(3) Sub-paragraph (2) shall not apply—

(*a*) in respect of any period during which the employee is incapable of work because of sickness or injury, or

(*b*) in respect of any period during which the employee is absent from work in accordance with the terms of his employment relating to holidays,

and any payment made to an employee by his employer in respect of such a period, whether by way of sick pay, holiday pay or otherwise, shall be taken into account for the purposes of this paragraph as if it were remuneration paid by the employer in respect of that period.

(4) Where the notice was given by the employee, the employer's liability under this paragraph shall not arise unless and until the employee leaves the service of the employer in pursuance of the notice.

Sickness or industrial injury benefit

4.—(1) The following provisions of this paragraph shall have effect where the arrangements in force relating to the employment are such that—

(*a*) payments by way of sick pay are made by the employer to employees to whom the arrangements apply, in cases where any such employees are incapable of work because of sickness or injury, and

(*b*) in calculating any payment so made to any such employee an amount representing, or treated as representing, sickness benefit or industrial injury benefit is taken into account, whether by way of deduction or by way of calculating the payment as a supplement to that amount.

(2) If during any part of the period of notice the employee is incapable of work because of sickness or injury, and—

(*a*) one or more payments, by way of sick pay are made to him by the employer in respect of that part of the period of notice, and

(*b*) in calculating any such payment such an amount as is referred to in sub-paragraph (1)(*b*) is taken into account as therein mentioned,

then for the purposes of this Schedule the amount so taken into account shall be treated as having been paid by the employer to the employee by way of sick pay in respect of that part of that period, and shall go towards meeting the liability of the employer under paragraph 2 or paragraph 3 accordingly.

Absence on leave granted at request of employee

5. The employer shall not be liable under the foregoing provisions of this Schedule to make any payment in respect of a period during which the employee is absent from work with the leave of the employer granted at the request of the employee (including any period of time off taken in accordnace with section 27, 28, 29 or 31).

Notice given before a strike

6. No payment shall be due under this Schedule in consequence of a notice to terminate a contract given by an employee if, after the notice is given and on or before the termination of the contract, the employee takes part in a strike of employees of the employer.

In this paragraph " strike " has the meaning given by paragraph 24 of Schedule 13.

Termination of employment during period of notice

7.—(1) If, during the period of notice, the employer breaks the contract of employment, payments received under this Schedule in respect of the part of the period after the breach shall go towards mitigating the damages recoverable by the employee for loss of earnings in that part of the period of notice.

(2) If, during the period of notice, the employee breaks the contract and the employer rightfully treats the breach as terminating the contract, no payment shall be due to the employee under this Schedule in respect of the part of the period of notice falling after the termination of the contract.

NOTES

Derivation: 1972, Sched 2, substituted by 1975, Sched 5.

Further provisions: note ss 110 (4), 137 and 149 (2).

Week's pay: this is calculated in accordance with Sched 14, Pt II: see s 152. Note Sched 14, para 7 (1) (*e*).

Paragraph 7: see notes to s 49 (5).

Definitions: 'employee' and 'employer': see note to s 1; 'contract of employment': see s 153 (1).

SCHEDULE 4

Calculation of Redundancy Payments

1. The amount of a redundancy payment to which an employee is entitled in any case shall, subject to the following provisions of this Schedule, be calculated by reference to the period, ending with the relevant date, during which he has been continuously employed.

2. Subject to paragraphs 3 and 4, the amount of the redundancy payment shall be calculated by reference to the period specified in paragraph 1 by starting at the end of that period and reckoning backwards the number of years of employment falling within that period, and allowing—

(*a*) one and a half week's pay for each such year of employment which consists wholly of weeks (within the meaning of Schedule 13) in which the employee was not below the age of forty-one;

(*b*) one week's pay for each such year of employment (not falling within the preceding sub-paragraph) which consists wholly of weeks (within the meaning of Schedule 13) in which the employee was not below the age of twenty-two; and

(*c*) half a week's pay for each such year of employment not falling within either of the preceding sub-paragraphs.

3. Where, in reckoning the number of years of employment in accordance with paragraph 2, twenty years of employment have been reckoned, no account shall be taken of any year of employment earlier than those twenty years.

4.—(1) Where in the case of an employee the relevant date is after the specified anniversary, the amount of the redundancy payment, calculated in accordance with the preceding provisions of this Schedule, shall be reduced by the appropriate fraction.

(2) In this paragraph " the specified anniversary ", in relation to a man, means the sixty-fourth anniversary of the day of his birth, and, in relation to a woman, means the fifty-ninth anniversary of the day of her birth, and " the appropriate fraction " means the fraction of which—

(*a*) the numerator is the number of whole months, reckoned from the specified anniversary, in the period beginning with that anniversary and ending with the relevant date, and

(*b*) the denominator is twelve.

5. For the purposes of any provision contained in Part VI whereby an industrial tribunal may determine that an employer shall be liable to pay to an employee either—

(*a*) the whole of the redundancy payment to which the employee would have been entitled apart from another provision therein mentioned, or

(*b*) such part of that redundancy payment as the tribunal thinks fit,

the preceding provisions of this Schedule shall apply as if in those provisions any reference to the amount of a redundancy payment were a reference to the amount of the redundancy payment to which the employee would have been so entitled.

6. The preceding provisions of this Schedule shall have effect without prejudice to the operation of any regulations made under section 98 whereby the amount of a redundancy payment, or part of a redundancy payment, may be reduced.

7. Where the relevant date does not occur on a Saturday, any reference in the preceding provisions of this Schedule to the relevant date shall be construed as a reference to the Saturday immediately following that date.

NOTES

Derivation: 1965, Sched 1, paras 1 to 4, 6 to 9; 1975, Sched 16, Pt I, paras 19, 20, 22.

General Note: see Sched 2, Pt II, para 4 (3) in relation to maternity, and Sched 6. Note ss 137 and 149.

Continuously employed: see s 151, and Sched 13. Note Sched 13, paras 11 (2) and (3), 12 and 13.

Week's pay: this is calculated in accordance with Sched 14, Part II: see s 152. Note Sched 14, para 7 (1) (*k*) and (*l*).

Definitions: 'relevant date': see s 153 (1) and s 90; 'continuously employed': see above; 'employment': see s 153 (1); 'week's pay': see above; 'employee' and 'employer': see note to s 1; 'redundancy payment': see s 153 (1); 'week': note para 2.

SCHEDULE 5

NATIONAL HEALTH SERVICE EMPLOYERS

1. A Regional Health Authority, Area Health Authority, special health authority, Health Board or the Common Services Agency for the Scottish Health Service.

2. The Dental Estimates Board.

3. Any joint committee constituted under section 13(8) of the National Health Service (Scotland) Act 1972.

4. The Public Health Laboratory Service Board.

NOTES

Derivation: 1965, Sched 3; National Health Service Reorganisation Act 1973, Sched 4, para 106; National Health Service (Scotland) Act 1972, Sched 6, para 130.

Further provisions: note the power given to the Secretary of State by s 149 (1) (*d*) to amend the provisions of this Schedule. Note also s 137.

SCHEDULE 6

CALCULATION OF REDUNDANCY REBATES

PART I

REBATES IN RESPECT OF REDUNDANCY PAYMENTS

1. Subject to sections 104(7) and 108 and to the following provisions of this Part, the amount of any redundancy rebate payable in respect of a redundancy payment shall be calculated by taking the number of years of employment by reference to which the redundancy payment falls to be calculated in accordance with Schedule 4 and allowing—

(*a*) 123/200 of one week's pay for each year of employment falling within sub-paragraph (*a*) of paragraph 2 of that Schedule;

(*b*) 41/100 of one week's pay for each year of employment falling within sub-paragraph (*b*) of that paragraph; and

(*c*) 41/200 of one week's pay for each year of employment falling within sub-paragraph (*c*) of that paragraph.

2. Where the amount of the redundancy payment, calculated in accordance with paragraphs 1, 2 and 3 of Schedule 4, is reduced by virtue of

paragraph 4 of that Schedule, the amount of the rebate shall be 41/100 of the amount of the redundancy payment as so reduced.

3.—(1) The provisions of this paragraph shall have effect in relation to any case where—

(*a*) under section 85, 92 and 110 an industrial tribunal is empowered to determine that an employer shall be liable to pay to an employee either the whole or part of the redundancy payment to which the employee would have been entitled apart from another provision therein mentioned, and

(*b*) the tribunal determines that the employer shall be liable to pay part (but not the whole) of that redundancy payment.

(2) There shall be ascertained what proportion that part of the redundancy payment bears to the whole of it (in this paragraph referred to as " the relevant proportion ").

(3) There shall also be ascertained what, in accordance with the preceding provisions of this Part, would have been the amount of the redundancy rebate payable in respect of that redundancy payment if the employer had been liable to pay the whole of it.

(4) Subject to paragraph 4, the amount of the rebate payable in that case shall then be an amount equal to the relevant proportion of the amount referred to in sub-paragraph (3).

4. Where the amount of a redundancy payment or part of a redundancy payment is reduced in accordance with regulations made under section 98,—

(*a*) the proportion by which it is so reduced shall be ascertained, and

(*b*) the amount of any redundancy rebate calculated by reference to that payment shall be reduced by that proportion.

PART II

REBATES IN RESPECT OF OTHER PAYMENTS

Introductory

5. The provisions of this Part shall have effect for the purpose of calculating the amount of any redundancy rebate payable in respect of an employer's payment which is not a redundancy payment or part of a redundancy payment (in this Part referred to as " the agreed payment ").

6. In this Part " the agreement ", in relation to the agreed payment, means the agreement referred to in paragraph (*b*) or paragraph (*c*) of section 104(1) by reference to which that payment is payable; and " the relevant provisions of the agreement " means those provisions of the agreement which relate to either of the following matters, that is to say—

(*a*) the circumstances in which the continuity of an employee's period of employment is to be treated as broken, and

(*b*) the weeks which are to count in computing a period of employment.

7. In this Part any reference to the amount of the relevant redundancy payment, in relation to the agreed payment, shall be construed as a reference to the amount of the redundancy payment which the employer would have been liable to pay to the employee if—

(*a*) the order referred to in paragraph (*b*) of subsection (1) of section 104, or (as the case may be) the order and the award referred to in paragraph (*c*) of that subsection, had not been made;

(*b*) the circumstances in which the agreed payment is payable had been such that the employer was liable to pay a redundancy payment to the employee in those circumstances;

(*c*) in relation to that redundancy payment, the relevant date had been the date on which the termination of the employee's contract of employment is treated for the purposes of the agreement as having taken effect; and

(*d*) in so far as the relevant provisions of the agreement are inconsistent with the provisions of Schedule 13 as to the matters referred to in sub-paragraphs (*a*) and (*b*) of paragraph 6, those provisions of the agreement were substituted for those provisions of that Schedule;

and " the assumed conditions " means the conditions specified in sub-paragraphs (*a*) to (*d*) of this paragraph.

Method of calculation

8. Subject to sections 104(7) and 108, and to the following provisions of this Part, the amount of any redundancy rebate payable in respect of the agreed payment shall be an amount calculated as follows, that is to say, by taking the number of years of employment by reference to which the amount of the relevant redundancy payment would fall to be calculated in accordance with Schedule 4 (as that Schedule would have applied if the assumed conditions were fulfilled), and allowing—

(*a*) 123/200 of one week's pay for each such year of employment falling within sub-paragraph (*a*) of paragraph 2 of that Schedule;

(*b*) 41/100 of one week's pay for each such year of employment falling within sub-paragraph (*b*) of that paragraph; and

(*c*) 41/200 of one week's pay for each such year of employment falling within sub-paragraph (*c*) of that paragraph.

9. For the purposes of paragraph 8, Schedule 13 shall have effect as if paragraphs 11(2), 12 and 14 were omitted.

10. Where the amount of the agreed payment is less than the amount of the relevant redundancy payment—

(*a*) the proportion which it bears to the amount of the relevant redundancy payment shall be ascertained, and

(*b*) the amount of the rebate shall (except as provided by the next following paragraph) be that proportion of the amount calculated in accordance with the preceding provisions of this Part of this Schedule.

11. Where the amount of the relevant redundancy payment calculated in accordance with paragraphs 1, 2 and 3 of Schedule 4 would (if the assumed conditions were fulfilled) have been reduced by virtue of paragraph 4 of that Schedule, the amount of the rebate shall be 41/100 of the amount of the relevant redundancy payment as so reduced.

Savings

12.—(1) This Schedule shall have effect in relation to redundancy rebates of a kind specified in sub-paragraph (2), as if—

(*a*) in paragraphs 1 and 8, for the reference to 123/200, 41/100 and 41/200 there were substituted a reference to 3/4, 1/2 and 1/4 respectively, and

(*b*) in paragraphs 2 and 11 for each reference to 41/100 there were substituted a reference to 1/2.

(2) The redundancy rebates referred to in sub-paragraph (1) are—

(*a*) any rebate payable in respect of the whole or part of a redundancy payment in relation to which the relevant date is or would but for the operation of section 90(3) be earlier than 14th August 1977;

(*b*) any rebate payable in respect of a payment to an employee on the termination of his contract of employment which is paid—

(i) in pursuance of an agreement in respect of which an order under section 96 is in operation; or

(ii) in pursuance of an award made under Schedule 11 to the Employment Protection Act 1975 in connection with such an agreement,

where, under the agreement in question, the employee's contract is treated for the purposes of the agreement as having been terminated on a date earlier than 14th August 1977.

Power to modify paragraphs 1, 2, 8 *and* 11

13.—(1) The Secretary of State may from time to time by order modify this Schedule—

(*a*) by substituting for the three fractions of a week's pay for the time being specified in sub-paragraphs (*a*), (*b*) and (*c*) of paragraphs 1 and 8 one of the other sets of three fractions specified in the following Table; and

(*b*) by substituting for the fraction for the time being specified in paragraphs 2 and 11 for the purpose of calculating the amount of the rebates in respect of reduced payments the like fraction as, by virtue of paragraph (*a*) is substituted for the fraction in paragraphs 1(*b*) and 8(*b*).

TABLE

	Fraction in paragraphs 1(*a*) *and* 8(*a*)	*Fraction in paragraphs* 1(*b*), 2, 8(*b*) and 11	*Fraction in paragraphs* 1(*c*) *and* 8(*c*)
1	21/40	7/20	7/40
2	123/200	41/100	41/200
3	27/40	9/20	9/40
4	3/4	1/2	1/4
5	33/40	11/20	11/40
6	9/10	3/5	3/10
7	39/40	13/20	13/40
8	21/20	7/10	7/20
9	9/8	3/4	3/8
10	6/5	4/5	2/5

In this Table—

(*a*) the three fractions specified in paragraph 2 are those which, at the passing of this Act, are specified in sub-paragraphs (*a*), (*b*) and (*c*) of paragraphs 1 and 8;

(*b*) the second of the fractions specified in paragraph 2 is the fraction which, at the passing of this Act, is specified in paragraphs 2 and 11.

(2) No order shall be made under sub-paragraph (1) unless a draft thereof has been laid before and approved by a resolution of each House of Parliament.

NOTES

Derivation: Paras 1, 2: 1965, Sched 5, paras 2, 3; 1977 Order, Art 3. Paras 3 to 7: 1965, Sched 5, paras 4 to 8. Para 8: 1965, Sched 5, para 9; 1977 Order, Art 3. Paras 9, 10: 1965, Sched 5, paras 10, 11. Para 11: 1965, Sched 5, para 12; 1977 Order, Art 3. Para 12: 1977 Order, Art 4. Para 13: Redundancy Rebates Act 1977, s 1 (1), (2), (4), Sched.

Further provisions: note ss 137 and 149.

Week's pay: this is calculated in accordance with Sched 14, Pt II: see s 152.

Years of employment: if a new employer takes on a redundant employee and leads the employee to understand that the rights which accrued with his previous employer will be carried over, and if the new employer makes the employee redundant, he will be estopped from disputing continuity of employment covering the period of employment with the previous employer and will have to make a redundancy payment covering both periods: see *Evenden* v *Guildford City Association Football Club* [1975] ICR 367. In such a situation, the Secretary of State will be liable to make a rebate from the Redundancy Fund covering both periods of employment, despite the fact that the continuity of employment arises not from the statutory provisions but from an estoppel: see *Secretary of State for Employment* v *Globe Elastic Thread Co Ltd*, The Times, July 19, 1978. See also the notes to s 104.

Definitions: 'redundancy rebate', 'redundancy payment' and 'employment': see s 153 (1); 'week's pay': see above; 'employee' and 'employer': see note to s 1; 'contract of employment': see s 153 (1); 'relevant date': see s 153 (1), and s 90.

SCHEDULE 7

CALCULATION OF PAYMENTS TO EMPLOYEES OUT OF REDUNDANCY FUND

1.—(1) Where the employer's payment is a redundancy payment, the sum referred to in section 106(2) is a sum equal to the amount of that payment.

(2) Where, in a case falling within section 104(6), the employer's payment is part of a redundancy payment, the sum referred to in section 106(2) is a sum equal to the amount of that part of the payment.

2.—(1) The provisions of this paragraph shall have effect for the purpose of determining the sum referred to in section 106(2) in relation to an employer's payment which is not a redundancy payment or part of a redundancy payment.

(2) Paragraphs 6 and 7 of Schedule 6 shall have effect for the purposes of this paragraph as they have effect for the purposes of Part II of that

Schedule; and in the application of those paragraphs in accordance with this sub-paragraph the employer's payment in relation to which the sum referred to in section 106(2) falls to be determined shall be taken to be the agreed payment.

(3) In relation to any such employer's payment, the sum in question shall be a sum equal to—

(*a*) the amount of the employer's payment, or

(*b*) the amount of the relevant redundancy payment,

whichever is the less.

NOTES

Derivation: 1965, Sched 6, paras 1, 2.

Further provisions: note ss 137 and 149.

Definitions: 'employer': see note to s 1.

SCHEDULE 8

EMPLOYEES PAID BY VIRTUE OF STATUTORY PROVISION BY PERSON OTHER THAN EMPLOYER

Provision of Act	*Reference to be construed as reference to the person responsible for paying the remuneration*
Section 81(1)	The second reference to the employer.
Section 85(3)	The reference to the employer in paragraph (*b*).
Section 85(4)	The last reference to the employer.
Section 88(4)	The reference to the employer.
Section 89(1)	The first reference to the employer.
Section 89(4) and (5)...	The references to the employer.
Section 92(3)	The second reference to the employer.
Section 98(3)	The reference to the employer.
Section 101(1) ...	The reference to the employer.
Section 102	The references to the employer.
Section 104	The references to the employer.
Section 106	The references to the employer.
Section 107(1) ...	The reference to the employer.
Section 108(1), (2), (4) and (5)	The references to the employer.
Section 110(2) ...	The third reference to the employer.
Section 110(5) and (6)	The reference to the employer.
Schedule 13, paragraph 12(3)	The references to the employer.

NOTES

Derivation: 1965, Sched 8.

Further provisions: note ss 137 and 149.

SCHEDULE 9

INDUSTRIAL TRIBUNALS

Regulations as to tribunal procedure

1.—(1) The Secretary of State may by regulations (in this Schedule referred to as " the regulations ") make such provision as appears to him to be necessary or expedient with respect to proceedings before industrial tribunals.

(2) The regulations may in particular include provision—

(*a*) for determining by which tribunal any appeal, question or complaint is to be determined;

(*b*) for enabling an industrial tribunal to hear and determine proceedings brought by virtue of section 131 concurrently with proceedings brought before the tribunal otherwise than by virtue of that section;

(*c*) for treating the Secretary of State (either generally or in such circumstances as may be prescribed by the regulations) as a party to any proceedings before an industrial tribunal, where he would not otherwise be a party to them, and entitling him to appear and to be heard accordingly;

(*d*) for requiring persons to attend to give evidence and produce documents, and for authorising the administration of oaths to witnesses;

(*e*) for granting to any person such discovery or inspection of documents or right to further particulars as might be granted by a county court in England and Wales or, in Scotland, for granting to any person such recovery or inspection of documents as might be granted by the sheriff;

(*f*) for prescribing the procedure to be followed on any appeal, reference or complaint or other proceedings before an industrial tribunal, including provisions as to the persons entitled to appear and to be heard on behalf of parties to such proceedings, and provisions for enabling an industrial tribunal to review its decisions, and revoke or vary its orders and awards, in such circumstances as may be determined in accordance with the regulations;

(*g*) for the appointment of one or more assessors for the purposes of any proceedings before an industrial tribunal, where the proceedings are brought under an enactment which provides for one or more assessors to be appointed;

(*h*) for the award of costs or expenses, including any allowances payable under paragraph 10 other than allowances payable to members of industrial tribunals or assessors;

(*i*) for taxing or otherwise settling any such costs or expenses (and, in particular, in England and Wales, for enabling such costs to be taxed in the county court); and

(*j*) for the registration and proof of decisions, orders and awards of industrial tribunals.

(3) In relation to proceedings on complaints under section 67 or any other enactment in relation to which there is provision for conciliation, the regulations shall include provision—

(*a*) for requiring a copy of any such complaint, and a copy of any notice relating to it which is lodged by or on behalf of the employer against whom the complaint is made, to be sent to a conciliation officer;

(*b*) for securing that the complainant and the employer against whom the complaint is made are notified that the services of a conciliation officer are available to them; and

(*c*) for postponing the hearing of any such complaint for such period as may be determined in accordance with the regulations for the purpose of giving an opportunity for the complaint to be settled by way of conciliation and withdrawn.

(4) In relation to proceedings under section 67—

(*a*) where the employee has expressed a wish to be reinstated or re-engaged which has been communicated to the employer at least seven days before the hearing of the complaint; or

(*b*) where the proceedings arise out of the employer's failure to permit the employee to return to work after an absence due to pregnancy or confinement,

regulations shall include provision for requiring the employer to pay the costs or expenses of any postponement or adjournment of the hearing caused by his failure, without a special reason, to adduce reasonable evidence as to the availability of the job from which the complainant was dismissed, or, as the case may be, which she held before her absence, or of comparable or suitable employment.

(5) Without prejudice to paragraph 2, the regulations may enable an industrial tribunal to sit in private for the purpose of hearing evidence which in the opinion of the tribunal relates to matters of such a nature that it would be against the interests of national security to allow the evidence to be given in public or of hearing evidence from any person which in the opinion of the tribunal is likely to consist of—

(*a*) information which he could not disclose without contravening a prohibition imposed by or under any enactment; or

(*b*) any information which has been communicated to him in confidence, or which he has otherwise obtained in consequence of the confidence reposed in him by another person; or

(*c*) information the disclosure of which would, for reasons other than its effect on negotiations with respect to any of the matters mentioned in section 29(1) of the Trade Union and Labour Relations Act 1974 (matters to which trade disputes relate) cause substantial injury to any undertaking of his or in which he works.

(6) The regulations may include provision authorising or requiring an industrial tribunal, in circumstances specified in the regulations, to send notice or a copy of any document so specified relating to any proceedings before the tribunal, or of any decision, order or award of the tribunal, to any government department or other person or body so specified.

(7) Any person who without reasonable excuse fails to comply with any requirement imposed by the regulations by virtue of sub-paragraph (2)(*d*) or any requirement with respect to the discovery, recovery or inspection of documents so imposed by virtue of sub-paragraph (2)(*e*) shall be liable on summary conviction to a fine not exceeding £100.

National security

2.—(1) If on a complaint under section 24 or 67 it is shown that the action complained of was taken for the purpose of safeguarding national security, the industrial tribunal shall dismiss the complaint.

(2) A certificate purporting to be signed by or on behalf of a Minister of the Crown, and certifying that the action specified in the certificate was taken for the purpose of safeguarding national security, shall for the purposes of sub-paragraph (1) be conclusive evidence of that fact.

Payment of certain sums into Redundancy Fund

3. Any sum recovered by the Secretary of State in pursuance of any such award as is mentioned in paragraph 1(2)(*h*) where the award was made in proceedings in pursuance of Part VI of this Act shall be paid into the Redundancy Fund.

Exclusion of Arbitration Act 1950

4. The Arbitration Act 1950 shall not apply to any proceedings before an industrial tribunal.

Presumption as to dismissal for redundancy

5. Where in accordance with the regulations an industrial tribunal determines in the same proceedings—

(*a*) a question referred to it under sections 81 to 102, and

(*b*) a complaint presented under section 67,

section 91(2) shall not have effect for the purposes of the proceedings in so far as they relate to the complaint under section 67.

Right of appearance

6. Any person may appear before an industrial tribunal in person or be represented by counsel or by a solicitor or by a representative of a trade union or an employers' association or by any other person whom he desires to represent him.

Recovery of sums awarded

7.—(1) Any sum payable in pursuance of a decision of an industrial tribunal in England and Wales which has been registered in accordance with the regulations shall, if a county court so orders, be recoverable by execution issued from the county court or otherwise as if it were payable under an order of that court.

(2) Any order for the payment of any sum made by an industrial tribunal in Scotland may be enforced in like manner as a recorded decree arbitral.

(3) In this paragraph any reference to a decision or order of an industrial tribunal—

(*a*) does not include a decision or order which, on being reviewed, has been revoked by the tribunal, and

(*b*) in relation to a decision or order which, on being reviewed, has been varied by the tribunal, shall be construed as a reference to the decision or order as so varied.

Constitution of tribunals for certain cases

8. An industrial tribunal hearing an application under section 77 or 79 may consist of a President of Industrial Tribunals, the chairman of the tribunal or a member of a panel of chairmen of such tribunals for the time being nominated by a President to hear such applications.

Remuneration for presidents and full-time chairmen of industrial tribunals

9. The Secretary of State may pay such remuneration as he may with the consent of the Minister for the Civil Service determine to the President of the Industrial Tribunals (England and Wales), the President of the Industrial Tribunals (Scotland) and any person who is a member on a full-time basis of a panel of chairmen of tribunals which is appointed in accordance with regulations under subsection (1) of section 128.

Remuneration etc. for members of industrial tribunals and for assessors and other persons

10. The Secretary of State may pay to members of industrial tribunals and to any assessors appointed for the purposes of proceedings before industrial tribunals such fees and allowances as he may with the consent of the Minister for the Civil Service determine and may pay to any other persons such allowances as he may with the consent of that Minister determine for the purposes of, or in connection with, their attendance at industrial tribunals.

Pensions for full-time presidents or chairmen of industrial tribunals

11.—(1) The Secretary of State may from time to time make to the Minister for the Civil Service, as respects any holder on a full-time basis of any of the following offices established by regulations under section 128 who is remunerated, apart from any allowances, on an annual basis, namely—

(*a*) President of the Industrial Tribunals (England and Wales);
(*b*) President of the Industrial Tribunals (Scotland);
(*c*) member of a panel of chairmen so established,

a recommendation that the Minister shall pay to that holder (hereafter in this paragraph referred to as " the pensioner ") out of moneys provided by Parliament an annual sum by way of superannuation allowance calculated in accordance with sub-paragraph (3).

(2) No such allowance shall be payable unless—

(*a*) the pensioner is at the time of his retirement over the age of seventy-two or, where he retires after fifteen years' service, over the age of sixty-five; or
(*b*) the Secretary of State is satisfied by means of a medical certificate that at the time of the pensioner's retirement the pensioner is, by reason of infirmity of mind or body, incapable of discharging the duties of his office and that the incapacity is likely to be permament.

(3) The said annual sum shall be a sum not exceeding such proportion of the pensioner's last annual remuneration (apart from any allowances) as in the following Table corresponds with the number of the pensioner's completed years of relevant service.

TABLE

Years of service	*Fraction of remuneration*
Less than 5	six-fortieths
5	ten-fortieths
6	eleven-fortieths
7	twelve-fortieths
8	thirteen-fortieths
9	fourteen-fortieths
10	fifteen-fortieths
11	sixteen-fortieths
12	seventeen-fortieths
13	eighteen-fortieths
14	nineteen-fortieths
15 or more	twenty-fortieths

(4) In this paragraph the expression " relevant service " means service on a full-time basis as holder of any of the offices referred to in sub-paragraph (1) (including such service remunerated otherwise than on an annual basis) or service in any such other capacity under the Crown as may be prescribed by regulations made by the Minister for the Civil Service; and regulations under this sub-paragraph—

(*a*) may be made generally or subject to specified exceptions or in relation to specified cases or classes of case and may make different provision for different cases or classes of cases; and

(*b*) may provide that in calculating relevant service either the whole of a person's prescribed service of any description shall be taken into account or such part thereof only as may be determined by or under the regulations.

(5) The decision of the Minister shall be final on any question arising as to—

(*a*) the amount of any superannuation allowance under sub-paragraph (1); or

(*b*) the reckoning of any service for the purpose of calculating such an allowance.

(6) Sections 2 to 8 of the Administration of Justice (Pensions) Act 1950 (which provide for the payment of lump sums on retirement or death and of widows' and children's pensions in the case of persons eligible for pensions for service in any of the capacities listed in Schedule 1 to that Act) shall have effect as if—

(*a*) the capacity of holder on a full-time basis of any of the offices referred to in sub-paragraph (1) were listed in the said Schedule 1; and

(*b*) in relation to that capacity the expression " relevant service " in the said sections 2 to 8 had the meaning assigned by sub-paragraph (4); and

(*c*) in relation to such a holder of such an office, any reference in the said section 2 to his last annual salary were a reference to his last annual remuneration apart from any allowances.

(7) Where the rate of the superannuation allowance payable to any person under sub-paragraph (1) is or would be increased by virtue of regulations made under sub-paragraph (4) in respect of relevant service in some capacity other than as holder of one of the offices referred to in sub-paragraph (1), and a pension payable to him wholly in respect of service in that other capacity would have been paid and borne otherwise than out of money's provided by Parliament, any pension benefits paid to or in respect of him as having been the holder of such an office shall, to such extent as the Minister for the Civil Service may determine, having regard to the relative length of service and rate of remuneration in each capacity, be paid and borne in like manner as that in which a pension payable to him wholly in respect of service in that other capacity would have been paid and borne.

(8) In this paragraph the expression " pension " includes any superannuation or other retiring allowance or gratuity, and the expression " pensionable " shall be construed accordingly, and the expression " pension benefits " includes benefits payable to or in respect of the pensioner by virtue of sub-paragraph (6).

NOTES

Derivation: Para 1: 1974, para 21 (1) to (3A), (5), (5A), (6); 1975, s 109 (6), Sched 16, Pt III, paras 18, 19, 22, 23. Para 2: 1975, s 55 (3), (4); 1974, para 18. Para 3: 1965, s 46 (6). Para 4: 1974, para 22. Para 5: 1974, para 23. Para 6: 1974, para 24. Para 7: 1974, para 25. Para 8: 1975, s 80 (4). Paras 9, 10: Industrial Training Act 1964, s 12 (2B), (3); 1965, s 46 (5); Employment and Training Act 1973, Sched 2, Pt I, para 15; Minister for the Civil Service Order 1971 (SI 1971 No 2099). Para 11: Superannuation (Miscellaneous Provisions) Act 1967, s 9; Minister for the Civil Service Order 1968 (SI 1968 No 1656).

Further provisions: note ss 138 (7) (*e*) and 139 (1) (*d*) in relation to para 1 (5) (*c*), and s 149 (2). Note also s 137.

Regulations under para 1*:* these are at present as follows:
Industrial Tribunals (Labour Relations) Regulations 1974 (SI 1974 No 1386) (as amended by SI 1976 No 661, SI 1977 No 911 and SI 1978 No 991); Industrial Tribunals (Labour Relations) (Scotland) Regulations 1974 (SI 1974 No 1387) (as amended by SI 1976 No 662, SI 1977 No 912 and SI 1978 No 992). See also the Industrial Tribunals (Non-Discrimination Notices Appeals) Regulations 1977 (SI 1977 No 1094) and the Industrial Tribunals (Non-Discrimination Notices Appeals) (Scotland) Regulations 1977 (SI 1977 No 1095).

Definitions: 'conciliation officer': see s 133; 'employee' and 'employer': see note to s 1; 'complaint': see s 67; 'reinstated' and 're-engaged': see s 69; 'confinement' : see s 153 (1); 'trade union' and 'employers' association': see s 153 (1) and s 28 of the Trade Union and Labour Relations Act 1974; 'employment': see s 153 (1).

SCHEDULE 10

STATUTORY PROVISIONS RELATING TO REFEREES AND BOARDS OF REFEREES

1. Regulations under section 37 of the Coal Industry Nationalisation Act 1946.

2. Regulations under section 67 of the National Insurance Act 1946.

3. Regulations under section 68 of the National Health Service Act 1946, and orders under section 11(9) or section 31(5) of that Act.

4. Regulations under section 67 of the National Health Service (Scotland) Act 1947.

5. Regulations under Schedule 5 to the Fire Services Act 1947.

6. Regulations under section 101 of the Transport Act 1947.

7. Subsections (3) and (5) of section 54 of the Electricity Act 1947, and regulations under section 55 of that Act or under that section as applied by section 27 of the Electricity Act 1957.

8. Regulations under section 140 of the Local Government Act 1948, and such regulations as applied by any local Act, whether passed before or after this Act.

9. Regulations under subsection (1) or subsection (2) of section 60 of the National Assistance Act 1948.

10. Rules under section 3 of the Superannuation (Miscellaneous Provisions) Act 1948.

11. Subsections (3) and (5) of section 58 of the Gas Act 1948, and regulations under section 60 of that Act.

12. Subsection (4) of section 6 of the Commonwealth Telegraphs Act 1949 and regulations under that section.

13. Regulations under section 25 of the Prevention of Damage by Pests Act 1949.

14. Regulations under section 42 of the Justices of the Peace Act 1949.

15. Regulations under section 27 or section 28 of the Transport Act 1953.

16. Regulations under section 24 of the Iron and Steel Act 1953.

17. Regulations under section 12 of the Electricity Reorganisation (Scotland) Act 1954.

18. Orders under section 23 of the Local Government Act 1958 and regulations under section 60 of that Act.

19. Regulations under section 1 of the Water Officers Compensation Act 1960.

20. Regulations under section 18(6) of the Land Drainage Act 1961.

21. Subsection (6) of section 74 of the Transport Act 1962 and orders under that section, regulations under section 81 of that Act, and paragraph 17(3) of Schedule 7 to that Act.

22. Orders under section 84 of the London Government Act 1963 and regulations under section 85 of that Act.

23. Regulations under section 106 of the Water Resources Act 1963.

NOTES

Derivation: 1965, Sched 7.

Further provisions: note ss 137 and 149.

SCHEDULE 11

EMPLOYMENT APPEAL TRIBUNAL

PART I

PROVISIONS AS TO MEMBERSHIP, SITTINGS, PROCEEDINGS AND POWERS

Tenure of office of appointed members of Appeal Tribunal

1. Subject to paragraphs 2 and 3, a member of the Appeal Tribunal appointed by Her Majesty under section 135(2)(*c*) (in this Schedule referred to as an " appointed member ") shall hold and vacate office as such a member in accordance with the terms of his appointment.

2. An appointed member may at any time resign his membership by notice in writing addressed to the Lord Chancellor and the Secretary of State.

3.—(1) If the Lord Chancellor, after consultation with the Secretary of State, is satisfied that an appointed member—

(*a*) has been absent from sittings of the Appeal Tribunal for a period longer than six consecutive months without the permission of the President of the Tribunal; or

(*b*) has become bankrupt or made an arrangement with his creditors; or (*c*) is incapacitated by physical or mental illness; or

(*d*) is otherwise unable or unfit to discharge the functions of a member;

the Lord Chancellor may declare his office as a member to be vacant and shall notify the declaration in such manner as the Lord Chancellor thinks fit; and thereupon the office shall become vacant.

(2) In the application of this paragraph to Scotland for the references in sub-paragraph (1)(*b*) to a member's having become bankrupt and to a member's having made an arrangement with his creditors there shall be substituted respectively references to a member's estate having been sequestrated and to a member's having made a trust deed for behoof of his creditors or a composition contract.

Temporary membership of Appeal Tribunal

4. At any time when the office of President of the Appeal Tribunal is vacant, or the person holding that office is temporarily absent or otherwise unable to act as President of the Tribunal, the Lord Chancellor may nominate another judge nominated under section 135(2)(*a*) to act temporarily in his place.

5. At any time when a judge of the Appeal Tribunal nominated by the Lord Chancellor is temporarily absent or otherwise unable to act as a judge of that Tribunal, the Lord Chancellor may nominate another person who is qualified to be nominated under section 135(2)(*a*) to act temporarily in his place.

6. At any time when a judge of the Appeal Tribunal nominated by the Lord President of the Court of Session is temporarily absent or otherwise unable to act as a judge of the Appeal Tribunal, the Lord President may nominate another judge of the Court of Session to act temporarily in his place.

7. At any time when an appointed member is temporarily absent or otherwise unable to act as a member of the Appeal Tribunal, the Lord Chancellor and the Secretary of State may jointly appoint a person appearing to them to have the qualifications for appointment as such a member to act temporarily in his place.

8.—(1) At any time when it appears to the Lord Chancellor that it is expedient to do so in order to facilitate in England and Wales the disposal of business in the Appeal Tribunal, he may appoint a qualified person to be a temporary additional judge of the Tribunal during such period or on such occasions as the Lord Chancellor thinks fit.

(2) In this paragraph " qualified person " means a person qualified for appointment as a puisne judge of the High Court under section 9 of the Supreme Court of Judicature (Consolidation) Act 1925 or any person who has held office as a judge of the Court of Appeal or of the High Court.

9. A person appointed to act temporarily in place of the President or any other member of the Appeal Tribunal shall, when so acting, have all the functions of the person in whose place he acts.

10. A person appointed to be a temporary additional judge of the Appeal Tribunal shall have all the functions of a judge nominated under section 135(2)(*a*).

11. No judge shall be nominated under paragraph 5 or 6 except with his consent.

Organisation and sittings of Appeal Tribunal

12. The Appeal Tribunal shall be a superior court of record and shall have an official seal which shall be judicially noticed.

13. The Appeal Tribunal shall have a central office in London.

14. The Appeal Tribunal may sit at any time and in any place in Great Britain.

15. The Appeal Tribunal may sit, in accordance with directions given by the President of the Tribunal, either as a single tribunal or in two or more divisions concurrently.

16. With the consent of the parties to any proceedings before the Appeal Tribunal, the proceedings may be heard by a judge and one appointed member, but, in default of such consent, any proceedings before the Tribunal shall be heard by a judge and either two or four appointed members, so that in either case there are equal numbers of persons whose experience is as representatives of employers and whose experience is as representatives of workers.

Rules

17.—(1) The Lord Chancellor, after consultation with the Lord President of the Court of Session, shall make rules with respect to proceedings before the Appeal Tribunal.

(2) Subject to those rules, the Tribunal shall have power to regulate its own procedure.

18. Without prejudice to the generality of paragraph 17 the rules may include provision—

(*a*) with respect to the manner in which an appeal may be brought and the time within which it may be brought;

(*b*) for requiring persons to attend to give evidence and produce documents, and for authorising the administration of oaths to witnesses;

(*c*) enabling the Appeal Tribunal to sit in private for the purpose of hearing evidence to hear which an industrial tribunal may sit in private by virtue of paragraph 1 of Schedule 9.

19.—(1) Without prejudice to the generality of paragraph 17 the rules may empower the Appeal Tribunal to order a party to any proceedings before the Tribunal to pay to any other party to the proceedings the whole or part of the costs or expenses incurred by that other party in connection with the proceedings, where in the opinion of the Tribunal—

(*a*) the proceedings were unnecessary, improper or vexatious, or

(*b*) there has been unreasonable delay or other unreasonable conduct in bringing or conducting the proceedings.

(2) Except as provided by sub-paragraph (1), the rules shall not enable the Appeal Tribunal to order the payment of costs or expenses by any party to proceedings before the Tribunal.

20. Any person may appear before the Appeal Tribunal in person or be represented by counsel or by a solicitor or by a representative of a trade union or an employers' association or by any other person whom he desires to represent him.

Powers of Tribunal

21.—(1) For the purpose of disposing of an appeal the Appeal Tribunal may exercise any powers of the body or officer from whom the appeal was brought or may remit the case to that body or officer.

(2) Any decision or award of the Appeal Tribunal on an appeal shall have the same effect and may be enforced in the same manner as a decision or award of a body or officer from whom the appeal was brought.

22.—(1) The Appeal Tribunal shall, in relation to the attendance and examination of witnesses, the production and inspection of documents and all other matters incidental to its jurisdiction, have the like powers, rights, privileges and authority—

(*a*) in England and Wales, as the High Court,

(*b*) in Scotland, as the Court of Session.

(2) No person shall be punished for contempt of the Tribunal except by, or with the consent of, a judge.

23.—(1) In relation to any fine imposed by the Appeal Tribunal for contempt of the Tribunal, section 14 of the Criminal Justice Act 1948 and section 47 of the Criminal Justice Act 1967 (which relate to fines imposed and recognizances forfeited at certain courts) shall have effect as if in those provisions any reference to the Crown Court included a reference to the Tribunal.

(2) A magistrates' court shall not remit the whole or any part of a fine imposed by the Appeal Tribunal except with the consent of a judge who is a member of the Tribunal.

(3) This paragraph does not extend to Scotland.

Staff

24. The Secretary of State may appoint such officers and servants of the Appeal Tribunal as he may determine, subject to the approval of the Minister for the Civil Service as to numbers and as to terms and conditions of service.

PART II

SUPPLEMENTARY

Remuneration and allowances

25. The Secretary of State shall pay the appointed members of the Appeal Tribunal, the persons appointed to act temporarily as appointed members, and the officers and servants of the Tribunal such remuneration and such travelling and other allowances as he may with the approval of the Minister for the Civil Service determine.

26. A person appointed to be a temporary additional judge of the Appeal Tribunal shall be paid such remuneration and allowances as the Lord Chancellor may, with the approval of the Minister for the Civil Service, determine.

Pensions, etc.

27. If the Secretary of State determines, with the approval of the Minister for the Civil Service, that this paragraph shall apply in the case of an appointed member, the Secretary of State shall pay such pension, allowance or gratuity to or in respect of that member on his retirement or death or make that member such payments towards the provision of such a pension, allowance or gratuity as the Secretary of State may with the like approval determine.

28. Where a person ceases to be an appointed member otherwise than on his retirement or death and it appears to the Secretary of State that there are special circumstances which make it right for him to receive compensation, the Secretary of State may make him a payment of such amount as the Secretary of State may, with the approval of the Minister for the Civil Service, determine.

NOTES

Derivation: 1975, Sched 6.

Further provisions: note ss 137 and 149.

Rules: see the Employment Appeal Tribunal Rules 1976 (SI 1976 No 322). See also Practice Direction (EAT: Appeals) [1978] ICR 621.

Definitions: 'employer': see note to s 1; 'worker': see s 30 (1) of the Trade Union and Labour Relations Act 1974; 'trade union' and 'employers' association': see s 153 (1).

SCHEDULE 12

DEATH OF EMPLOYEE OR EMPLOYER

PART I

GENERAL

Introductory

1. In this Schedule " the relevant provisions " means Part I (so far as it relates to itemised pay statements), section 53 and Parts II, III, V, VI and VII of this Act and this Schedule.

Institution or continuance of tribunal proceedings

2. Where an employee or employer has died, tribunal proceedings arising under any of the relevant provisions may be instituted or continued by a personal representative of the deceased employee or, as the case may be, defended by a personal representative of the deceased employer.

3.—(1) If there is no personal representative of a deceased employee, tribunal proceedings arising under any of the relevant provisions (or proceedings to enforce a tribunal award made in any such proceedings) may be instituted or continued on behalf of the estate of the deceased employee by such other person as the industrial tribunal may appoint being either—

(*a*) a person authorised by the employee to act in connection with the proceedings before the employee's death; or

(*b*) the widower, widow, child, father, mother, brother or sister of the deceased employee, and references in this Schedule to a personal representative shall be construed as including such a person.

(2) In such a case any award made by the industrial tribunal shall be in such terms and shall be enforceable in such manner as may be provided by regulations made by the Secretary of State.

4.—(1) Subject to any specific provision of this Schedule to the contrary, in relation to an employee or employer who has died—

(*a*) any reference in the relevant provisions to the doing of anything by or in relation to an employee or employer shall be construed as including a reference to the doing of that thing by or in relation to any personal representative of the deceased employee or employer; and

(*b*) any reference in the said provisions to a thing required or authorised to be done by or in relation to an employee or employer shall be construed as including a reference to any thing which, in accordance with any such provision as modified by this Schedule (including sub-paragraph (*a*)), is required or authorised to be done by or in relation to any personal representative of the deceased employee or employer.

(2) Nothing in this paragraph shall prevent references in the relevant provisions to a successor of an employer from including a personal representative of a deceased employer.

Rights and liabilities accruing after death

5. Any right arising under any of the relevant provisions as modified by this Schedule shall, if it had not accrued before the death of the employee in question, nevertheless devolve as if it had so accrued.

6. Where by virtue of any of the relevant provisions as modified by this Schedule a personal representative of a deceased employer is liable to pay any amount and that liability had not accrued before the death of the employer, it shall be treated for all purposes as if it were a liability of the deceased employer which had accrued immediately before the death.

NOTES

Derivation: the provisions of this Schedule in general are derived from 1975, Sched 12, and 1965, Sched 4, amended by 1975, Sched 16, Pt I, paras 23 to 34. The derivations of each paragraph in Pt I are set forth below:
para 1: —;
para 2: 1975, Sched 12, para 2;
para 3: 1975, Sched 12, para 3; 1965, Sched 4, para 21A (1), (2);
para 4: 1975, Sched 12, para 4; 1965, Sched 4, paras 14, 21;
para 5: 1975, Sched 12, para 5; 1965, Sched 4, para 22 (1);
para 6: 1975, Sched 12, para 6; 1965, Sched 4, para 15.

General Note: see Sched 2, Pt II, para 4 (3) in relation to maternity, and Sched 13, para 17 (4). Note ss 137 and 149.

Paragraph 3 (2): regulations: see the Industrial Tribunals Awards (Enforcement in Case of Death) Regulations 1976 (SI 1976 No 663).

Definitions: 'employee' and 'employer': see note to s 1; 'relevant provisions': note para 1; 'successor': see s 153 (1) and s 30 (3) and (4) of the Trade Union and Labour Relations Act 1974.

PART II

UNFAIR DISMISSAL

Introductory

7. In this Part of this Schedule "the unfair dismissal provisions" means Part V of this Act and this Schedule.

Death during notice period

8. Where an employer has given notice to an employee to terminate his contract of employment and before that termination the employee or the employer dies, the unfair dismissal provisions shall apply as if the contract had been duly terminated by the employer by notice expiring on the date of the death.

9. Where the employee's contract of employment has been terminated by the employer and by virtue of section 55(5) a date later than the effective date of termination as defined by subsection (4) of that section is to be treated as the effective date of termination for the purposes of certain of the unfair dismissal provisions, and before that later date the employee or the employer dies, section 55(5) shall have effect as if the notice referred to in that subsection as required to be given by the employer would have expired on the date of the death.

Remedies for unfair dismissal

10. Where an employee has died, then, unless an order for reinstatement or re-engagement has already been made, section 69 shall not apply; and accordingly if the industrial tribunal finds that the grounds of the complaint are well-founded the case shall be treated as falling within section 68(2) as a case in which no order is made under section 69.

11. If an order for reinstatement or re-engagement has been made and the employee dies before the order is complied with—

(*a*) if the employer has before the death refused to reinstate or re-engage the employee in accordance with the order, section 71(2) and (3) shall apply and an award shall be made under section 71(2)(*b*) unless the employer satisfies the tribunal that it was not practicable at the time of the refusal to comply with the order;

(*b*) if there has been no such refusal, section 71(1) shall apply if the employer fails to comply with any ancillary terms of the order which remain capable of fulfilment after the employee's death as it would apply to such a failure to comply fully with the terms of an order where the employee had been reinstated or re-engaged.

NOTES

Derivation: 1975, Sched 12, paras 8 to 12.

Reinstatement, Re-engagement: see s 69.

Definitions: 'employee' and 'employer': see note to s 1; 'contract of employment': see s 153 (1); 'unfair dismissal provisions': note para 7; 'effective date of termination': see s 55 (4); 'order for reinstatement or re-engagement': see above.

Part III

Redundancy Payments: Death of Employer

Introductory

12. The provisions of this Part shall have effect in relation to an employee where his employer (in this Part referred to as " the deceased employer ") dies.

13. Section 94 shall not apply to any change whereby the ownership of the business, for the purposes of which the employee was employed by the deceased employer, passes to a personal representative of the deceased employer.

Dismissal

14. Where by virtue of subsection (1) of section 93 the death of the deceased employer is to be treated for the purposes of Part VI of this Act as a termination by him of the contract of employment, section 84 shall have effect subject to the following modifications:—

(*a*) for subsection (1) there shall be substituted the following subsection—

" (1) If an employee's contract of employment is renewed, or he is re-engaged under a new contract of employment, by a personal representative of the deceased employer and the renewal or re-engagement takes effect not later than eight weeks after the death of the deceased employer, then, subject to subsections (3) and (6), the employee shall not be regarded as having been dismissed by reason of the ending of his employment under the previous contract.";

(*b*) in subsection (2), paragraph (*a*) shall be omitted and in paragraph (*b*) for the words " four weeks " there shall be substituted the words " eight weeks ";

(*c*) in subsections (5) and (6), references to the employer shall be construed as references to the personal representative of the deceased employer.

15. Where by reason of the death of the deceased employer the employee is treated for the purposes of Part VI of this Act as having been dismissed by him, section 82 shall have effect subject to the following modifications—

(*a*) for subsection (3) there shall be substituted the following subsection—

" (3) If a personal representative of the deceased employer makes an employee an offer (whether in writing or not) to renew his contract of employment, or to re-engage him under a new contract of employment, so that the renewal or re-engagement would take effect not later than eight weeks after the death of the deceased employer the provisions of subsections (5) and (6) shall have effect.";

(*b*) in subsection (4), paragraph (*a*) shall be omitted and in paragraph (*b*) for the words " four weeks " there shall be substituted the words " eight weeks ";

(*c*) in subsection (5), the reference to the employer shall be construed as a reference to the personal representative of the deceased employer.

16. For the purposes of section 82 as modified by paragraph 15—

(*a*) an offer shall not be treated as one whereby the provisions of the contract as renewed, or of the new contract, as the case may be, would differ from the corresponding provisions of the contract as in force immediately before the death of the decesased employer by reason only that the personal representative would be substituted as the employer for the deceased employer, and

(*b*) no account shall be taken of that substitution in determining whether the refusal of the offer was unreasonable, or, as the case may be, whether the employee acted reasonably in terminating the renewed, or new, employment during the trial period referred to in section 84.

Lay-off and short-time

17. Where the employee has before the death of the deceased employer been laid off or kept on short-time for one or more weeks, but has not given to the deceased employer notice of intention to claim, then if after the death of the deceased employer—

(*a*) his contract of employment is renewed, or he is re-engaged under a new contract by a personal representative of the deceased employer, and

(*b*) after the renewal or re-engagement, he is laid off or kept on short-time for one or more weeks by the personal representaive of the deceased employer,

the provisions of sections 88 and 89 shall apply as if the week in which the deceased employer died and the first week of the employee's employment by the personal representative were consecutive weeks, and any reference in those sections to four weeks or thirteen weeks shall be construed accordingly.

18. The provisions of paragraph 19 or (as the case may be) paragraph 20 shall have effect where the employee has given to the deceased employer notice of intention to claim, and—

(*a*) the deceased employer has died before the end of the next four weeks after the service of that notice, and

(*b*) the employee has not terminated the contract of employment by notice expiring before the death of the deceased employer.

19. If in the circumstances specified in paragraph 18 the employee's contract of employment is not renewed by a personal representative of the deceased employer before the end of the next four weeks after the service of the notice of intention to claim, and he is not re-engaged under a new contract by such a personal representative before the end of those four weeks, section 88(1) and (2) and (in relation to subsection (1) of that section) section 89(2) and (3) shall apply as if—

(*a*) the deceased employer had not died, and

(*b*) the employee had terminated the contract of employment by a week's notice (or, if under the contract he is required to give more than a week's notice to terminate the contract, he had terminated it by the minimum notice which he is so required to give) expiring at the end of those four weeks,

but sections 88(3) and (4) and 89(1) and (4) shall not apply.

20.—(1) The provisions of this paragraph shall have effect where, in the circumstances specified in paragraph 18, the employee's contract of employment is renewed by a personal representative of the deceased employer before the end of the next four weeks after the service of the notice of intention to claim, or he is re-engaged under a new contract by such a personal representative before the end of those four weeks, and—

(*a*) he was laid off or kept on short-time by the deceased employer for one or more of those weeks, and

(*b*) he is laid off or kept on short-time by the personal representative for the week, or for the next two or more weeks, following the renewal or re-engagement.

(2) Where the conditions specified in sub-paragraph (1) are fulfilled, sections 88 and 89 shall apply as if—

(*a*) all the weeks for which the employee was laid off or kept on short-time as mentioned in sub-paragraph (1) were consecutive weeks during which he was employed (but laid off or kept on short-time) by the same employer, and

(*b*) each of the periods specified in paragraphs (*a*) and (*b*) of sub-section (5) of section 89 were extended by any week or weeks any part of which was after the death of the deceased employer and before the date on which the renewal or re-engagement took effect.

Continuity of period of employment

21. For the purposes of the application, in accordance with section 100(1), of any provisions of Part VI of this Act in relation to an employee who was employed as a domestic servant in a private household, any reference to a personal representative in—

(*a*) this Part of this Schedule, or

(*b*) paragraph 17 of Schedule 13,

shall be construed as including a reference to any person to whom, otherwise than in pursuance of a sale or other disposition for valuable consideration, the management of the household has passed in consequence of the death of the deceased employer.

NOTES

Derivation: 1965, Sched 4, paras 1 to 5, 7 to 10, 13; 1975, Sched 16, Pt I, paras 23 to 27.

Paras 14 *and* 15: see *Ranger* v *Brown* [1978] ICR 603.

Definitions: 'employee' and 'employer': see note to s 1; 'contract of employment' and 'week': see s 153 (1); 'laid off' and 'short-time': see s 87; 'notice of intention to claim': see s 88 (1).

PART IV

REDUNDANCY PAYMENTS: DEATH OF EMPLOYEE

22.—(1) Where an employer has given notice to an employee to terminate his contract of employment, and before that notice expires the employee dies, the provisions of Part VI of this Act shall apply as if the contract had been duly terminated by the employer by notice expiring on the date of the employee's death.

(2) Where the employee's contract of employment has been terminated by the employer and by virtue of section 90(3) a date later than the relevant date as defined by subsection (1) of that section is to be treated as the relevant date for the purposes of certain provisions of Part VI of this Act, and before that later date the employee dies, section 90(3) shall have effect as if the notice referred to in that subsection as required to be given by an employer would have expired on the employee's death.

23.—(1) Where an employer has given notice to an employee to terminate his contract of employment, and has offered to renew his contract of employment, or to re-engage him under a new contract, then if—

(*a*) the employee dies without having either accepted or refused the offer, and

(*b*) the offer has not been withdrawn before his death,

section 82 shall apply as if for the words " the employee unreasonably refuses " there were substituted the words " it would have been unreasonable on the part of the employee to refuse ".

(2) Where an employee's contract of employment has been renewed, or he has been re-engaged under a new contract of employment, and during the trial period the employee dies without having terminated or having given notice to terminate the contract, subsection (6) of that section shall apply as if for the words from " and during the trial period " to " terminated " there were substituted the words " and it would have been unreasonable for the employee, during the trial period referred to in section 84, to terminate or give notice to terminate the contract ".

24. Where an employee's contract of employment has been renewed, or he has been re-engaged under a new contract of employment, and during the trial period he gives notice to terminate the contract but dies before the expiry of that notice, sections 82(6) and 84(6)(*a*) shall have effect as if the notice had expired and the contract had thereby been terminated on the date of the employee's death.

25.—(1) Where, in the circumstances specified in paragraphs (*a*) and (*b*) of subsection (1) of section 85, the employee dies before the notice given by him under paragraph (*b*) of that subsection is due to expire and before the employer has given him notice under subsection (3) of that section, subsection (4) of that section shall apply as if the employer had given him such notice and he had not complied with it.

(2) Where, in the said circumstances, the employee dies before his notice given under section 85(1)(*b*) is due to expire but after the employer has given him notice under subsection (3) of section 85, subsections (3) and (4) of that section shall apply as if the circumstances were that the employee had not died, but did not comply with the last-mentioned notice.

26.—(1) Where an employee has given notice of intention to claim and dies before he has given notice to terminate his contract of employment and before the period allowed for the purposes of subsection (2)(*a*) of section 88 has expired, the said subsection (2)(*a*) shall not apply.

(2) Where an employee, who has given notice of intention to claim, dies within seven days after the service of that notice, and before the employer has given a counter-notice, the provisions of sections 88 and 89 shall apply as if the employer had given a counter-notice within those seven days.

(3) In this paragraph " counter-notice " has the same meaning as in section 89(1).

27.—(1) In relation to the making of a claim by a personal representative of a deceased employee who dies before the end of the period of six months beginning with the relevant date, subsection (1) of section 101 shall apply with the substitution for the words " six months ", of the words " one year ".

(2) In relation to the making of a claim by a personal representative of a deceased employee who dies after the end of the period of six months beginning with the relevant date and before the end of the following period of six months, subsection (2) of section 101 shall apply with the substitution for the words " six months ", of the words " one year ".

28. In relation to any case where, under any provision contained in Part VI of this Act as modified by this Schedule, an industrial tribunal has power to determine that an employer shall be liable to pay to a personal representative of a deceased employee either—

(*a*) the whole of a redundancy payment to which he would have been entitled apart from another provision therein mentioned, or

(*b*) such part of such a redundancy payment as the tribunal thinks fit,

any reference in paragraph 5 to a right shall be construed as including a reference to any right to receive the whole or part of a redundancy payment if the tribunal determines that the employer shall be liable to pay it.

NOTES

Derivation: 1965, Sched 4, paras 16 to 20, 22 (2); 1975, Sched 16, Pt I, paras 28 to 33.

Definitions: 'employee' and 'employer': see note to s 1; 'contract of employment': see s 153 (1); 'trial period': see s 83 (3) to (6); 'notice of intention to claim': see s 88 (1); 'relevant date': see s 153 (1) and s 90; 'redundancy payment': see s 153 (1).

SCHEDULE 13

COMPUTATION OF PERIOD OF EMPLOYMENT

General Note: the provisions contained in this Schedule are used for two different purposes: (i) to ascertain whether the employee has the minimum period of employment to qualify him to make a claim under the provisions of the Act; and (ii) to calculate certain payments according to the length of continuous service.

Essentially, the concept of continuous employment involves two elements: (i) the existence of an unbroken (ie continuous) employment relationship over a period of time; and (ii) the duration of that relationship for the requisite period of time. The provisions of this Schedule, therefore, help to ascertain whether the relationship has been continuous and how many weeks the employee is to be credited with.

It should be noted, as was pointed out by Pennycuick, J in *Re Mack Trucks (Britain) Ltd* [1967] 1 WLR 780, that continuity of employment does not require that the employment should be pursuant to a single contract of service. See also *Wood* v *York City Council* [1978] IRLR 228.

Note s 7, which gives the Secretary of State power to amend paras 3 to 7, 137, 139, 145 (4) and 149 (2).

NB: to assist cross-referring, derivations will be appended to each paragraph.

Preliminary

1.—(1) Where an employee's period of employment is, for the purposes of any enactment (including any enactment contained in this Act), to be computed in accordance with this Schedule, it shall be computed in weeks, and in any such enactment which refers to a period of employment expressed in years, a year means fifty-two weeks (whether continuous or discontinuous) which count in computing a period of employment.

(2) For the purpose of computing an employee's period of employment (but not for any other purpose), the provisions of this Schedule apply, subject to paragraph 14, to a period of employment notwithstanding that during that period the employee was engaged in work wholly or mainly outside Great Britain or was excluded by or under this Act from any right conferred by this Act.

NOTES

Derivation: 1972, Sch 1, para 1 (1) (as substituted by 1975, Sched 16, Pt II, para 12), and (2).

Engaged in work wholly or mainly outside Great Britain: see note to s 141.

Definitions: 'employee': see note to s 1; 'employment' and 'week': see s 153 (1).

2. Except so far as otherwise provided by the following provisions of this Schedule, any week which does not count under paragraphs 3 to 13 breaks the continuity of the period of employment.

NOTES

Derivation: 1972, Sched 1, para 2.

Normal working weeks

3. Any week in which the employee is employed for sixteen hours or more shall count in computing a period of employment.

NOTES

Derivation: 1972, Sched 1, para 3, as amended by 1975, Sched 16, Pt II, para 13.

General Note: under s 7, the Secretary of State has power to amend this paragraph: see para 8.

See also *Bromsgrove Casting and Machinery Ltd* v *Martin* [1977] ICR 417; *Bullock* v *Merseyside County Council* [1978] ICR 419; and *Lake* v *Essex County Council* [1978] IRLR 24, and the cases mentioned in the note to para 4.

Definitions: 'employee' and 'employer': see note to s 1; 'week': see s 153 (1).

Employment governed by contract

4. Any week during the whole or part of which the employee's relations with the employer are governed by a contract of employment which normally involves employment for sixteen hours or more weekly shall count in computing a period of employment.

NOTES

Derivation: 1972, Sched 1, para 4, as amended by 1975, Sched 16, Pt II, para 13.

General Note: under s 7, the Secretary of State has power to amend this paragraph: see para 8.

Normally involves employment: presumably, therefore, if the employee is away ill for a considerable period of time, his continuity will be preserved, and the weeks of his absence will continue to be counted towards the period of employment, at any rate until the time when the illness causes the contract of employment to be frustrated. See also *Coulson* v *City of London Polytechnic* [1976] ICR 433; *Dean* v *Eastbourne Fishermen's and Boatmen's Protection Society & Club Ltd* [1977] ICR 556; *ITT Components* v *Kolah* [1977] ICR 740; and *Mailway (Southern) Ltd* v *Willsher* [1978] ICR 511 and the cases mentioned in the note to para 3.

Definitions: 'week': see s 153 (1); 'employee' and 'employer': see note to s 1; 'employment' and 'contract of employment': see s 153 (1).

5.—(1) If the employee's relations with his employer cease to be governed by a contract which normally involves work for sixteen hours or more weekly and become governed by a contract which normally involves employment for eight hours or more, but less than sixteen hours, weekly and, but for that change, the later weeks would count in computing a period of employment, or would not break the continuity of a period of employment, then those later weeks shall count in computing a period of employment or, as the case may be, shall not break the continuity of a period of employment, notwithstanding that change.

(2) Not more than twenty-six weeks shall count under this paragraph between any two periods falling under paragraph 4, and in computing the said figure of twenty-six weeks no account shall be taken of any week which counts in computing a period of employment, or does not break the continuity of a period of employment, otherwise than by virtue of this paragraph.

NOTES

Derivation: 1972, Sched 1, para 4A (inserted by 1975, Sched 16, Pt II, para 14).

General Note: under s 7, the Secretary of State has power to amend this paragraph: see para 8.

Definitions: 'employee' and 'employer': see note to s 1; 'employment': see s 153 (1).

6.—(1) An employee whose relations with his employer are governed, or have been from time to time governed, by a contract of employment which normally involves employment for eight hours or more, but less than sixteen hours, weekly shall nevertheless, if he satisfies the condition referred to in sub-paragraph (2), be treated for the purposes of this Schedule (apart from this paragraph) as if his contract normally involved employment for sixteen hours or more weekly, and had at all times at which there was a contract during the period of employment of five years or more referred to in sub-paragraph (2) normally involved employment for sixteen hours or more weekly.

(2) Sub-paragraph (1) shall apply if the employee, on the date by reference to which the length of any period of employment falls to be ascertained in accordance with the provisions of this Schedule, has been continuously employed within the meaning of sub-paragraph (3) for a period of five years or more.

(3) In computing for the purposes of sub-paragraph (2) an employee's period of employment, the provisions of this Schedule (apart from this paragraph) shall apply but as if, in paragraphs 3 and 4, for the words " sixteen hours " wherever they occur, there were substituted the words " eight hours ".

NOTES

Derivation: 1972, Sched 1, para 4B (inserted by 1975, Sched 16, Pt II, para 14).

General Note: under s 7, the Secretary of State has power to amend this paragraph: see para 8.

Definitions: 'employee' and 'employer': see note to s 1; 'contract of employment' and 'employment': see s 153 (1).

7.—(1) If an employee has, at any time during the relevant period of employment, been continuously employed for a period which qualifies him for any right which requires a qualifying period of continuous employment computed in accordance with this Schedule, then he shall be regarded for the purposes of qualifying for that right as continuing to satisfy that requirement until the condition referred to in sub-paragraph (3) occurs.

(2) In this paragraph the relevant period of employment means the period of employment ending on the date by reference to which the length of any period of employment falls to be ascertained which would be continuous (in accordance with the provisions of this Schedule) if at all relevant times the employee's relations with the employer had been governed by a contract of employment which normally involved employment for sixteen hours or more weekly.

(3) The condition which defeats the operation of sub-paragraph (1) is that in a week subsequent to the time at which the employee qualified as referred to in that sub-paragraph—

(*a*) his relations with his employer are governed by a contract of employment which normally involves employment for less than eight hours weekly; and

(*b*) he is employed in that week for less than sixteen hours.

(4) If, in a case in which an employee is entitled to any right by virtue of sub-paragraph (1), it is necessary for the purpose of ascertaining the amount of his entitlement to determine for what period he has been continuously employed, he shall be regarded for that purpose as having been continuously employed throughout the relevant period.

NOTES

Derivation: 1972, Sched 1, para 4c (inserted by 1975, Sched 16, Pt II, para 14).

General Note: under s 7, the Secretary of State has power to amend this paragraph: see para 8.

Definitions: 'employee' and 'employer': see note to s 1; 'employment' and 'contract of employment': see s 153 (1); 'relevant period of emploment': note sub-para (2).

Orders under section 7

8. The foregoing provisions of this Schedule shall have effect subject to any order made under section 7 and an order under that section shall affect the operation of this Schedule as respects periods before the order takes effect as well as respects later periods.

NOTES

Derivation: 1972, s 10 (2).

Periods in which there is no contract of employment

9.—(1) If in any week the employee is, for the whole or part of the week—

(*a*) incapable of work in consequence of sickness or injury, or (*b*) absent from work on account of a temporary cessation of work, or

(*c*) absent from work in circumstances such that, by arrangement or custom, he is regarded as continuing in the employment of his employer for all or any purposes, or

(*d*) absent from work wholly or partly because of pregnancy or confinement,

that week shall, notwithstanding that it does not fall under paragraph 3, 4 or 5, count as a period of employment.

(2) Not more than twenty-six weeks shall count under paragraph (*a*) or, subject to paragraph 10, under paragraph (*d*) of sub-paragraph (1) between any periods falling under paragraph 3, 4 or 5.

NOTES

Derivation: 1972, Sched 1, para 5 (1), (2), as amended by 1975, Sched 16, Pt II, para 15.

General Note: this paragraph has the effect of saving an employee from the general rule stated in para 2. The effect of the heading is not entirely clear: see *Fitzgerald* v *Hall, Russell & Co Ltd* [1970] AC 780, at 1000.

Sub-paragraph (1) (*a*): see *Kolatsis* v *Rockware Glass Ltd* [1974] ICR 580, though the main issue in that case does not arise under (1) (*a*).

Sub-paragraph (1) (*b*): this sub-paragraph in effect poses three questions: (i) was there a cessation of the employee's work or job; (ii) was the employee absent on account of that cessation; and (ii) was the cessation temporary? see *Bentley Engineering Co Ltd* v *Crown* [1976] ICR 225.

'Cessation of work' means a cessation of work available for the particular employee to do: see *Fitzgerald* v *Hall, Russell & Co Ltd* and *Kolatsis* v *Rockware Glass Ltd.*

'Temporary': this is essentially a question of fact, and the tribunal must look at the original dismissal with hindsight, taking into account all relevant evidence and all relevant factors: see *Fitzgerald's* case and *Bentley Engineering Co Ltd v Crown.*

'Absent': the fact that the employee takes another job does not necessarily lead to the inference that he is not absent on account of a temporary cessation of work: see *Thompson* v *Bristol Channel Ship Repairers and Engineers Ltd* (1969) 4 ITR 262 and (1970) 5 ITR 85 and *Bentley Engineering Co Ltd* v *Crown.* A supply teacher who is appointed to a school for a term cannot be said to be absent on account of a temporary cessation of work during the holidays; he is absent because his contract has come to an end: see *Rashid* v *ILEA* [1977] ICR 157. *Quaere* whether this case might have been decided under sub-paragraph (1) (*c*).

Sub-paragraph (1) (*c*): it is not sufficient that the employee is customarily reinstated after an absence; the employment relationship must be regarded as continuing: see *Rhodes* v *Pontins Ltd* (1970) 6 ITR 88. The retention of the employee as a member of the employer's pension scheme may give rise to the inference that there was a custom or implied arrangement within this sub-paragraph: see *Wishart* v *NCB* [1974] ICR 460. See also *SEB* v *Collins* [1970] 1 QB 83.

Sub-paragraph (2): presumably, if an employee is absent for more than twenty-six weeks, his continuity will be broken.

Definitions: 'employee' and 'employer': see note to s 1; 'week', 'employment', and 'confinement': see s 153 (1).

Maternity

10. If an employee returns to work in accordance with section 47

after a period of absence from work wholly or partly occasioned by pregnancy or confinement, every week during that period shall count in computing a period of employment, notwithstanding that it does not fall under paragraph 3, 4 or 5.

NOTES

Derivation: 1972, Sched 1, para 5A (inserted by 1975, Sched 16, Pt II, para 17).

Definitions: 'employee': see note to s 1; 'week' and 'confinement': see s 153 (1).

Intervals in employment where section 55(5) *or* 84(1) *or* 90(3) *applies*

11.—(1) In ascertaining, for the purposes of section 64(1)(*a*) and of section 73(3), the period for which an employee has been continuously employed, where by virtue of section 55(5) a date is treated as the effective date of termination which is later than the effective date of termination as defined by section 55(4), the period of the interval between those two dates shall count as a period of employment notwithstanding that it does not otherwise count under this Schedule.

(2) Where by virtue of section 84(1) an employee is treated as not having been dismissed by reason of a renewal or re-engagement taking effect after an interval, then, in determining for the purposes of section 81(1) or Schedule 4 whether he has been continuously employed for the requisite period, the period of that interval shall count as a period of employment except in so far as it is to be disregarded under paragraphs 12 to 14 (notwithstanding that it does not otherwise count under this Schedule).

(3) Where by virtue of section 90(3) a date is to be treated as the relevant date for the purposes of section 81(4) which is later than the relevant date as defined by section 90(1), then in determining for the purposes of section 81(1) or Schedule 4 whether the employee has been continuously employed for the requisite period, the period of the interval between those two dates shall count as a period of employment except in so far as it is to be disregarded under paragraphs 12 to 14 (notwithstanding that it does not otherwise count under this Schedule).

NOTES

Derivation: 1974, Sched 1, para 30 (1A); 1975, s 74 (4); 1965, s 8 (3), (3A), (4), Sched 1, para 1 (1) (*b*) and (*c*); 1975, Sched 16, Pt I, paras 5, 19, 20, Pt III, para 29.

General Note: see Sched 2, Pt I, para 2 (4), in relation to maternity, and 6, para 9.

Definitions: 'employee': see note to s 1; 'employment': see s 153 (1).

Payment of previous redundancy payment or equivalent payment

12.—(1) Where the conditions mentioned in sub-paragraph (2)(*a*) or (2)(*b*) are fulfilled in relation to a person, then in determining, for the purposes of section 81(1) or Schedule 4, whether at any subsequent time he has been continuously employed for the requisite period, or for what period he has been continuously employed, the continuity of the period of employment shall be treated as having been broken—

(*a*) in so far as the employment was under a contract of employment, at the date which was the relevant date in relation to the payment mentioned in sub-paragraph (2)(*a*) or, as the case may be, sub-paragraph (2)(*b*); or (*b*) in so far as the employment was otherwise than under a contract of employment, at the date which would have been the relevant date in relation to that payment had the employment been under a contract of employment,

and accordingly no account shall be taken of any time before that date.

(2) Sub-paragraph (1) has effect—

(*a*) where—

(i) a redundancy payment is paid to an employee, whether in respect of dismissal or in respect of lay-off or short-time; and

(ii) the contract of employment under which he was employed (in this section referred to as " the previous contract ") is renewed, whether by the same or another employer, or he is re-engaged under a new contract of employment, whether by the same or another employer; and

(iii) the circumstances of the renewal or re-engagement are such that, in determining for the purposes of section 81(1) or Schedule 4 whether at any subsequent time he has been continuously employed for the requisite period, or for what period he has been continuously employed, the continuity of his period of employment would, apart from this paragraph, be treated as not having been broken by the termination of the previous contract and the renewal or re-engagement; or

(*b*) where—

(i) a payment has been made, whether in respect of the termination of any person's employment or in respect of lay-off or short-time, either in accordance with any provisions of a scheme under section 1 of the Superannuation Act 1972 or in accordance with any such arrangements as are mentioned in section 111(3); and

(ii) he commences new, or renewed, employment; and

(iii) the circumstances of the commencement of the new, or renewed, employment are such that, in determining for the purposes of section 81(1) or Schedule 4 whether at any subsequent time he has been continuously employed for the requisite period, or for what period he has been continously employed, the continuity of his period of employment would, apart from this paragraph, be treated as not having been broken by the termination of the previous employment and the commencement of the new, or renewed, employment.

(3) For the purposes of this paragraph, a redundancy payment shall be treated as having been paid if—

(*a*) the whole of the payment has been paid to the employee by the employer, or, in a case where a tribunal has determined that the employer is liable to pay part (but not the whole) of the redundancy payment, that part of the redundancy payment has been paid in full to the employee by the employer, or

(*b*) the Secretary of State has paid a sum to the employee in respect of the redundancy payment under section 106.

NOTES

Derivation: 1965, s 24, 24A; 1975, s 120 (3).

General Note: the effect of this provision is that where a redundancy (or equivalent) payment is paid to a person, the period in respect of which the payment is made cannot be taken into account for the purpose of a subsequent determination whether the employee has the requisite amount of continuous employment to qualify for a redundancy payment and how much the payment should be. Note s 117 (2) and Sched 6, para 9 and Sched 8. Note also para 20 of this Schedule.

Sub-paragraph (3): note s 117 and Sched 8, which make provision for employees paid by a person other than the employer.

Definitions: 'employment' and 'contract of employment': see s 153(1); 'relevant date': see s 153 (1) and s 90; 'lay-off' and 'short-time': see s 87; 'renewed' and 're-engaged': see s 84; 'employee' and 'employer': see note to s 1; 'requisite period': see s 81(4); 'redundancy payment': see s 153(1).

Certain weeks of employment to be disregarded for purposes of Schedule 4

13. In ascertaining for the purposes of Schedule 4 the period for which an employee has been continuously employed, any week which began before he attained the age of eighteen shall not count under this Schedule.

NOTES

Derivation: 1965, Sched 1, para 1 (1) (*a*).

Definitions: 'employee': see note to s 1; 'week': see s 153 (1).

Redundancy payments: employment wholly or partly abroad

14.—(1) In computing in relation to an employee the period specified in section 81(4) or the period specified in paragraph 1 of Schedule 4, a week of employment shall not count if—

(*a*) the employee was employed outside Great Britain during the whole or part of that week, and

(*b*) he was not during that week, or during the corresponding contribution week,—

(i) where the week is a week of employment after 1st June 1976, an employed earner for the purposes of the Social Security Act 1975 in respect of whom a secondary Class 1 contribution was payable under that Act; or

(ii) where the week is a week of employment after 6th April 1975 and before 1st June 1976, an employed earner for the purposes of the Social Security Act 1975; or

(iii) where the week is a week of employment before 6th April 1975, an employee in respect of whom an employer's contribution was payable in respect of the corresponding contribition week;

whether or not the contribution mentioned in paragraph (i) or (iii) of this sub-paragraph was in fact paid.

(2) For the purposes of the application of sub-paragraph (1) to a week of employment where the corresponding contribution week began before 5th July 1948, an employer's contribution shall be treated as payable as mentioned in sub-paragraph (1) if such a contribution would

have been so payable if the statutory provisions relating to national insurance which were in force on 5th July 1948 had been in force in that contribution week.

(3) Where by virtue of sub-paragraph (1) a week of employment does not count in computing such a period as is mentioned in that sub-paragraph, the continuity of that period shall not be broken by reason only that that week of employment does not count in computing that period.

(4) Any question arising under this paragraph whether—

(*a*) an employer's contribution was or would have been payable, as mentioned in sub-paragraph (1) or (2), or

(*b*) a person was an employed earner for the purposes of the Social Security Act 1975 and if so whether a secondary Class 1 contribution was payable in respect of him under that Act,

shall be determined by the Secretary of State; and any legislation (including regulations) as to the determination of questions which under that Act the Secretary of State is empowered to determine (including provisions as to the reference of questions for decision, or as to appeals, to the High Court or the Court of Session) shall apply to the determination of any question by the Secretary of State under this paragraph.

(5) In this paragraph " employer's contribution " has the same meaning as in the National Insurance Act 1956, and " corresponding contribution week ", in relation to a week of employment, means a contribution week (within the meaning of the said Act of 1965) of which so much as falls within the period beginning with midnight between Sunday and Monday and ending with Saturday also falls within that week of employment.

(6) The provisions of this paragraph shall not apply in relation to a person who is employed as a master or seaman in a British ship and is ordinarily resident in Great Britain.

NOTES

Derivation: 1965, ss 17 (3) to (8), 20 (1), (3); 1975, Sched 16, Pt I, para 8.

General Note: note the provisions of s 137, particularly subs (3) (*g*), which enable the provisions of this Act to be extended by Order in Council to employment for the purposes of activities in the territorial waters of the United Kingdom or connected with the exploration of the sea bed or subsoil. See also the notes to that section. Note Sched 6, para 9.

Ordinarily resident: see note to s 141. Note sub-para (6).

Definitions: 'employee' and 'employer': see note to s 1; 'employment' and 'week': see s 153 (1); 'ordinarily resident': see above.

Industrial disputes

15.—(1) A week shall not count under paragraph 3, 4, 5, 9 or 10 if in that week, or any part of that week, the employee takes part in a strike.

(2) The continuity of an employee's period of employment is not broken by a week which does not count under this Schedule, and which begins after 5th July 1964 if in that week, or any part of that week, the employee takes part in a strike.

(3) Sub-paragraph (2) applies whether or not the week would, apart from sub-paragraph (1), have counted under this Schedule.

(4) The continuity of the period of employment is not broken by a week which begins after 5th July 1964 and which does not count under this Schedule, if in that week, or any part of that week, the employee is absent from work because of a lock-out by the employer.

NOTES

Derivation: 1972, Sched 1, paras 6, 7.

General Note: it is generally thought that these provisions apply to preserve the employee's continuity of employment without it being necessary for the tribunal to inquire whether the strike is unlawful or not, but there are dicta to the contrary: see *Soutar* v *Fisher* (1975) 10 ITR 38. In *Bloomfield* v *Springfield Hosiery Co Ltd* [1972] 1 WLR 386, it was held that the dismissal of employees while they were on strike did not take them outside the category of 'employees' unless and until they took other permanent work, or their employers engaged other persons on a permanent basis to do the work that they had been doing, or permanently discontinued the activity in which they were employed. Strikers who returned to work with the employers had their continuity preserved. This case was distinguished by the tribunal in *Soutar* v *Fisher*, which is a case of doubtful utility.

Definitions: 'week': see s 153 (1) and para 24 (1); 'employee' and 'employer': see note to s 1; 'strike' and 'lock-out': see paragraph 24 (1).

Reinstatement after service with the armed forces, etc.

16.—(1) If a person who is entitled to apply to his former employer under Part II of the National Service Act 1948 (reinstatement in civil employment) enters the employment of that employer not later than the end of the six month period mentioned in section 35(2)(*b*) of that Act, his previous period of employment with that employer (or if there was more than one such period, the last of those periods) and the period of employment beginning in the said period of six months shall be treated as continuous.

(2) The reference in this paragraph to Part II of the National Service Act 1948 includes a reference to that Part of that Act as amended, applied or extended by any other Act passed before or after this Act.

NOTE:

Derivation: 1972, Sched 1, para 8.

Definitions: 'employer': see note to s 1; 'employment': see s 153 (1).

Change of employer

17.—(1) Subject to this paragraph and paragraph 18, the foregoing provisions of this Schedule relate only to employment by the one employer.

(2) If a trade or business or an undertaking (whether or not it be an undertaking established by or under an Act of Parliament) is transferred from one person to another, the period of employment of an employee in the trade or business or undertaking at the time of the transfer shall count as a period of employment with the transferee, and the transfer shall not break the continuity of the period of employment.

(3) If by or under an Act of Parliament, whether public or local and whether passed before or after this Act, a contract of employment between any body corporate and an employee is modified and some other body

corporate is substituted as the employer, the employee's period of employment at the time when the modification takes effect shall count as a period of employment with the second-mentioned body corporate, and the change of employer shall not break the continuity of the period of employment.

(4) If on the death of an employer the employee is taken into the employment of the personal representatives or trustees of the deceased, the employee's period of employment at the time of the death shall count as a period of employment with the employer's personal representatives or trustees, and the death shall not break the continuity of the period of employment.

(5) If there is a change in the partners, personal representatives or trustees who employ any person, the employee's period of employment at the time of the change shall count as a period of employment with the partners, personal representatives or trustees after the change, and the change shall not break the continuity of the period of employment.

NOTES

Derivation: 1972, Sched 1, para 9.

Further provisions: note Sched 12, Pt III, para 21.

Sub-paragraph (2): the word 'transfer' does not include the transfer of the mere ownership of premises used in the course of carrying on a business: see *Dallow Industrial Properties Ltd* v *Else* [1967] 2 QB 449. The transfer of a trade, business or undertaking from one person to another covers and includes the transfer of any trade or business or undertaking run by the owner as a separate and self-contained part of his operations in which assets, stock-in-trade etc are engaged: *ibid.* The essential question is whether the effect of the transaction is to put the purchaser of the business into possession of a going concern: see *Kenmir Ltd* v *Frizzell* [1968] 1 WLR 329. Express assignment of goodwill is strong evidence of a transfer of the business, though the absence of such assignment is not conclusive if the transferree has effectively deprived himself of the power to complete; similarly, the absence of transfer of goodwill, current liabilities or contracts is not conclusive: see *Lloyd* v *Brassey* [1969] 2 QB 98. The fact that the working environment of the employees is the same does not mean that there has not been a transfer of the business, if the machines on which they work are used to manufacture different products: see *Woodhouse* v *Peter Brotherhood Ltd* [1972] ICR 197 and *Crompton* v *Truly Fair Ltd* [1975] ICR 359. If, on the transfer of a business, the new employer tells the employee that his service with the previous employer will count in computing his length of service with the new employer, the latter will be bound by that representation: see *Evenden* v *Guildford City Association Football Club* [1975] ICR 367. See also *Port Talbot Engineering Co Ltd* v *Passmore* [1975] ICR 234; *Dhami* v *Top Spot Night Club* [1977] IRLR 231; *Young* v *Daniel Thwaites & Co Ltd* [1977] ICR 877; and *Hector Powe Ltd v Melon* [1978] IRLR 258.

Sub-paragraph (4): see *Rowley, Holmes & Co* v *Barber* [1977] ICR 387.

Definitions: 'employment' and 'business': see s 153 (1); 'employee' and 'employer': see note to s 1; 'contract of employment': see s 153 (1).

18. If an employee of an employer is taken into the employment of another employer who, at the time when the employee enters his employment is an associated employer of the first-mentioned employer, the employee's period of employment at that time shall count as a period of employment with the second-mentioned employer and the change of employer shall not break the continuity of the period of employment.

NOTES

Derivation: 1972, Sched 1, para 10.

Associated employer: see *SEB* v *Collins* [1970] 1 QB 83; *Spanlite Structures Ltd* v *Jarrett* [1973] ICR 465; and *Zarb* v *British & Brazilian Produce Co (Sales) Ltd* [1978] IRLR 78. See also s 153 (4).

Definitions: 'employee' and 'employer': see note to s 1; 'employment': see s 153 (1); 'associated employer': see above.

Crown employment

19.—(1) Subject to the following provisions of this paragraph, the provisions of this Schedule shall have effect (for the purpose of computing an employee's period of employment, but not for any other purpose) in relation to Crown employment and to persons in Crown employment as they have effect in relation to other employment and to other employees, and accordingly, except where the context otherwise requires, references to an employer shall be construed as including a reference to the Crown.

(2) In this paragraph, subject to sub-paragraph (3), " Crown employment " means employment under or for the purposes of a government department or any officer or body exercising on behalf of the Crown functions conferred by any enactment.

(3) This paragraph does not apply to service as a member of the naval, military or air forces of the Crown, or of any women's service administered by the Defence Council, but does apply to employment by any association established for the purposes of the Auxiliary Forces Act 1953.

(4) In so far as a person in Crown employment is employed otherwise than under a contract of employment, references in this Schedule to an employee's relations with his employer being governed by a contract of employment which normally involves employment for a certain number of hours weekly shall be modified accordingly.

(5) The reference in paragraph 17(2) to an undertaking shall be construed as including a reference to any function of (as the case may require) a Minister of the Crown, a government department, or any other officer or body performing functions on behalf of the Crown.

NOTES

Derivation: 1972, Sched 1, para 10A; 1975, s 120 (1).

Crown employment: see also s 138.

Definitions: 'employee': see note to s 1; 'employment', 'employer' and 'contract of employment': see s 153 (1).

Reinstatement or re-engagement of dismissed employee

20.—(1) Regulations made by the Secretary of State may make provision—

(*a*) for preserving the continuity of a person's period of employment for the purposes of this Schedule or for the purposes of this Schedule as applied by or under any other enactment specified in the regulations, or

(*b*) for modifying or excluding the operation of paragraph 12 subject to the recovery of any such payment as is mentioned in sub-paragraph (2) of that paragraph, in cases where, in consequence of action to which sub-paragraph (2) applies, a dismissed employee is reinstated or re-engaged by his employer or by a successor or associated employer of that employer.

(2) This sub-paragraph applies to any action taken in relation to the dismissal of an employee which consists—

(*a*) of the presentation by him of a complaint under section 67, or

(*b*) of his making a claim in accordance with a dismissal procedures agreement designated by an order under section 65, or

(*c*) of any action taken by a conciliation officer under section 134(3).

NOTES

Derivation: 1974, para 30 (3), (4); 1975, Sched 16, Pt III, para 30.

Regulations: see the Labour Relations (Continuity of Employment) Regulations 1976 (SI 1976 No 660).

Definitions: 'employee' and 'employer': see note to s 1; 'reinstated' and 're-engaged': see s 69; 'successor': see s 153 (1); 'associated employer': see s 153 (4).

Employment before the commencement of Act

21. Save as otherwise expressly provided, the provisions of this Schedule apply to periods before it comes into force as they apply to later periods.

NOTES

Derivation: Contracts of Employment Act 1963, Sched 1, para 1 (2); 1972, s 13 (5).

22. If, in any week beginning before 6th July 1964, the employee was, for the whole or any part of the week, absent from work—

(*a*) because he was taking part in a strike, or

(*b*) because of a lock-out by the employer,

the week shall count as a period of employment.

NOTES

Derivation: Contracts of Employment Act 1963, Sched 1, para 6; 1972, s 13 (5).

Definitions: 'employee': see note to s 1; 'week': see s 153 (1) and para 24 (1); 'strike' and 'lock-out': see para 24 (1).

23. Without prejudice to the foregoing provisions of this Schedule, any week which counted as a period of employment in the computation of a period of employment in accordance with the Contracts of Employment Act 1972 whether for the purposes of that Act, the Redundancy Payments Act 1965, the Trade Union and Labour Relations Act 1974 or the Employment Protection Act 1975, shall count as a period of employment for the purposes of this Act, and any week which did not break the continuity of a person's employment for the purposes of those Acts shall not break the continuity of a period of employment for the purposes of this Act.

NOTES

Derivation: 1972, s 13 (5).

Definitions: 'week': see s 153 (1) and para 24 (1).

Interpretation

24.—(1) In this Schedule, unless the context otherwise requires,—

"lock-out" means the closing of a place of employment, or the suspension of work, or the refusal by an employer to continue to employ any number of persons employed by him in consequence of a dispute, done with a view to compelling those persons, or to aid another employer in compelling persons employed by him, to accept terms or conditions of or affecting employment;

"strike" means the cessation of work by a body of persons employed acting in combination, or a concerted refusal or a refusal under a common understanding of any number of persons employed to continue to work for an employer in consequence of a dispute, done as a means of compelling their employer or any person or body of persons employed, or to aid other employees in compelling their employer or any person or body of persons employed, to accept or not to accept terms or conditions of or affecting employment;

"week" means a week ending with Saturday.

(2) For the purposes of this Schedule the hours of employment of an employee who is required by the terms of his employment to live on the premises where he works shall be the hours during which he is on duty or during which his services may be required.

NOTES

Derivation: 1972, Sched 1, para 11.

Persons employed: see *Bloomfield* v *Springfield Hosiery Co Ltd* [1972] 1 WLR 386 and *Soutar* v *Fisher* (1975) 10 ITR 38.

Definitions: 'employment': see s 153 (1); 'persons employed': see above; 'employee' and 'employer': see note to s 1.

SCHEDULE 14

CALCULATION OF NORMAL WORKING HOURS AND A WEEK'S PAY

General Note: note the power given to the Secretary of State by s 16 (4) to modify this Schedule. Note also ss 137 and 149.

PART I

NORMAL WORKING HOURS

1. For the purposes of this Schedule the cases where there are normal working hours include cases where the employee is entitled to overtime pay when employed for more than a fixed number of hours in a week or other period, and, subject to paragraph 2, in those cases that fixed number of hours shall be the normal working hours.

2. If in such a case—

(*a*) the contract of employment fixes the number, or the minimum number, of hours of employment in the said week or other period (whether or not it also provides for the reduction of that number or minimum in certain circumstances), and

(*b*) that number or minimum number of hours exceeds the number of hours without overtime,

that number or minimum number of hours (and not the number of hours without overtime) shall be the normal working hours.

NOTES

Derivation: 1975, Sched 4, paras 1, 2.

General Note: many of the provisions in this Act make it necessary to calculate an employee's normal working hours and a week's pay. Before determining a week's pay, it is first necessary to ascertain whether there are normal working hours. One of the problems that has most frequently arisen in this context has concerned whether overtime should count towards an employee's normal working hours. One can say that it will only count in exceptional circumstances, where the overtime requirement is obligatory on both employer and employee: see *Tarmac Roadstone Holdings Ltd* v *Peacock* [1973] ICR 273. Paragraph 2 will not apply, therefore, where the overtime is voluntary or where the employee is obliged to and does work overtime but there is no corresponding obligation on the employer to provide overtime or payment in lieu: *ibid.* See also *Gascol Conversions Ltd* v *Mercer* [1974] ICR 420; *Friend* v *PMA Holdings Ltd* [1976] ICR 330; *Ogden* v *Ardphalt Asphalt Ltd* [1977] ICR 604; and *Fox* v *C Wright* (*Farmers*) *Ltd* [1978] ICR 98.

Definitions: 'employee': see note to s 1; 'week' and 'contract of employment': see s 153 (1).

PART II

A WEEK'S PAY

Employments for which there are normal working hours

3.—(1) This paragraph and paragraph 4 shall apply if there are normal working hours for an employee when employed under the contract of employment in force on the calculation date.

(2) Subject to paragraph 4, if an employee's remuneration for employment in normal working hours, whether by the hour or week or other period, does not vary with the amount of work done in the period, the amount of week's pay shall be the amount which is payable by the employer under the contract of employment in force on the calculation date if the employee works throughout his normal working hours in a week.

(3) Subject to paragraph 4, if sub-paragraph (2) does not apply, the amount of a week's pay shall be the amount of remuneration for the number of normal working hours in a week calculated at the average hourly rate of remuneration payable by the employer to the employee in respect of the period of twelve weeks—

(*a*) where the calculation date is the last day of a week, ending with that week;

(*b*) in any other case, ending with the last complete week before the calculation date.

(4) References in this paragraph to remuneration varying with the amount of work done include references to remuneration which may include any commission or similar payment which varies in amount.

4.—(1) This paragraph shall apply if there are normal working hours for an employee when employed under the contract of employment in force on the calculation date, and he is required under that contract to work during those hours on days of the week or at times of the day which differ from week to week or over a longer period so that the remuneration payable for, or apportionable to, any week varies according to the incidence of the said days or times.

(2) The amount of a week's pay shall be the amount of remuneration for the average weekly number of normal working hours (calculated in accordance with sub-paragraph (3)) at the average hourly rate of remuneration (calculated in accordance with sub-paragraph (4)).

(3) The average number of weekly hours shall be calculated by dividing by twelve the total number of the employee's normal working hours during the period of twelve weeks—

(*a*) where the calculation date is the last day of a week, ending with that week;

(*b*) in any other case, ending with the last complete week before the calculation date.

(4) The average hourly rate of remuneration shall be the average hourly rate of remuneration payable by the employer to the employee in respect of the period of twelve weeks—

(*a*) where the calculation date is the last day of a week, ending with that week;

(*b*) in any other case, ending with the last complete week before the calculation date.

5.—(1) For the purpose of paragraphs 3 and 4, in arriving at the average hourly rate of remuneration only the hours when the employee was working, and only the remuneration payable for, or apportionable to, those hours of work, shall be brought in; and if for any of the twelve weeks mentioned in either of those paragraphs no such remuneration was payable by the employer to the employee, account shall be taken of remuneration in earlier weeks so as to being the number of weeks of which account is taken up to twelve.

(2) Where, in arriving at the said hourly rate of remuneration, account has to be taken of remuneration payable for, or apportionable to, work done in hours other than normal working hours, and the amount of that remuneration was greater than it would have been if the work had been done in normal working hours, account shall be taken of that remuneration as if—

(*a*) the work had been done in normal working hours; and

(*b*) the amount of that remuneration had been reduced accordingly.

(3) For the purpose of the application of sub-paragraph (2) to a case falling within paragraph 2, sub-paragraph (2) shall be construed as if for the words " had been done in normal working hours ", in each place where those words occur, there were substituted the words " had been done in normal working hours falling within the number of hours without overtime ".

Employments for which there are no normal working hours

6.—(1) This paragraph shall apply if there are no normal working hours for an employee when employed under the contract of employment in force on the calculation date.

(2) The amount of a week's pay shall be the amount of the employee's average weekly remuneration in the period of twelve weeks—

(*a*) where the calculation date is the last day of a week, ending with that week;

(*b*) in any other case, ending with the last complete week before the calculation date.

(3) In arriving at the said average weekly rate of remuneration no account shall be taken of a week in which no remuneration was payable by the employer to the employee and remuneration in earlier weeks shall be brought in so as to bring the number of weeks of which account is taken up to twelve.

The calculation date

7.—(1) For the purposes of this Part, the calculation date is,—

(*a*) where the calculation is for the purposes of section 14, the day in respect of which the guarantee payment is payable, or, where an employee's contract has been varied, or a new contract entered into, in connection with a period of short-time working, the last day on which the original contract was in force;

(*b*) where the calculation is for the purposes of section 21, the day before that on which the suspension referred to in section 19(1) begins;

(*c*) where the calculation is for the purposes of section 31, the day on which the employer's notice was given;

(*d*) where the calculation is for the purposes of section 35, the last day on which the employee worked under the contract of employment in force immediately before the beginning of her absence;

(*e*) where the calculation is for the purposes of Schedule 3, the day immediately preceding the first day of the period of notice required by section 49(1) or, as the case may be, section 49(2);

(*f*) where the calculation is for the purposes of section 53 or 71(2)(*b*) and the dismissal was with notice, the date on which the employer's notice was given;

(*g*) where the calculation is for the purposes of section 53 or 71(2)(*b*) but sub-paragraph (*f*) does not apply, the effective date of termination;

(*h*) where the calculation is for the purposes of section 73 and by virtue of section 55(5) a date is to be treated as the effective date of termination for the purposes of section 73(3) which is later than the effective date of termination as defined by section 55(4), the effective date of termination as defined by section 55(4);

(*i*) where the calculation is for the purposes of section 73 but section 55(5) does not apply in relation to the date of termination, the date on which notice would have been given had the conditions referred to in sub-paragraph (2) been fulfilled (whether those conditions were in fact fulfilled or not);

(*j*) where the calculation is for the purposes of section 87(2), the day immediately preceding the first of the four or, as the case may be, the six weeks referred to in section 88(1);

(*k*) where the calculation is for the purposes of Schedule 4 and by virtue of section 90(3) a date is to be treated as the relevant date for the purposes of certain provisions of this Act which is later than the relevant date as defined by section 90(1), the relevant date as defined by section 90(1);

(*l*) where the calculation is for the purposes of Schedule 4 but sub-paragraph (*k*) does not apply, the date on which notice would have been given had the conditions referred to in sub-paragraph (2) been fulfilled (whether those conditions were in fact fulfilled or not).

(2) The conditions referred to in sub-paragraphs (1)(*i*) and (*l*) are that the contract was terminable by notice and was terminated by the employer giving such notice as is required to terminate that contract by section 49 and that the notice expired on the effective date of termination or on the relevant date, as the case may be.

Maximum amount of week's pay for certain purposes

8.—(1) Notwithstanding the preceding provisions of this Schedule, the amount of a week's pay for the purpose of calculating—

(*a*) an additional award of compensation (within the meaning of section 71(2)(*b*)), shall not exceed £100;

(*b*) a basic award of compensation (within the meaning of section 72) shall not exceed £100;

(*c*) a redundancy payment shall not exceed £100;

(2) The Secretary of State may after a review under section 148 vary the limit referred to in sub-paragraph (1)(*a*) or (*b*) or (*c*) by an order made in accordance with that section.

(3) Without prejudice to the generality of the power to make transitional provision in an order under section 148, such an order may provide that it shall apply in the case of a dismissal in relation to which the effective date of termination for the purposes of this sub-paragraph, as defined by section 55(5), falls after the order comes into operation, notwithstanding that the effective date of termination, as defined by section 55(4), for the purposes of other provisions of this Act falls before the order comes into operation.

(4) Without prejudice to the generality of the power to make transitional provision in an order under section 148, such an order may provide that it shall apply in the case of a dismissal in relation to which the relevant date for the purposes of this sub-paragraph falls after the order comes into operation, notwithstanding that the relevant date for the purposes of other provisions of this Act falls before the order comes into operation.

Supplemental

9. In any case in which an employee has not been employed for a sufficient period to enable a calculation to be made under any of the foregoing provisions of this Part, the amount of a week's pay shall be an amount which fairly represents a week's pay; and in determining that amount the tribunal shall apply as nearly as may be such of the foregoing provisions of this Part as it considers appropriate, and may have regard to such of the following considerations as it thinks fit, that is to say—

(*a*) any remuneration received by the employee in respect of the employment in question;

(*b*) the amount offered to the employee as remuneration in respect of the employment in question;

(*c*) the remuneration received by other persons engaged in relevant comparable employment with the same employer;

(*d*) the remuneration received by other persons engaged in relevant comparable employment with other employers.

10. In arriving at an average hourly rate or average weekly rate of remuneration under this Part account shall be taken of work for a former employer within the period for which the average is to be taken if, by virtue of Schedule 13, a period of employment with the former employer counts as part of the employee's continuous period of employment with the later employer.

11. Where under this Part account is to be taken of remuneration or other payments for a period which does not coincide with the periods for which the remuneration or other payments are calculated, then the remuneration or other payments shall be apportioned in such manner as may be just.

12. The Secretary of State may by regulations provide that in prescribed cases the amount of a week's pay shall be calculated in such manner as the regulations may prescribe.

NOTES

Derivation: Paras 3 to 6: 1975, Sched 4, paras 3 to 6. Para 7 (1): 1975, ss 24 (3), (4), 31 (2), 37 (5), 61 (5); 1972, Sched 2, para 1 (2); 1975, ss 75 (3), 75 (1), 70 (6), 72 (7); 1965, s 5 (2A), Sched 1, para 5 (1), (2), (3); 1975, Sched 5, para 1 (2), Sched 16, Pt I, paras 4, 21. Para 7 (2): 1975, s 75 (2); 1965, Sched 1, para 5 (2); 1975, Sched 16, Pt I, para 21. Para 8: 1975, ss 75 (4) to (6), 72 (8), 86; 1965, Sched 1, para 5 (4), (5), (7); 1975, Sched 16, Pt I, para 21; 1977 Order (No 2), Art 2. Para 9: 1975, Sched 4, para 7. Para 10: 1975, Sched 4, para 8 (*a*). Paras 11, 12: 1975, Sched 4, paras 9, 10.

General Note: see *Ogden* v *Ardphalt Asphalt Ltd* [1977] ICR 604; *A and B Marcusfield Ltd* v *Melhuish* [1977] IRLR 484; and *Fox* v *C Wright (Farmers) Ltd* [1978] ICR 98. See also Sched 2, Pt I, para 2 (5) and Pt II, para 4 (4) in relation to maternity.

Para 6: 'remuneration': remuneration includes commission: see *Weevsmay Ltd* v *Kings* [1977] ICR 244. The method of calculating the amount of commission owed to the employee will depend upon how it is paid, but, if the employer calculates it annually, the tribunal should take the amount of commission earned over the full year and apportion it rateably according to the number of weeks in the financial year which the employee has actually worked: see *J and S Bickley* v *Washer* [1977] ICR 425.

Paras 7 *and* 8: note Sched 2, Pt I, para 2 (4) and Pt II, para 4 (3) in relation to maternity. Note also ss 55 (5) and 90 (3).

Para 8 (1): note s 148.

Regulations: none had been made at the time of going to press.

Definitions: 'employee' and 'employer': see note to s 1; 'contract of employment': see s 153 (1); 'calculation date': note para 7; 'week': see s 153 (1); 'guarantee payment': see s 12.

SCHEDULE 15

TRANSITIONAL PROVISIONS AND SAVINGS

General

1. So far as anything done or treated as done under or for the purposes of any enactment repealed by this Act could have been done under a corresponding provision of this Act it shall not be invalidated by the repeal but shall have effect as if done under or for the purposes of that provision.

2. Where any period of time specified in an enactment repealed by this Act is current immediately before the corresponding provision of this Act comes into force, this Act shall have effect as if the corresponding provision had been in force when that period began to run.

3. Nothing in this Act shall affect the enactments repealed by this Act in their operation in relation to offences committed before the commencement of this Act.

4. Any reference in an enactment or document, whether express or implied, to—

(*a*) an enactment which is re-enacted in a corresponding provision of this Act;

(*b*) an enactment replaced or amended by a provision of the Employment Protection Act 1975 which is re-enacted in a corresponding provision of this Act;

(*c*) an enactment in the Industrial Relations Act 1971 which was re-enacted with or without amendment in a corresponding provision in Schedule 1 to the Trade Union and Labour Relations Act 1974 and that corresponding provision is re-enacted by a corresponding provision of this Act;

shall, except so far as the context otherwise requires, be construed as, or as including, a reference to the corresponding provision of this Act.

5. Paragraphs 1 to 4 have effect subject to the following provisions of this Schedule.

Guarantee payments

6. Section 15(1) shall have effect in relation to any day before 1st February 1978 as if for " £6·60 " there were substituted " £6 ".

Maternity pay

7. No employee is entitled to receive maternity pay in respect of a payment period or payment periods beginning before 6th April 1977.

Termination of employment

8. Sections 49 and 50 apply in relation to any contract made before the commencement of this Act.

Unfair dismissal

9.—(1) The repeal by this Act of the provisions relating to unfair dismissals of the Employment Protection Act 1975, of Schedule 1 to the Trade Union and Labour Relations Act 1974 and of the Trade Union and Labour Relations (Amendment) Act 1976 shall not have effect in relation to dismissals where the effective date of termination is earlier than 1st October 1976 and, accordingly, those provisions shall continue to apply to such dismissals as they applied thereto before this Act came into force.

(2) Without prejudice to the generality of sub-paragraph (1), the provisions of paragraphs 17(2) and (3) and 19 of Schedule 1 to the said Act of 1974 shall, notwithstanding the repeal of those provisions by the Employment Protection Act 1975, continue to apply to dismissals where the effective date of termination falls before 1st June 1976.

(3) Where the notice required to be given by an employer to terminate a contract of employment by section 49(1) would, if duly given when

notice of termination was given by the employer, or (where no notice was given) when the contract of employment was terminated by the employer, expire on a date later than the effective date of termination as defined by section 55(4), that later date shall be treated as the effective date of termination for the purposes of sub-paragraphs (1) and (2).

10.—(1) Section 54 does not apply to a dismissal from employment under a contract for a fixed term of two years or more, where the contract was made before 28th February 1972 and is not a contract of apprenticeship, and the dismissal consists only of the expiry of that term without its being renewed.

(2) Sub-paragraph (1) in its application to an employee treated as unfairly dismissed by virtue of subsection (1) or (2) of section 60 shall have effect as if for the reference to 28th February 1972 there were substituted a reference to 1st June 1976.

Redundancy

11.—(1) The repeal by this Act of any provision of the Redundancy Payments Act 1965 and of any enactment amending that Act shall not have effect in relation to dismissals and to lay-off and short-time where the relevant date falls before 1st June 1976, and, accordingly, a person's entitlement to or the computation of a redundancy payment or the reference of questions to industrial tribunals concerning such entitlement or computation in cases where the relevant date falls before 1st June 1976 shall continue to be determined as if this Act were not in force.

(2) Where the notice required to be given by an employer to terminate a contract of employment by section 49 would, if duly given when notice of termination was given by the employer, or (where no notice was given) when the contract of employment was terminated by the employer, expire on a date later than the relevant date as defined by section 90(1), that later date shall be treated as the relevant date for the purposes of sub-paragraph (1).

12. Section 81 shall not apply to an employee who immediately before the relevant date (within the meaning of section 90) is employed under a contract of employment for a fixed term of two years or more, if that contract was made before 6th December 1965 and is not a contract of apprenticeship.

13. Sections 104 and 107 shall have effect in relation to an offence committed before 17th July 1978 as if—

(*a*) for each reference to the prescribed sum in subsection (9) of section 104 and subsection (4) of section 107 there were substituted a reference to £100, and

(*b*) subsection (10) of section 104 and subsection (5) of section 107 were omitted.

14. Schedule 5 shall have effect as if there were added at the end the following paragraph—

"5. The Boards of Governors of the hospitals specified in Schedule 1 to the National Health Service (Preservation of Boards of Governors) Order 1974.".

This paragraph shall cease to have effect on 22nd February 1979 or, if the said Order of 1974 is revoked on an earlier date, on that date.

Insolvency

15.—(1) Subject to sub-paragraph (2), the provisions of sections 122 and 123 shall apply in relation to an employer who becomes insolvent (within the meaning of section 127) after 19th April 1976, and shall in such a case apply to any debts mentioned in section 122 and to any unpaid relevant contribution (within the meaning of section 123), whether falling due before or after that date.

(2) Section 122 shall have effect in relation to any case where the employer became insolvent before 1st February 1978 as if for each reference to £100 there were substituted a reference to £80.

Calculation of a week's pay

16. Paragraph 8 of Schedule 14 shall have effect—

(*a*) for the purpose of calculating an additional award of compensation in any case where the date by which the order for re-instatement or re-engagement was required to be complied with fell before 1st February 1978;

(*b*) for the purpose of calculating a basic award of compensation in any case where the effective date of determination (as defined by subsection (5) of section 55 or, if the case is not within that subsection, by subsection (4) of that section) fell before 1st February 1978;

(*c*) in relation to a claim for a redundancy payment, where the relevant date fell before 1st February 1978,

as if for each reference to £100 there were substituted a reference to £80.

Computation of period of continuous employment

17. For the purposes of the computation of a period of continuous employment falling to be made before 1st February 1977—

(*a*) paragraphs 3 and 4 of Schedule 13 shall have effect as if for the word " sixteen " there were substituted the word " twenty-one ", and

(*b*) paragraphs 5, 6 and 7 of that Schedule shall not apply.

Legal proceedings

18. Notwithstanding the repeal of any enactment by this Act, the Employment Appeal Tribunal and the industrial tribunals may continue to exercise the jurisdiction conferred on them by or under any enactment which is repealed by this Act with respect to matters arising out of or in connection with the repealed enactments.

House of Commons staff

19. Section 122 of the Employment Protection Act 1975 shall, until 1st January 1979, have effect as if it applied the enactments which are mentioned in subsection (1) of section 139 of this Act to relevant members of the House of Commons staff (within the meaning of the said section 122).

NOTES

Derivation:

paras 1 to 3: —;
para 4: 1975, Sched 17, para 18; 1974, Sched 4, para 7; 1972, s 13 (6);
para 5: —;

para 6: 1977 Order (No 2), Art 3 (1);
para 7: Employment Protection Act 1975 (Commencement No 4) Order 1976 (SI 1976 No 530); Employment Protection Act 1975 (Commencement No 5) Order 1976 (SI 1976 No 1379);
para 8: 1972, s 13 (2);
para 9: 1975, Sched 17, para 7;
para 10 (1): 1974, para 12 (*a*);
para 10 (2): 1975, s 34 (6);
para 11: 1975, Sched 17, para 16;
para 12: 1965, s 15 (1);
para 13: —;
para 14: National Health Service (Preservation of Boards of Governors) Order 1974 (SI 1974 No 281);
para 15 (1): 1975, Sched 17, para 8;
para 15 (2): 1977 Order (No 2), Art 3 (2);
para 16: 1977 Order (No 2), Art 3 (3), (4), (5);
para 17: 1975, Sched 17, para 17;
para 18: —.

Para 9: note Sched 2, Pt I, para 2 (4) in relation to maternity.

SCHEDULE 16

CONSEQUENTIAL AMENDMENTS

House of Commons Offices Act 1846 (9 & 10 *Vict. c.* 77)

1. In section 5 of the House of Commons Offices Act 1846, after the words " Employment Protection Act 1975 " there are inserted the words " the Employment Protection (Consolidation) Act 1978 ".

Trade Union Act 1913 (2 & 3 *Geo.* 5. *c.* 30)

2. In section 5A of the Trade Union Act 1913, for the words " section 88(2) of the Employment Protection Act 1975 " there are substituted the words " section 136(2) of the Employment Protection (Consolidation) Act 1978 ".

Iron and Steel Act 1949 (12, 13 & 14 *Geo.* 6. *c.* 72)

3.—(1) In section 40 of the Iron and Steel Act 1949, in subsection (3), for the words from " a tribunal " to the end there are substituted the words " an industrial tribunal.".

(2) In section 41 of the said Act of 1949, in subsection (3), for the words from " a tribunal " to the end there are substituted the words " an industrial tribunal ".

Industrial Training Act 1964 (*c.* 16)

4.—(1) In section 4(7) of the Industrial Training Act 1964, for the words from " a tribunal " to " Act " there are substituted the words " an industrial tribunal ".

(2) For subsection (1) of section 12 of the said Act of 1964 there is substituted the following subsection—

> " (1) A person assessed to levy imposed under this Act may appeal to an industrial tribunal.".

Trade Union (*Amalgamation, etc.*) *Act* 1964 (*c.* 24)

5. In section 4(8) of the Trade Union (Amalgamations, etc.) Act 1964, for the words " section 88(2) of the Employment Protection Act

1975 " there are substituted the words " section 136(2) of the Employment Protection (Consolidation) Act 1978 ".

Transport Act 1968 (*c.* 73)

6. In section 135(4)(*b*) of the Transport Act 1968, for the words from " a tribunal " to the end there are substituted the words " an industrial tribunal.".

Transport (*London*) *Act* 1969 (*c.* 35)

7.—(1) In section 37(4)(*b*) of the Transport (London) Act 1969, for the words from " a tribunal " to the end there are substituted the words " an industrial tribunal.".

(2) In paragraph 6 of Schedule 2 to the said Act of 1969, for the words " paragraph 10(3) of Schedule 1 to the Contracts of Employment Act 1963 and section 8(2) of the Redundancy Payments Act 1965, for the purposes of those Acts " there are substituted the words " section 151(1) of and paragraph 17(3) of Schedule 13 to the Employment Protection (Consolidation) Act 1978, for the purposes of that Act ".

Post Office Act 1969 (*c.* 48)

8. In paragraph 33 of Schedule 9 to the Post Office Act 1969—

(*a*) in sub-paragraph (1) for the words " sections 1 and 2 of the Contracts of Employment Act 1963, Schedule 1 " there are substituted the words " sections 49 and 50 and Part VI of the Employment Protection (Consolidation) Act 1978, Schedule 13 ", for the words " the said Act of 1963 " there are substituted the words " the said Act of 1978 "; and for the words " twenty-one hours " there are substituted the words " sixteen hours ";

(*b*) in sub-paragraph (2), for the words " Schedule 1 to the said Act of 1963 " there are substituted the words " Schedule 13 to the said Act of 1978 ";

(*c*) in sub-paragraph (3), for the words " 7 of Schedule 2 to the said Act of 1963 " there are substituted the words " 10 of Schedule 14 to the said Act of 1978 " and for the words from " paragraph 10 " to the end there are substituted the words " Schedule 13 to that Act shall be construed as a reference to that Schedule as it has effect by virtue of sub-paragraph (1) above.";

(*d*) in sub-paragraph (4), for the words " the said Act of 1963 " and " Schedule 1 " there are substituted respectively the words " the said Act of 1978 " and " Schedule 13 ";

(*e*) at the end there is added the following sub-paragraph—

" (6) This paragraph applies notwithstanding the provisions of section 99 of the Employment Protection (Consolidation) Act 1978.".

Income and Corporation Taxes Act 1970 (*c.* 10)

9.—(1) In section 412(6) of the Income and Corporation Taxes Act 1970, for the words " section 32 of the Redundancy Payments Act 1965 " there are substituted the words " section 106 of the Employment Protection (Consolidation) Act 1978 ".

(2) In section 412(7) of the said Act of 1970—

(*a*) for the words " Part II of the Redundancy Payments Act 1965 " there are substituted the words " the Employment Protection (Consolidation) Act 1978 ";

(*b*) for the words " section 30(2) of the Redundancy Payments Act 1965 " there are substituted the words " section 104(2) of the Employment Protection (Consolidation) Act 1978 ";

(*c*) for the words " Schedule 5 to the Redundancy Payments Act 1965 " there are substituted the words " Schedule 6 to the Employment Protection (Consolidation) Act 1978 ";

(*d*) for the words " the Redundancy Payments Act 1965 " in paragraph (*c*) of the said section 412(7), there are substituted the words " the Employment Protection (Consolidation) Act 1978 ".

Atomic Energy Authority Act 1971 (*c.* 11)

10.—(1) In subsection (1) of section 10 of the Atomic Energy Authority Act 1971, for the words " section 22 of the Redundancy Payments Act 1965 " there are substituted the words " section 93 of the Employment Protection (Consolidation) Act 1978 ".

(2) In subsection (2) of the said section 10—

(*a*) for the words " section 4 of the Contracts of Employment Act 1963 " there are substituted the words " sections 1 to 4 of the Employment Protection (Consolidation) Act 1978 ";

(*b*) for the words " subsection (8) of that section ", in both places where they occur, there are substituted the words " section 5 of the said Act of 1978 ";

(*c*) for the words " the said section 4 " there are substituted the words " the said sections 1 to 4 ".

(3) In subsection (3) of the said section 10—

(*a*) for the words " Section 4A(1) of the Contracts of Employment Act 1963 " there are substituted the words " Section 11 of the Employment Protection (Consolidation) Act 1978 ";

(*b*) for the words " section 4 " there are substituted the words " sections 1 to 4 ".

(4) In subsection (4) of the said section 10—

(*a*) for the words from the beginning to " Redundancy Payments Act 1965 " there are substituted the words " For the purposes of Schedule 13 to the said Act of 1978 (computation of period of employment) ";

(*b*) for the words " paragraph 10 " there are substituted the words " paragraph 17 ".

Tribunals and Inquiries Act 1971 (*c.*62)

11. In section 13 of the Tribunals and Inquiries Act 1971, the following subsection is inserted after subsection (1)—

" (1A) Subsection (1) of this section shall not apply in relation to proceedings before industrial tribunals which arise under or by virtue of any of the enactments mentioned in section 136(1) of the Employment Protection (Consolidation) Act 1978.".

Civil Aviation Act 1971 (*c.*75)

12.—(1) In paragraph 1 of Schedule 9 to the Civil Aviation Act 1971—

(*a*) in sub-paragraph (1) for the words " sections 1 and 2 of the

Contracts of Employment Act 1963, Schedule 1 " there are substituted the words " sections 49 and 50 and Part VI of the Employment Protection (Consolidation) Act 1978, Schedule 13 ", for the words " the said Act of 1963 " there are substituted the words " the said Act of 1978 "; and for the words " twenty-one hours " there are substituted the words " sixteen hours ";

(*b*) in sub-paragraph (2), for the words " Schedule 1 to the said Act of 1963 " there are substituted the words " Schedule 13 to the said Act of 1978 ";

(*c*) in sub-paragraph (3), for the words " 7 of Schedule 2 to the said Act of 1963 " there are substituted the words " 10 of Schedule 14 to the said Act of 1978 " and for the words from " paragraph 10 " to the end there are substituted the words " Schedule 13 to that Act shall be construed as a reference to that Schedule as it has effect by virtue of sub-paragraph (1) above.";

(*d*) in sub-paragraph (4), for the words " the said Act of 1963 " and " Schedule 1 " there are substituted respectively the words " the said Act of 1978 " and " Schedule 13 ";

(*e*) at the end there is added the following sub-paragraph—

" (6) This paragraph applies notwithstanding the provisions of section 99 of the Employment Protection (Consolidation) Act 1978.".

(2) In paragraph 4 of the said Schedule 9—

(*a*) for the words " paragraph 10(2) of Schedule 1 to the Contracts of Employment Act 1963 and section 13(1) of the Redundancy Payments Act 1965 " there are substituted the words " section 94(1) of and paragraph 17(2) of Schedule 13 to the Employment Protection (Consolidation) Act 1978 ";

(*b*) for the words " the said section 13(1) " there are substituted the words " the said section 94(1) ";

(*c*) for the words from " the said Act of 1963 " to " Act of 1965 " there are substituted the words " the said paragraph 17(2) and the references to the said section 94(1) ", and after the words " a reference " there are inserted the words " to paragraph 10(2) of Schedule 1 ".

Transport Holding Company Act 1972 (*c*.14)

13.—(1) In section 2(3)(*c*) of the Transport Holding Company Act 1972, for the words from " a tribunal " to the end there are substituted the words " an industrial tribunal.".

(2) In section 2(7) of the said Act of 1972, for the words " a tribunal established under section 12 of the Industrial Training Act 1964 " there are substituted the words " an industrial tribunal ".

Finance Act 1972 (*c*.41)

14. In paragraph 1(*b*) of Part V of Schedule 12 to the Finance Act 1972, for the words " Redundancy Payments Act 1965 " there are substituted the words " Employment Protection (Consolidation) Act 1978 ".

British Library Act 1972 (*c*.54)

15. In paragraph 13(3)(*a*) of the Schedule to the British Library Act 1972, for the words " the Acts of 1963 and 1965 " there are substituted the words " the Employment Protection (Consolidation) Act 1978 ".

Gas Act 1972 (*c*.60)

16. In section 36(5) of the Gas Act 1972, for the words from " a tribunal " to the end there are substituted the words " an industrial tribunal.".

Health and Safety at Work etc. Act 1974 (*c*.37)

17. The following subsection is inserted in section 80 of the Health and Safety at Work etc. Act 1974 after subsection (2)—

" (2A) Subsection (1) above shall apply to provisions in the Employment Protection (Consolidation) Act 1978 which re-enact provisions previously contained in the Redundancy Payments Act 1965, the Contracts of Employment Act 1972 or the Trade Union and Labour Relations Act 1974 as it applies to provisions contained in Acts passed before or in the same Session as this Act.".

Trade Union and Labour Relations Act 1974 (*c*.52)

18. In section 8(7) of the Trade Union and Labour Relations Act 1974, for the words " section 88(3) of the Employment Protection Act 1975 " there are substituted the words " section 136(3) of the Employment Protection (Consolidation) Act 1978 ".

Social Security Act 1975 (*c*.14)

19.—(1) In section 114 of the Social Security Act 1975, the following subsection is inserted after subsection (2)—

" (2A) It is hereby declared for the avoidance of doubt that the power to make regulations under subsection (1) above includes power to make regulations for the determination of any question arising as to the total or partial recoupment of unemployment benefit in pursuance of regulations under section 132 of the Employment Protection (Consolidation) Act 1978 (including any decision as to the amount of benefit).".

(2) In section 139 of the said Act of 1975, after subsection (2) there is inserted the following subsection—

" (2A) Subsection (1) above does not apply to regulations made under this Act and contained in a statutory instrument which states that the regulations provide only that a day in respect of which there is payable a particular description of any payment to which section 132 of the Employment Protection (Consolidation) Act 1978 (recoupment of unemployment and supplementary benefits) applies shall not be treated as a day of unemployment for the purposes of entitlement to unemployment benefit.".

Sex Discrimination Act 1975 (*c*.65)

20.—(1) In section 65(2) of the Sex Discrimination Act 1975, for the words " paragraph 20 of Schedule 1 to the Trade Union and Labour Relations Act 1974 " there are substituted the words " section 75 of the Employment Protection (Consolidation) Act 1978 ".

(2) In section 75(5)(*c*) of the said Act of 1975 for the words " paragraph 21 of Schedule 1 to the Trade Union and Labour Relations Act 1974." there are substituted the words " paragraph 1 of Schedule 9 to the Employment Protection (Consolidation) Act 1978.".

Scottish Development Agency Act 1975 (*c.* 69)

21. In paragraph 6 of Schedule 3 to the Scottish Development Agency Act 1975, for sub-paragraphs (*a*), (*b*) and (*c*) there are substituted the words " the Employment Protection (Consolidation) Act 1978 ".

Welsh Development Agency Act 1975 (*c.* 70)

22. In paragraph 7 of Schedule 2 to the Welsh Development Agency Act 1975, for sub-paragraphs (*a*), (*b*) and (*c*) there are substituted the words " the Employment Protection (Consolidation) Act 1978 ".

Employment Protection Act 1975 (*c.* 71)

23.—(1) The Employment Protection Act 1975 shall be amended in accordance with the following provisions of this paragraph.

(2) In section 6(2)—

(*a*) the words from " in relation to " to " that is to say " shall be omitted;

(*b*) for the words " section 57 below; and " there are substituted the words " section 27 of the Employment Protection (Consolidation) Act 1978, including guidance on the circumstances in which a trade union official is to be permitted to take time off under that section in respect of duties connected with industrial action; and ";

(*c*) for the words " section 58 below " there are substituted the words " section 28 of the said Act of 1978, including guidance on the question whether, and the circumstances in which, a trade union member is to be permitted to take time off under that section for trade union activities connected with industrial action.".

(3) In section 8(9), for the words " section 88(3) below " there are substituted the words " section 136(3) of the Employment Protection (Consolidation) Act 1978 ".

(4) In section 102(4), for the words " Schedule 2 to the Contracts of Employment Act 1972 " there are substituted the words " Schedule 3 to the Employment Protection (Consolidation) Act 1978 ", and for the words " section 1(1) " there are substituted the words " section 49(1) ".

(5) In section 104(1)(*a*), for the words " section 30(1) of the Redundancy Payments Act 1965 " there are substituted the words " section 104(1) of the Employment Protection (Consolidation) Act 1978 ".

(6) In section 106(3), for the words from the beginning to " Redundancy Payments Act 1965 " there are substituted the words " Schedule 14 to the Employment Protection (Consolidation) Act 1978 shall apply for the calculation of a week's pay for the purposes of section 102 above, and, for the purposes of Part II of that Schedule, the calculation date is—

(*a*) in the case of an employee who was dismissed before the date on which the protective award was made, the date which by virtue of paragraph 7(1)(*k*) or (*l*) of the said Schedule 14 ".

(7) In section 108(1), for the words " paragraph 21 of Schedule 1 to the 1974 Act " there are substituted the words " paragraph 1 of Schedule 9 to the Employment Protection (Consolidation) Act 1978 ".

(8) In section 119(1), for the words " Parts II and IV of this Act apply " there are substituted the words " Part IV of this Act applies ".

(9) In section 119, the following subsection is added at the end—

" (17) Schedule 13 to the Employment Protection (Consolidation) Act 1978 and, so far as they modify that Schedule, any order under section 7 of that Act and any regulations under paragraph 20 of that Schedule, shall have effect for the purposes of this section in determining for what period an employee has been continuously employed; and, for the purposes of any proceedings brought under or by virtue of this Act, a person's employment during any period shall, unless the contrary is shown, be presumed to have been continuous.".

(10) In section 121(5), for the words " Schedule 3 to the Redundancy Payments Act 1965 " there are substituted the words " Schedule 5 to the Employment Protection (Consolidation) Act 1978 ".

(11) In section 121(6) and (7), for the words " section 41(3) of the Redundancy Payments Act 1965 " there are substituted the words " section 111(3) of the Employment Protection (Consolidation) Act 1978 ".

(12) In section 125(1) for the words from the beginning to " Part III of that Schedule " there are substituted the words " The provisions of the 1974 Act specified in Part III of Schedule 16 to this Act ".

(13) In section 126(1), for the words " paragraph 5 of Schedule 1 to the 1974 Act " there are substituted the words " section 55 of the Employment Protection (Consolidation) Act 1978 ".

New Towns (Amendment) Act 1976 (*c.* 68)

24. In section 13 of the New Towns (Amendment) Act 1976—

(*a*) in subsection (5), for the words " Schedule 1 to the Contracts of Employment Act 1972 " there are substituted the words " Schedule 13 to the Employment Protection (Consolidation) Act 1978 ";

(*b*) in subsection (6), for the words " section 13 of the Redundancy Payments Act 1965 " there are substituted the words " section 94 of the Employment Protection (Consolidation) Act 1978 ".

Race Relations Act 1976 (*c.* 74)

25.—(1) The Race Relations Act 1976 shall be amended in accordance with the following provisions of this paragraph.

(2) In section 56(2) for the words " paragraph 20 of Schedule 1 to the Trade Union and Labour Relations Act 1974 " there are substituted the words " section 75 of the Employment Protection (Consolidation) Act 1978 ".

(3) In section 66(7) for the words " paragraph 21 of Schedule 1 to the Trade Union and Labour Relations Act 1974 " there are substituted the words " paragraph 1 of Schedule 9 to the Employment Protection (Consolidation) Act 1978 ".

(4) In paragraph 11 of Schedule 2—

(*a*) in sub-paragraph (3) for the words " the Redundancy Payments Act 1965 " there are substituted the words " Part VI of the Employment Protection (Consolidation) Act 1978 ";

(*b*) for sub-paragraph (4)(*a*) and (*b*) there is substituted the following paragraph—

" (*a*) the Employment Protection (Consolidation) Act 1978 except Part VI of that Act; ".

Development of Rural Wales Act 1976 (*c.* 75)

26. In both paragraph 6 of Schedule 2 and paragraph 6 of Schedule 6 to the Development of Rural Wales Act 1976, for sub-paragraphs (*a*) (*b*) and (*c*) there are substituted the words " the Employment Protection (Consolidation) Act 1978 ".

Dock Work Regulation Act 1976 (*c.* 79)

27.—(1) In section 14(7) of the Dock Work Regulation Act 1976 for the words " subsections (1), (5) and (6) above " there are substituted the words " subsection (6) above ".

(2) In paragraph 17(1) of Schedule 1 to the said Act of 1976, for the words " Schedule 1 to the Contracts of Employment Act 1972 " there are substituted the words " Schedule 13 to the Employment Protection (Consolidation) Act 1978 ".

Aircraft and Shipbuilding Industries Act 1977 (*c.* 3)

28. In both section 49(10) and section 50(3)(*b*) of the Aircraft and Shipbuilding Industries Act 1977, for the words " a tribunal established under section 12 of the Industrial Training Act 1964 or, as the case may require " there are substituted the words " an industrial tribunal or, as the case may require, a tribunal established under ".

Social Security (*Miscellaneous Provisions*) *Act* 1977 (*c.* 5)

29. In section 18 of the Social Security (Miscellaneous Provisions) Act 1977—

(*a*) in subsection (1)(*c*), for " Act 1975 " there shall be substituted " (Consolidation) Act 1978 ";

(*b*) in subsection (2)(*a*), for the words " section 43 of the Employment Protection Act 1975 " there are substituted the words " section 40 of the Employment Protection (Consolidation) Act 1978 ";

(*c*) in subsection (2)(*b*), for " 64(3)(*a*) " and " 45(1) " there are substituted " 122(3)(*a*) " and " 42(1) " respectively;

(*d*) in subsection (2)(*e*), for the words " that Act " there are substituted the words " the Employment Protection Act 1975 ".

New Towns (*Scotland*) *Act* 1977 (*c.* 16)

30. In section 3(6) of the New Towns (Scotland) Act 1977 for paragraphs (*a*), (*b*) and (*c*) there are substituted the words " Parts I, IV, V and VI of the Employment Protection (Consolidation) Act 1978 ".

Housing (*Homeless Persons*) *Act* 1977 (*c.* 48)

31. In section 14(4) of the Housing (Homeless Persons) Act 1977—

(*a*) in paragraph (*a*), for the words " section 13 of the Redundancy Payments Act 1965 " there are substituted the words " section 94 of the Employment Protection (Consolidation) Act 1978 ";

(*b*) in paragraph (*b*), for the words " Schedule 1 to the Contracts of Employment Act 1972 " there are substituted the words " Schedule 13 to the said Act of 1978 ", and the words " sections 1 and 2 of " shall cease to have effect.

National Health Service Act 1977 (*c.* 49)

32. In paragraph 13(1)(*b*) of Schedule 14 to the National Health Service Act 1977, the reference to paragraph 106 of Schedule 4 to the National Health Service Reorganisation Act 1973 shall cease to have effect, and, accordingly, for that reference to paragraph 106 there is substituted a reference to paragraph 107 of the said Schedule 4.

Scotland Act 1978 (*c.* [51])

33. In section 33 of the Scotland Act 1978—

(*a*) in subsection (1), for paragraphs (*a*) and (*b*) there is substituted the following paragraph—

" (*a*) Parts I (so far as it relates to itemised pay statements), II, III (except section 44), V, VIII and IX and section 53 of the Employment Protection (Consolidation) Act 1978; and ",

and for the words " section 121 of the Employment Protection Act 1975 " there are substituted the words " section 138 of the Employment Protection (Consolidation) Act 1978 ";

(*b*) in subsection (2), for the words " paragraph 21(5)(*c*) of Schedule 1 to the Act of 1974 " there are substituted the words " paragraph 1(5)(*c*) of Schedule 9 to the Employment Protection (Consolidation) Act 1978 ".

House of Commons (*Administration*) *Act* 1978 (*c.* 36)

34. In paragraph 1 of Schedule 2 to the House of Commons (Administration) Act 1978, after the words " the Employment Protection Act 1975 " there are inserted the words " and section 139 of the Employment Protection (Consolidation) Act 1978 ".

SCHEDULE 17

REPEALS

Chapter	Short title	Extent of repeal
1964 c. 16.	Industrial Training Act 1964.	Section 12(2B), (3) and (4).
1965 c. 62.	Redundancy Payments Act 1965.	Sections 1 to 26. Sections 30 to 44. Sections 46 to 55 except section 55(6)(*b*). Sections 56 to 58. In section 59, subsection (2) and in subsection (3) the words " except the last preceding section ". Schedules 1 to 9.
1967 c. 17.	Iron and Steel Act 1967.	In section 31, in subsection (3), paragraph (*c*) and all the words following paragraph (*c*), and subsections (4)(*b*) and (6).
1967 c. 28.	Superannuation (Miscellaneous Provisions) Act 1967.	Section 9.
1968 c. 13.	National Loans Act 1968.	In Schedule 1, the paragraph relating to the Redundancy Payments Act 1965.
1969 c. 8.	Redundancy Rebates Act 1969.	The whole Act.
1969 c. 48.	Post Office Act 1969.	In Schedule 9, paragraph 34.
1970 c. 41.	Equal Pay Act 1970.	Section 2(7).
1971 c. 75.	Civil Aviation Act 1971.	In Schedule 9, paragraph 2.
1972 c. 11.	Superannuation Act 1972.	In Schedule 6, paragraphs 54 and 55.
1972 c. 53.	Contracts of Employment Act 1972.	The whole Act.
1972 c. 54.	British Library Act 1972.	In paragraph 13(2) of the Schedule, the definition of " the Act of 1963 ".
1972 c. 58.	National Health Service (Scotland) Act 1972.	In Schedule 6, paragraph 130.
1973 c. 32.	National Health Service Reorganisation Act 1973.	In Schedule 4, paragraph 106.
1973 c. 38.	Social Security Act 1973.	In Schedule 27, paragraphs 54 to 59.
1973 c. 50.	Employment and Training Act 1973.	In Schedule 2 in Part I, paragraph 15.
1974 c. 52.	Trade Union and Labour Relations Act 1974.	In section 1(2), paragraphs (*b*) and (*c*) and, in paragraph (*d*), the references to sections 146, 148, 149, 150 and 151 of the 1971 Act. In section 30(1), the definitions of " dismissal procedures agreement ", " position " and " job ".

Chapter	Short title	Extent of repeal
1974 c. 52—*cont.*	Trade Union and Labour Relations Act 1974—*cont.*	In Schedule 1, paragraphs 4 to 16, 17(1), 18, 20 to 27 and 30, in paragraph 32, sub-paragraphs (1)(*b*) and (2)(*b*) to (*e*) and, in paragraph 33, sub-paragraphs (3)(*c*) and (*d*) and (4A). In Schedule 3, paragraph 16. In Schedule 4, paragraphs 1, 3 and 6(4).
1975 c. 18.	Social Security (Consequential Provisions) Act 1975.	In Schedule 2, paragraphs 19 to 23.
1975 c. 60.	Social Security Pensions Act 1975.	Section 30(5).
1975 c. 71.	Employment Protection Act 1975.	Part II except section 40. Section 108(2) to (8). Section 109. Section 112. In section 118(2), in paragraph (*a*) the words " section 22 above or " and " section 28 or, as the case may be," and paragraphs (*b*) and (*c*). In section 119— subsection (2); in subsection (3) the figures from " 22 " to " 70 "; in subsection (4) the figures from " 22 " to " 81 "; in subsection (5), the figures from " 22 " to " 81 "; in subsection (7) the figures " 22 " and " 29 "; subsections (8) to (11); in subsection (12) the figures from " 59 " to " 81 ". Section 120. In section 121— in subsection (1), the reference to sections 47 and 63 to 69; in subsection (5), the reference to sections 47(3) and (4) and 68(3) and (4); subsection (8). In section 122(1), the words " Schedule 1 to the Contracts of Employment Act 1972 and Parts I and II of Schedule 1 to the 1974 Act "; and in paragraph (*d*), the words " paragraph 21(5)(*c*) of Schedule 1 to the 1974 Act and ".

Chapter	Short title	Extent of repeal
1975 c. 71—*cont.*	Employment Protection Act 1975—*cont.*	In section 122, subsection (3), in subsection (4) the definition of " civil employment claim " and in subsection (5) the words from " and of the Redundancy " to " employment claim ". In section 123(2)(*b*) the words " 28 or ". In section 124, subsections (2) to (4). In section 126— in subsection (1), the definitions of " guarantee payment " and " maternity pay "; subsections (3) and (5). In section 127— in subsection (1), paragraphs (*c*) and (*d*); in subsection 3(*g*), the words from " the following " to " also of ". In section 128— in subsection (1), the words " or of the 1974 Act so far as it relates to unfair dismissal " and " and the 1974 Act "; subsection (2); in subsection (3), the words " and the relevant provisions of the 1974 Act " in both places where they occur, and the words " or the relevant provisions of the 1974 Act ". Section 129(2). Schedules 2 to 6. In Schedule 12— in paragraph 1, the words from " and " to the end; paragraphs 8 to 12. In Schedule 16— Parts I and II; in Part III, paragraphs 8 to 30 and 34; in Part IV, paragraph 14. In Schedule 17, paragraphs 7 to 10, 16 and 17.
1976 c. 7.	Trade Union and Labour Relations (Amendment) Act 1976.	Section 1(*e*). Section 3(5) and (6).
1976 c. 68.	New Towns (Amendment) Act 1976.	In section 13(5), the words " sections 1 and 2 of ".
1976 c. 71.	Supplementary Benefits Act 1976.	In Schedule 7, paragraph 40.

Chapter	Short title	Extent of repeal
1976 c. 74.	Race Relations Act 1976.	In Schedule 3, paragraphs 1(2), (3) and (4).
1976 c. 79.	Dock Work Regulation Act 1976.	In section 14, subsections (1) to (5) and in subsection (6), paragraph (*a*) and so much of paragraph (*b*) as relates to sections 22, 29, 61, 64, 65 and 70 of the Employment Protection Act 1975. In Schedule 1, paragraph 17(2).
1977 c. 5.	Social Security (Miscellaneous Provisions) Act 1977.	Section 16.
1977 c. 22.	Redundancy Rebates Act 1977.	The whole Act.
1977 c. 38.	Administration of Justice Act 1977.	Section 6. Section 32(11).
1977 c. 48.	Housing (Homeless Persons) Act 1977.	In section 14(4)(*b*), the words " sections 1 and 2 of ".

INDEX